Network+
Practice Tests

Robert Gradante

The Coriolis Group, LLC
14455 N. Hayden Road, Suite 220
Scottsdale, Arizona 85260

480/483-0192
FAX 480/483-0193
http://www.coriolis.com

Library of Congress Cataloging-in-Publication Data
Gradante, Robert.
   Network+ practice tests exam cram/by Robert Gradante
      p. cm.
   ISBN 1-57610-484-2
   1. Electronic data processing personnel--Certification.
2. Computer networks--Examinations Study guides. I. Title.
QA76.3.G752 1999
004.6--dc21   99-25862
                                                  CIP

Printed in the United States of America
10 9 8 7 6 5 4 3 2

Publisher
Keith Weiskamp

Acquisitions Editor
Shari Jo Hehr

Marketing Specialist
Cynthia Caldwell

Project Editor
Sharon Sanchez McCarson

Technical Reviewer
Shawn McNutt

Production Coordinator
Wendy Littley

Cover Design
Jody Winkler
Thomas Shinkel

Layout Design
April Nielsen

CD-ROM Developer
Robert Clarfield

14455 North Hayden Road, Suite 220 • Scottsdale, Arizona 85260

Coriolis: The Training And Certification Destination ™

Thank you for purchasing one of our innovative certification study guides, just one of the many members of the Coriolis family of certification products.

Certification Insider Press™ has long believed that achieving your IT certification is more of a road trip than anything else. This is why most of our readers consider us their *Training And Certification Destination*. By providing a one-stop shop for the most innovative and unique training materials, our readers know we are the first place to look when it comes to achieving their certification. As one reader put it, "I plan on using your books for all of the exams I take."

To help you reach your goals, we've listened to others like you, and we've designed our entire product line around you and the way you like to study, learn, and master challenging subjects. Our approach is *The Smartest Way To Get Certified*™.

In addition to our highly popular *Exam Cram* and *Exam Prep* guides, we have a number of new products. We recently launched Exam Cram Live!, two-day seminars based on *Exam Cram* material. We've also developed a new series of books and study aides—*Practice Tests Exam Crams* and *Exam Cram Flash Cards*—designed to make your studying fun as well as productive.

Our commitment to being the *Training And Certification Destination* does not stop there. We just introduced *Exam Cram Insider*, a biweekly newsletter containing the latest in certification news, study tips, and announcements from Certification Insider Press. (To subscribe, send an email to **eci@coriolis.com** and type "subscribe insider" in the body of the email.) We also recently announced the launch of the Certified Crammer Society and the Coriolis Help Center—two new additions to the Certification Insider Press family.

We'd like to hear from you. Help us continue to provide the very best certification study materials possible. Write us or email us at **cipq@coriolis.com** and let us know how our books have helped you study, or tell us about new features that you'd like us to add. If you send us a story about how we've helped you, and we use it in one of our books, we'll send you an official Coriolis shirt for your efforts.

Good luck with your certification exam and your career. Thank you for allowing us to help you achieve your goals.

Keith Weiskamp
Publisher, Certification Insider Press

For Lil and Olivia, the reason I do everything.

About The Author

Robert Gradante works as a technical trainer and technical training manager of New Horizons Computer Learning Center of Long Island, part of the largest computer training organization in the world. He currently holds the MCP+I, MCSE+I, CCNA, A+, and Network+ certifications, as well as 16 MCT certifications.

Acknowledgments

I am very excited about the way this book turned out, and I must give all the credit to the people at the Coriolis Group for making this happen. I'd like to thank Shari Jo Hehr for making this all possible in the first place, and for surrounding me with great people. Special thanks to Sharon McCarson, my project editor, who did a great job of coordinating all phases of this project and was a pleasure to deal with. Thanks also to the rest of the team at Coriolis who worked on this book: Wendy Littley, Cynthia Caldwell, April Nielsen, Jody Winkler, Jesse Dunn, and Thom Schinkel. Many thanks to Bonnie Smith for an excellent copyediting job and also for providing valuable technical input. Thanks also to my technical reviewer, Shawn McNutt. His technical expertise added depth and clarity to this work.

Table Of Contents

Introduction

You Spoke

Welcome to *Network+ Practice Tests Exam Cram*! A recent survey of Coriolis readers showed us how important practice questions are in your efforts to prepare to take and pass certification exams. You asked us to give you more practice tests on a variety of certification topics, including MCSE Core Four, MCSE+I, A+, Network+, and others.

We Responded

The *Practice Tests Exam Cram* series is our answer to your requests, and provides you with entirely new practice tests for many certification topics. Each practice test appears in its own chapter, followed by a corresponding answer and explanation chapter, in the same format as the Sample Test and Answer Key chapters at the end of each of our *Exam Cram* books. We not only tell you which answers are correct, but we also explain why the right answers are right and why the wrong answers are wrong. That's because we're convinced that you can learn as much from understanding the wrong answers as you can from knowing the right ones!

This book makes a perfect companion to any study material you may own that covers the exam subject matter. For those of you who already own *Network+ Exam Cram*, we have included a time-saving study feature. At the end of each answer, you will find a reference to an appropriate chapter in the *Network+ Exam Cram*, or to another valuable resource. That way, if you want to review the material on which the question is based in more depth, you will be able to quickly locate that information.

But Wait, There's More!

This book also includes a CD-ROM that contains one more exam. This additional exams are built using an interactive format that allows you to practice in an exam environment similar to CompTIA's own testing formats.

Thus, this book gives you access to a pool of over 300 questions. Thorough review of these materials should provide you with a reasonably complete view of the numerous topics and types of questions you're likely to see on a real Network+ exam. We can't claim total coverage, but we have designed these question pools to deal with the topics and concepts that are most likely to appear on a real exam in some form or fashion.

Using This Book To Prepare For An Exam

You should begin your preparation process by working through the materials in the book to guide your studies. As you discover topics or concepts that may be unfamiliar or unclear, be sure to consult additional study materials to increase your knowledge and familiarity with the materials involved. In fact, you should employ this particular technique on any practice test questions you come across that may expose areas in your knowledge base that may need further development or elaboration.

To help you increase your knowledge base, we suggest that you work with whatever materials you have at hand. Certainly, we can't help but recommend our own *Exam Cram* and *Exam Prep* books, but you will find that the *Exam Crams* also cite numerous other sources of information as well.

An outstanding source of free information about networking can be found online at **www.webopedia.com**. Webopedia contains a searchable encyclopedia of networking terminology and concepts, as well as useful links to find additional information.

Once you've worked your way through the text-based practice tests in the book, use the interactive exam on the CD to assess your test readiness. That way, you can build confidence in your ability to sit for and pass these exams, as you master the subject material for each one.

Tell Us What You Think

Feel free to share your feedback on the book with us. We'll carefully consider your comments. Please be sure to include the title of the book in your message; otherwise, we'll be forced to guess which book you are writing about. Please send your comments and questions to us at **cipq@coriolis.com**.

Visit our Web site at **www.certificationinsider.com** for the latest on what's happening in the world of certification, updates, and new *Exam Prep* and *Exam Cram* titles. For the latest information on CompTIA certification exams, visit CompTIA's Web site at **www.comptia.org**. Good luck with your exams!

Network+
Practice Test #1

Question 1

Which networking topology is characterized by a continuous line of cable with termination at both ends?

○ a   Bus

○ b. Star

○ c. Ring

○ d. Mesh

Question 2

Due to recent problems with data loss, your company has asked you to implement a fault tolerance solution on their servers. Which of the following provides fault tolerance?

○ a. Volume set

○ b. Mirror set

○ c. Stripe set without parity

○ d. RAID 0

Question 3

You are the network administrator for a small sporting goods manufacturer. Your network is comprised of 35 computers. Twenty computers are
running Windows 98, and 15 computers are running NT Workstation. The
only server in your network is an NT Server. Your boss has been research-
ing print servers and decides to purchase a NetWare server to act as a
print server in your network. You are asked to install the NetWare server
and configure all clients to utilize it for printing. Which of the following
best describes how you will proceed?

○ a. Tell your boss no problem; Windows 98, Windows NT
Workstation, and NT Server can all be configured to access
resources on a NetWare server.

○ b. Tell your boss to return the server, because NetWare is
manufactured by Novell, a competitor of Microsoft.

○ c. Tell your boss that all the client computers will be able to
access the NetWare server, but not the NT Server.

○ d. Tell your boss that the Windows 98 clients will be able to use
the NetWare server, but the NT Workstation computers will
not.

Question 4

Which of the following protocols are routable? [Choose the three best
answers]

❑ a. NetBEUI

❑ b. TCP/IP

❑ c. IPX/SPX

❑ d. NWLink

Question 5

Your company, Marcus Pet Supply, has a 30-user server-based network. The client computers are running Windows 98, and there is one server running NT Server. The managers have expressed their concerns about data loss. To address this issue, you implement fault tolerance on the server. Emily, one of your assistants, asks you if she will still have to perform the daily tape backup on the server. What should you tell Emily?

- a. That's correct, because fault tolerance provides redundancy of data; it can be used as an alternative to tape backup.

- b. Are you kidding? Although fault tolerance does provide for redundancy, it should not be used as a replacement for tape backup.

- c. You can't be serious! Fault tolerance refers to internal processor speed and has nothing to do with redundancy.

- d. Because we have fault tolerance, tape backup is no longer needed, but do it anyway to get the overtime pay.

Question 6

Paul's dental company is planning a new network and has hired you as a consultant. They have 30 users and wish to have all users networked together. The client computers will be running Windows 98. You recommend a 10BaseT network. You need to select a cable type for this network. The cable must be inexpensive, easy to install, support 10BaseT, and allow room for upgrading the network speed to 100Mbps in the future without having to rewire the building. Which cable type will you recommend?

- a. Category 3 twisted-pair

- b. Category 4 twisted-pair

- c. Category 5 twisted-pair

- d. Fiber optic

Question 7

One of the most common network topologies in use today is 10BaseT. Which of the following statements are true about 10BaseT? [Choose the two best answers]

- ❏ a. A 10BaseT network uses twisted-pair cable.
- ❏ b. A 10BaseT network transmits at 100Mbps.
- ❏ c. A 10BaseT is part of the token ring standard.
- ❏ d. A 10BaseT is part of the Ethernet standard.

Question 8

What is the main difference between a WAN and a LAN?

- ○ a. A WAN uses a bus topology and a LAN uses a star topology.
- ○ b. A WAN is used in Microsoft networks, and a LAN is used in Novell NetWare networks.
- ○ c. A LAN is a number of computers connected together in a single location, and a WAN connects LANs together.
- ○ d. A WAN is a number of computers connected together in a single location, and a LAN connects WANs together.

Question 9

Robert is the sergeant at his police station in New York. His precinct needs to connect its internal 10BaseT network to the main Federal Bureau of Investigation (FBI) network in Maryland. Which of the following is the best connectivity device Robert could use to make this connection?

- ○ a. A hub
- ○ b. A router
- ○ c. A repeater
- ○ d. A token ring

Question 10

Which of the following correctly describes the functionality of full duplex versus half duplex?

○ a. Full duplex allows data to travel in two directions simulta-neously. Half duplex can only transfer data in one direction at a time.

○ b. Half duplex allows data to travel in two directions simulta-neously. Full duplex can only transfer data in one direction at a time.

○ c. Full duplex is used in LANs. Half duplex is used in WANs.

○ d. There is no difference between full and half duplex.

Question 11

Which of the following are network operating systems? [Choose the three best answers]

❑ a. Windows NT

❑ b. Novell NetWare

❑ c. DOS

❑ d. OS/2

Question 12

You are the network administrator for a small manufacturing company. The network consists of 15 users who all need access to a database that is located on a server on the local network. The database contains sensi-tive information, so access to this database should only be given to specific individuals. You are asked to implement a security model for your network that will provide a high level of control over the users that can access this database. What security model will you implement?

○ a. User-level security

○ b. Share-level security

○ c. Password-protected, share-level security

○ d. No access share-implemented resource distribution (NASIRD)

Question 13

What is the default username of the administrator's account created by Microsoft's NT Server upon installation?

○ a   Admin

○ b.   Administrator

○ c.   Supervisor

○ d.   Manager

Question 14

You have been asked to recommend a network topology for a Helena's real estate company. The company has done some research on the available technologies and asks you to implement a topology that guarantees there will not be any collisions of packets sent over the network. Which topology is the customer thinking of?

○ a.   Bus

○ b.   Star

○ c.   Token ring

○ d.   Carrier Sense Multiple Access with Collision Detection (CSMA/CD)

Question 15

You are the network administrator for a small 10BaseT network of 14 computers, all connected to a single hub. The computers all run Windows 98. Jenny, a user in the accounting department, complains that she cannot connect to the network. Everything was working fine until yesterday, when Jenny added a sound card to her computer. Since then, she has been unable to use the network. All other users can access the network. You check the con-figuration of her computer and notice that the sound card and the network card are both configured to use IRQ 5. Given this information, what is the most likely reason Jenny cannot connect to the network?

○ a.   There is an IRQ conflict between the network card and the sound card.

○ b.   The fact that the network card and the sound card share the same IRQ is irrelevant. The problem must exist elsewhere.

○ c.   Jenny must have kicked the plug out from the hub.

○ d.   The cable must have fallen out of the back of Jenny's computer last week sometime.

Question 16

Connectivity devices are commonly used to connect computers together in a network. Which of the following statements best describes the difference between a hub and a multistation access unit (MAU)?

○ a. A hub can be used in Ethernet networks, and an MAU is used in token ring networks.

○ b. An MAU is used to connect wide area networks; a hub is used to connect metropolitan area networks.

○ c. A hub and an MAU refer to the same device.

○ d. A hub is known as an "active" connector, and an MAU is known as a "passive" connector.

Question 17

On what layer of the Open System Interconnection (OSI) model does a bridge reside?

○ a. Transport

○ b. Network

○ c. Physical

○ d. Data Link

Question 18

The Institute for Electrical and Electronics Engineers (IEEE) publishes standards used in networking. A subgroup of IEEE is Project 802, which defines network standards for the physical components of a network. Which of the following statements are true of Project 802 standards? [Choose the two best answers]

❑ a. Project 802.5 defines standards for token ring networks.

❑ b. Project 802.2 defines standards for CSMA/CD (Ethernet).

❑ c. Project 802.3 defines standards for CSMA/CD (Ethernet).

❑ d. Project 802.3 defines standards for the Logical Link Control (LLC).

Question 19

Which of the following best describes the difference between a router and a brouter ?

○ a. A router is used in Ethernet networks, and a brouter is used in token ring networks.

○ b. A router can route Network layer protocols; a brouter can route Network layer protocols and bridge nonroutable protocols.

○ c. A router resides at the Transport layer of the OSI model, and a brouter resides at the Session layer of the OSI model.

○ d. A router resides at the Presentation layer of the OSI model, and a brouter resides at the Application layer of the OSI model.

Question 20

At what layers of the OSI model does a brouter reside?

○ a. Application and Transport

○ b. Session and Network

○ c. Transport and Data Link

○ d. Network and Data Link

Question 21

You are the network administrator for your company in New York. Your office is connected to another office located in Florida. Routers are used to connect the two locations. Which of the following protocols could you use for communication between the users in Florida and New York? [Choose the two best answers]

❑ a. TCP/IP

❑ b. NetBIOS Enhanced User Interface (NetBEUI)

❑ c. Internetwork Packet Exchange/Sequenced Packet Exchange (IPX/SPX)

❑ d. Local Area Transport (LAT)

Question 22

Which of the following topologies is the most expensive to implement?

○ a. Bus

○ b. Star

○ c. Ring

○ d. Mesh

Question 23

You are configuring the settings for TCP/IP on your LAN. Users need to use TCP/IP to communicate with each other in the local network. Currently, there is no connection outside of your office. What TCP/IP parameters must you configure on each computer in this scenario?

○ a. IP address and subnet mask

○ b. IP address, subnet mask, and default gateway

○ c. IP address only

○ d. No configuration is necessary; this is a LAN, and TCP/IP only requires configuring in a WAN

Question 24

You are brought in as a consultant to assist in implementing TCP/IP for a large network. The network consists of 747 computers, all of which require communication with each other, as well as other offices through a router. The company asks you to configure TCP/IP configuration information on all clients.

Required result:

- All client computers should have their IP address information dynamically assigned.

First optional result:

- You need to provide for efficient name resolution of hostnames to IP addresses.

Second optional result:

- You need to provide for efficient name resolution of NetBIOS names to IP addresses.

Proposed solution:

- Implement Dynamic Host Configuration Protocol (DHCP), Domain Name System (DNS), and Address Resolution Protocol (ARP).

Which of the following is true about the proposed solution?

- ○ a. The proposed solution meets the required result and both optional results.
- ○ b. The proposed solution meets the required result and only one of the optional results.
- ○ c. The proposed solution meets the required result and none of the optional results.
- ○ d. The proposed solution does not meet the required result or any of the optional results.

Question 25

Which TCP/IP utility is used to resolve NetBIOS names to IP addresses?

- ○ a. Windows Internet Naming Service (WINS)
- ○ b. Domain Name System (DNS)
- ○ c. Dynamic Host Configuration Protocol (DHCP)
- ○ d. Address Resolution Protocol (ARP)

Question 26

You are setting up a small network of four Unix computers to use TCP/IP. All the Unix computers will have a unique hostname. You want to provide for name resolution of hostnames to IP addresses. Which of the following can you choose?

- ○ a. Set up a WINS server and configure all clients to use it.
- ○ b. Manually configure the HOSTS files on each computer.
- ○ c. Set up a DHCP server.
- ○ d. Manually configure the LMHOSTS files on each computer.

Question 27

TCP/IP is a widely used industry-standard routable protocol. TCP/IP is made up of an entire suite of protocols. Two key components of the TCP/IP protocol suite are TCP and User Datagram Protocol (UDP). Which of the following correctly states the difference between TCP and UDP?

- ○ a. TCP is a connection-oriented protocol; UDP is a connectionless protocol.
- ○ b. TCP is a connectionless protocol; UDP is a connection-oriented protocol.
- ○ c. TCP does not guarantee delivery of packets; UDP guarantees delivery of packets.
- ○ d. There is no difference between TCP and UDP.

Question 28

You are configuring the client computers in your network to access Internet mail. They all have an Internet mail account and an incoming and outgoing mail server provided by your ISP. Your ISP has given you the IP address of their Post Office Protocol (POP) 3 server and their Simple Mail Transfer Protocol (SMTP) server. Which of the following best describes how you will configure the email clients on your users' computers?

- ○ a. Specify the POP3 server as the incoming mail server and the SMTP server as the outgoing mail server.

- ○ b. Specify the SMTP server as the incoming mail server and the POP3 server as the outgoing mail server.

- ○ c. Specify the SMTP server as the incoming mail server and the outgoing mail server.

- ○ d. Specify the POP3 server as the incoming mail server and the outgoing mail server.

Question 29

Which of the following components of the TCP/IP protocol suite makes use of a Management Information Base (MIB)?

- ○ a. POP3

- ○ b. SMTP

- ○ c. Simple Network Management Protocol (SNMP)

- ○ d. TCP

Question 30

Which of the following components of the TCP/IP protocol suite makes use of agent and manager software?

- ○ a. POP3

- ○ b. SMTP

- ○ c. SNMP

- ○ d. TCP

Question 31

You are a master chef connected to the Internet from your computer at home. You find a cool site that offers free downloads of files that contain recipes. You download several exciting recipes. What protocol were you most likely using to download these files?

○ a. SMTP

○ b. SNMP

○ c. FTP

○ d. POP3

Question 32

Keyshawn, a network administrator, needs to implement a fault tolerance strategy on his NT Server computer. The server has two physical disks, each with a single partition. The disks are 1GB each in size and each contains only one partition. He decides to implement a stripe set with parity. He soon runs into difficulty attempting to implement this strategy and calls you for help. What will you tell Keyshawn?

○ a. You cannot implement a stripe set with parity on an NT Server. NT does not support it.

○ b. You cannot implement a stripe set with parity on a disk larger than 100MB.

○ c. You cannot implement a stripe set with parity on two disks. The minimum number of disks required is three.

○ d. You cannot implement a stripe set with parity on an NT Server unless you first reset the disk counters using DISKPERF –Y.

Question 33

Which of the following statements is true about operating systems' support of the use of TCP/IP?

○ a. Microsoft Windows 98 and Unix support TCP/IP; Novell NetWare 5 does *not* support TCP/IP.

○ b. Microsoft Windows NT and Novell NetWare 5 support TCP/IP; Unix does *not* support TCP/IP.

○ c. Microsoft Windows 95 and Unix support TCP/IP; Novell NetWare 5 does *not* support TCP/IP.

○ d. Microsoft Windows 9X and NT operating systems, Unix, and Novell NetWare 5 *all* support TCP/IP.

Question 34

What is the address range for TCP/IP Class C addresses?

○ a. 1 through 126

○ b. 128 through 191

○ c. 192 through 223

○ d. Both a and c

Question 35

What is the default subnet mask for a Class B IP address?

○ a. 255.0.0.0

○ b. 255.255.0.0

○ c. 255.255.255.0

○ d. 255.255.255.255

Question 36

Your network is a LAN of 30 computers in a single subnet and uses TCP/IP as the communication protocol. Your computer is configured with the IP address 131.50.50.72. What is the correct default subnet mask for this network?

○ a. 255.255.0.0

○ b. 255.0.0.0

○ c. 255.255.255.0

○ d. 255.255.255.255

Question 37

The File Transfer Protocol (FTP) is part of the TCP/IP protocol suite. It is considered a well-known protocol. What port number does FTP use?

○ a. 21

○ b. 25

○ c. 80

○ d. 110

Question 38

You are the network administrator for your company. You are configuring the email clients on your users' computers, so they can access Internet email. Your ISP has given you the IP address of the POP3 and SMTP mail servers to be used in this configuration, but they did not give you the port numbers that the servers are using. You call the ISP back and ask what port numbers you should use. They tell you to use the well-known port numbers of each server. Which of the following best describes what you should do next?

○ a. Configure the POP3 server to use port 80 and the SMTP server to use port 21.

○ b. Configure the POP3 server to use port 110 and the SMTP server to use port 25.

○ c. Configure the POP3 server to use port 25 and the SMTP server to use port 110.

○ d. Tell the ISP, "Those port numbers might be well known to you, but I'm not a mind reader. You'll have to tell me what they are."

Question 39

Which network topology provides equal access for all computers?

○ a. Bus

○ b. Star

○ c. Token ring

○ d. Ethernet

Question 40

You want to provide all users on your network with Internet access. Performance and security are of the utmost importance. Users need improved speed when retrieving Web pages, and you want to provide a measure of security to protect your local network from potential hackers on the Internet. What should you install?

○ a. A DHCP server

○ b. A POP3 server

○ c. An IP proxy server

○ d. A WINS server

Question 41

You are configuring DHCP for use in your TCP/IP network. Which of the following can a DHCP server assign to clients in a TCP/IP network?

○ a. DHCP can provide clients with the IP address of a DNS server.

○ b. DHCP can provide clients with the IP address of a WINS server.

○ c. DHCP can provide clients with the IP address of their default gateway.

○ d. All of the above.

Question 42

You are the administrator of a bus network that contains 75 computers. The network uses coaxial cable to connect all users and is spread out over the first two floors of a building. Lillian, one of the users on the first floor, experiences a system crash and turns off her computer. Which of the following best describes the effect this will have on the other users of the network?

- ○ a. All users will not be able to communicate as long as Lillian's computer remains off.

- ○ b. All users on the first floor will not be able to communicate until Lillian's computer is fixed.

- ○ c. All users will not be able to communicate until Lillian's computer is turned back on.

- ○ d. All users will be able to communicate whether or not Lillian's computer is turned back on, as long as the network cable is still attached to her computer and the bus network maintains a continuous line of cable that is terminated at both ends.

Question 43

The POP3 protocol is part of the TCP/IP protocol suite. It is considered a well-known protocol. What port number does POP3 use?

- ○ a. 21
- ○ b. 25
- ○ c. 80
- ○ d. 110

Question 44

What TCP/IP command line utility would you use to display the IP address-to-media access control (MAC) address names that a TCP/IP computer has resolved during a session?

- ○ a. ARP
- ○ b. TRACERT
- ○ c. NBTSTAT
- ○ d. NETSTAT

Question 45

You are the network administrator for your company in New York. Your office is connected to another office located in Florida. Routers are used to connect the two locations. The routers you are using automatically update their own routing tables. What type of routing table are your routers using?

○ a. Dynamic

○ b. Automatic mid-distance vectoring

○ c. Static

○ d. NY-to-FL link states

Question 46

You are troubleshooting a computer on your network. The computer is using TCP/IP as the only protocol. You need to display a list of the NetBIOS names in use by this computer. What TCP/IP command line utility can give you this information?

○ a. ARP

○ b. TRACERT

○ c. NBTSTAT

○ d. NETSTAT

Question 47

You are troubleshooting a Windows NT Server computer on your network. The computer is using TCP/IP as the only protocol. You need to display the IP address, subnet mask, and default gateway parameters that this computer is using. What TCP/IP command line utility can give you this information?

○ a. WINIPCFG

○ b. IPCONFIG

○ c. Both a and b

○ d. None of the above

Question 48

The IPX/SPX protocol is commonly used in the Novell NetWare network. Like TCP/IP, the IPX/SPX protocol also uses an addressing scheme to identify the computers on a network. Which of the following statements is true about an IPX/SPX address?

- ○ a. An IPX/SPX address is made up of an internal address and an external network address.

- ○ b. An IPX/SPX address is made up of a network ID and a subnet mask.

- ○ c. An IPX/SPX address is made up of an external network address in a WAN and an internal address in a LAN.

- ○ d. An IPX/SPX address is made up of an external network address in a LAN and an internal address in a WAN.

Question 49

The TCP/IP protocol contains utilities useful when troubleshooting. Which of the following best describes the use of the PING utility?

- ○ a. PING is used to obtain a MAC address on behalf of a client.

- ○ b. PING is used to display IP configuration information.

- ○ c. PING is used in troubleshooting to test connectivity between hosts.

- ○ d. PING is not used in TCP/IP.

Question 50

What terminal emulation program is used in TCP/IP to connect to a server on a remote network?

- ○ a. PING

- ○ b. IPCONFIG

- ○ c. TRACERT

- ○ d. Telnet

Question 51

You are asked to look at the following that is displayed on the screen of a user's TCP/IP computer:

```
Active Connections
Proto  Local Address            Foreign Address
       State
TCP    208.100.50.109:1033      208.100.50.4:80
       TIME_WAIT
TCP    208.100.50.109:1034      208.100.50.4:80
       TIME_WAIT
UDP    208.100.50.109:1043      208.100.50.14:80
       TIME_WAIT
UDP    208.100.50.109:1044      208.100.50.11:139
       TIME_WAIT
UDP    208.100.50.109:1045      208.100.50.12:139
       TIME_WAIT
```

What TCP/IP utility was used to produce this information?

○ a. ARP

○ b. TRACERT

○ c. NBTSTAT

○ d. NETSTAT

Question 52

Which of the following best describes the difference between Point-to-Point Protocol (PPP) and Serial Line Internet Protocol (SLIP)?

○ a. PPP is used as a dial-up protocol; SLIP is not.

○ b. SLIP is used as a dial-up protocol; PPP is not.

○ c. PPP is a newer, more efficient dial-up protocol than SLIP.

○ d. SLIP is a newer, more efficient dial-up protocol than PPP.

Question 53

Which network topology will cause computers to "beacon" when one of the computers goes down?

○ a. Bus

○ b. Star

○ c. Token ring

○ d. Mesh

Question 54

You are the network administrator for a sales company in California. Your company has a branch office located in New York. You need to set up a virtual private network (VPN) to connect these two locations. Both offices will be connecting to each other through the Internet. Your boss is concerned about the security risk of connecting your private networks through the Internet. What protocol of the TCP/IP protocol suite could you use in this scenario to provide secure communications between your two offices over the Internet?

○ a. PPP

○ b. SLIP

○ c. PPTP

○ d. WINS

Question 55

The Law offices of Boy, Dewy, Cheatem, and Howe asks for your help in configuring their TCP/IP network. They currently have 235 computers connected together in one location. The network uses TCP/IP as the only protocol. They connect to their home office through a router. When configuring the TCP/IP configuration of this network, which of the following statements are true? [Choose the three best answers]

❏ a. All computers in this scenario should be configured with a subnet mask.

❏ b. All computers in this scenario should be configured with a default gateway.

❏ c. All computers in this scenario should be configured with a unique IP address.

❏ d. All computers in this scenario should be configured with the same IP address.

Question 56

The users on your network need to access the Internet. You are deciding on a connection method to use. You want a digital connection that is capable of transmission speeds of more than 100Kbps. You have the choice of either ISDN or PSTN. Which of these can you choose to meet your requirement?

O a. ISDN

O b. PSTN

O c. Both ISDN and PSTN meet the requirement

O d. Neither ISDN nor PSTN meet the requirement

Question 57

Which of the following best describes the difference between user-level security and share-level security? [Choose the two best answers]

❑ a. User-level security is considered a more secure method of controlling resource access than share-level security.

❑ b. Share-level security is considered a more secure method of controlling resource access than user-level security.

❑ c. User-level security assigns permissions to users; share-level security assigns passwords to resources.

❑ d. Share-level security assigns permissions to users; user-level security assigns passwords to resources.

Question 58

You are the newly hired network administrator for Scott's Tea Company. The office consists of 35 computers networked together. The office is on the fifth floor of a large office building. On the fourth floor of this building is Don's Tea Company, a competitor of yours. Your boss suspects that Don's Tea Company is tapping into your network's coaxial cable and reading sensitive information about your company. He asks you to implement a solution. Which of the following is the best solution you could recommend?

○ a. Implement user-level security on all network resources.

○ b. Implement share-level security on all network resources.

○ c. Implement data encryption on all sensitive data that passes across the network.

○ d. Send a fish wrapped in newspaper to Don's Tea Company. That will definitely send the "message."

Question 59

Which of the following is an example of data encryption?

○ a. Data Eletro Propagation (DEP)

○ b. Secure Sockets Layer (SSL)

○ c. User-level security

○ d. Share-level security

Question 60

Which connectivity device resides at the Data Link layer of the OSI model and uses the MAC address of the packets it receives to direct network traffic?

○ a. Router

○ b. Bridge

○ c. Hub

○ d. Gateway

Question 61

You administer a server-based network of 20 computers. All servers are located in a small utility room. Lately, network performance has become erratic, and the servers are intermittently failing. You go into the utility room and observe the room temperature to be 60 degrees Fahrenheit, and the humidity level is 99 percent. What observations can you make about the room conditions these servers are in?

○ a. These conditions are suitable for computers.

○ b. These conditions are not suitable for computers. The room is too cold.

○ c. These conditions are not suitable for computers. The humidity is too low.

○ d. These conditions are not suitable for computers. The humidity is too high.

Question 62

A TCP/IP network requires planning to be implemented correctly. TCP/IP provides a number of utilities to assist administrators with this task. An important TCP/IP utility is DHCP. Which of the following circumstances describes a good example of the use of a DHCP server?

○ a. Use DHCP when you need to provide name resolution on the local network.

○ b. Use DHCP when you need to provide name resolution on the Internet.

○ c. Use DHCP when you need to automatically assign IP configuration information to TCP/IP hosts.

○ d. Use DHCP when you need to find out the MAC address of all TCP/IP hosts on a network.

Question 63

Small Computer System Interface (SCSI) is a parallel interface standard for attaching peripheral devices to a computer. Which of the following connectors are supported by SCSI?

- ○ a. SCSI supports the use of Centronics 50 connectors.
- ○ b. SCSI supports the use of Centronics 68 HP connectors.
- ○ c. SCSI supports the use of DB-25 connectors.
- ○ d. All of the above.

Question 64

Which of the following are examples of peripherals?

- ○ a. Printer
- ○ b. Display monitor
- ○ c. Scanner
- ○ d. All of the above

Question 65

You need to extend of a 130-meter length of Thinnet coaxial cable. You decide to use a patch cable without a repeater and manually splice the cables together. How long can the length of the patch cable be if you are to remain within specification?

- ○ a. 185 meters
- ○ b. 40 meters
- ○ c. 45 meters
- ○ d. 55 meters

Question 66

Performing regular tape backups are an important part of data protection. Which of the following backup methods will reset or clear the archive bit of files?

- ○ a. Incremental and differential
- ○ b. Differential and full backup
- ○ c. Full backup and incremental
- ○ d. Incremental, differential, and full backup

Question 67

You need to expand your 10BaseT network. You are deciding between using a hub or a switch for this upgrade. Which of the following best describes the difference between a hub and a switch? [Choose the two best answers]

- ❑ a. A hub passes packets out of all ports; a switch provides for full-bandwidth utilization by passing packets only to the destination port.
- ❑ b. A switch passes packets out of all ports; a hub provides for full-bandwidth utilization by passing packets only to the destination port.
- ❑ c. A hub resides at the Data Link layer of the OSI model.
- ❑ d. A switch resides at the Data Link layer of the OSI model.

Question 68

Performing regular tape backups are an important part of data protection. Common backup methods rely on the use of an "archive bit." Which of the following statements best describes an "archive bit?"

- ○ a. An archive bit is the attribute of a file used to determine its backup status.
- ○ b. An archive bit is the name of the tape device used in a tape backup.
- ○ c. An archive bit is the "oldest" bit in your computer.
- ○ d. An archive bit is not used by any backup method.

Question 69

You are configuring a newly purchased printer for use on your network. You connect the printer to your computer and share the printer using the share name "PRINT." Your computer's name on the network is "JETS." The users on your network will be using DOS-based programs when printing to this network printer. Which of the following is the best way to configure your client computers to connect to this network printer *and* to be able to print to it using their DOS-based programs?

- ○ a. Connect to the printer with the UNC \\JETS\PRINT and capture a virtual port like LPT3 so DOS programs can print to it.

- ○ b. Connect to the printer with the UNC \\JETS\PRINT and do nothing more.

- ○ c. Connect to the printer with the UNC \\PRINT\JETS and capture a virtual port like LPT3 so DOS programs can print to it.

- ○ d. Connect to the printer with the UNC \\PRINT\JETS and do nothing more.

Question 70

You are working as an assistant in the management information system (MIS) department for your company. The network administrator needs you to perform an upgrade of the operating system on one of the network's NT Servers. Which of the following will you need to perform this operation?

- ○ a. You only need a valid user account on the server.

- ○ b. You need a valid group account on the server.

- ○ c. You only need administrative rights, not a valid user account.

- ○ d. You need a valid user account on the server that has been assigned administrative rights.

Question 71

When using a modem to connect to a remote network, a dial-up protocol is required. Which dial-up protocols can be used when using a modem to make a remote connection to the Internet?

○ a. PPP, not SLIP

○ b. SLIP, not PPP

○ c. Both PPP and SLIP

○ d. Neither SLIP nor PPP can be used as dial-up protocols

Question 72

You need to implement a tape backup strategy for your NT Server. This NT server contains a directory called "client data" that is used by all of your users to store their important files. Which of the following items should you include in your daily tape backup if you are to have an effective tape-backup strategy?

○ a. The "client data" directory

○ b. User accounts/groups/profile/policy information

○ c. NT server systems files and the Registry of the server

○ d. All of the above

Question 73

An important part of a network administrator's responsibilities is to assign rights to users on a network. What is the purpose of assigning rights to users on a network?

○ a. Rights are the permissions given to users to access network resources.

○ b. Rights are used to preserve a user's personal settings, such as a screen saver and shortcuts.

○ c. Rights are used to execute a series of commands when a user logs into a server.

○ d. Rights are only used when profiles are not in place.

Question 74

You want to implement tighter security on your network. One of your objectives is to install antivirus software. Which of the following best describes antivirus software?

○ a. Antivirus software can only be installed on a computer that has been infected with a virus.

○ b. Antivirus software is used to restore a formatted hard disk back to a normal state.

○ c. Antivirus software can only protect server computers from viruses.

○ d. Antivirus software is used to search a disk for the presence of a known virus and remove it.

Question 75

You have two and only two computers that need to be networked together. The computers each have a 10BaseT network adapter card installed. Which of the following is true about the use of a crossover cable when connecting these two computers together?

○ a. A hub is required to connect two 10BaseT computers together. A crossover cable will not work without a hub.

○ b. At least six crossover cables and a hub are required to connect two 10BaseT computers together.

○ c. A crossover cable can be used to connect two 10BaseT computers together without the use of a hub.

○ d. None of the above.

Network+
Answer Key #1

2

1. a	16. a	31. c	46. c	61. d
2. b	17. d	32. c	47. b	62. c
3. a	18. a, c	33. d	48. a	63. d
4. b, c, d	19. b	34. c	49. c	64. d
5. b	20. d	35. b	50. d	65. d
6. c	21. a, c	36. a	51. d	66. c
7. a, d	22. d	37. a	52. c	67. a, d
8. c	23. a	38. b	53. c	68. a
9. b	24. b	39. c	54. c	69. a
10. a	25. a	40. c	55. a, b, c	70. d
11. a, b, d	26. b	41. d	56. a	71. c
12. a	27. a	42. d	57. a, c	72. d
13. b	28. a	43. d	58. c	73. a
14. c	29. c	44. a	59. b	74. d
15. a	30. c	45. a	60. b	75. c

Question 1

Answer a is correct. A bus topology is configured by connecting nodes together with a continuous line of cable that is terminated at both ends. The cable used in a bus topology must be continuous and terminated at both ends, or the entire network will fail. Bus networks support the use of Thinnet coaxial cable, categorized as RG-58 cable. When using RG58 Thinnet coaxial cable in a bus network, the cable attaches to the network card with a T-connector. Both ends of a bus network are terminated using a 50-ohm resistor, known as a "terminator." A terminator is used in a bus network to absorb a signal and prevent it from remaining on the cable. When using Thicknet coaxial cable in a bus network, the Thinnet is tapped with a drop cable (vampire tap) and connects to the network card with a DEC-Intel-Xerox (DIX) or Attachment Unit Interface (AUI) connector. In a star topology, computers connect directly to a hub, and the hub handles termination. In a ring topology, computers are connected in a single circle, and each computer boosts the signal around the network. A mesh topology features multiple links that can provide alternate routes to a host in the event of a single line failure.

For more information, see Chapter 2 of *Network+ Exam Cram*.

Question 2

Answer b is correct. Fault tolerance refers to the ability of a system to recover from a failure. Standards for implementing fault tolerance on hard disks are defined by redundant arrays of independent disks (RAID). A mirror set, defined as RAID level 1, consists of two disks: a primary and a mirror. When data is written to the primary member of a mirror set, it also is written to the mirrored copy, providing fault tolerance. If the primary member of a mirror set fails, the mirrored disk can replace it. A volume set is created by combining 2 to 32 areas of free disk space into one logical drive. A stripe set without parity, defined by RAID level 0, is created by combining the free disk space of 2 to 32 disks into a single logical drive, where data is written evenly across all members of the set. Stripe sets without parity and volume sets do not provide fault tolerance, meaning that if a single disk in a volume set or stripe set without parity fails, all data will be lost.

For more information, see Chapter 5 of *Network+ Exam Cram*.

Question 3

Answer a is correct. Windows 95, 98, NT Workstation, and NT Server can all access file and printer resources on NetWare servers. Both Novell and Microsoft have software that can be added to an operating system to do this. This software is referred to as "client software" or a "redirector." The key to interoperability in a network that contains different computers is the use of the appropriate redirector. Novell NetWare's redirector is called Client32. Windows 9X's is called Client for NetWare Networks, and NT's is called Client and Gateway Services for NetWare.

For more information, see Chapter 3 of *Network+ Exam Cram.*

Question 4

Answers b, c, and d are correct. NetBEUI is a small, fast, nonroutable protocol used in Microsoft networking. All other protocols listed here are routable, meaning that their packets can pass through a router and can, therefore, be used in a wide area network (WAN). The fact that NetBEUI is not routable limits its use to a local area network (LAN). Novell NetWare networks use Internetwork Packet Exchange/Sequenced Packet Exchange (IPX/SPX) as the communication protocol. NWlink is Windows NT's implementation of the IPX/SPX protocol. TCP/IP is the protocol used on the Internet and is supported by all Microsoft networks and Novell NetWare 5.

For more information, see Chapter 4 of *Network+ Exam Cram.*

Question 5

Answer b is correct. Fault tolerance is the ability to recover from a failure. A standard created for implementing fault-tolerant strategies on hard disks is known as RAID. Although fault tolerance does provide for redundancy, it should *never* be used as a replacement for tape backup. Tape backups should be done regularly, in addition to a fault tolerance disk strategy, and an extra copy of recent tape backups should be kept in a remote location in the event of physical damage to the premises.

For more information, see Chapter 5 of *Network+ Exam Cram.*

Question 6

Answer c is correct. 10BaseT networks support the use of twisted-pair cable. Although 10BaseT supports categories 3, 4, and 5 twisted-pair, only category 5 supports transmission speeds up to 100Mbps. Categories 3 (10Mbps) and 4 (16Mbps) are older implementations of twisted-pair. Twisted-pair is relatively inexpensive. Fiber optic cable is a very fast media that is impervious to interference, but it is very costly to implement. A common reason for beginning a basic network with category 5 twisted-pair is the ability to upgrade to the 100BaseT standard without rewiring. If Paul's dental company wanted to upgrade their network to 100MB, only the network cards and hubs would have to be replaced.

For more information, see Chapter 2 of *Network+ Exam Cram*.

Question 7

Answers a and d are correct. The 10BaseT is a standard defined by Ethernet (802.3). 10BaseT uses twisted-pair cable in a star/bus topology and transmits at 10Mbps. Token ring is defined by the 802.5 standard. The Ethernet standard for 100Mbps with twisted-pair is 100BaseT.

For more information, see Chapter 2 of *Network+ Exam Cram*.

Question 8

Answer c is correct. A LAN is a term used to describe computers connected together in a single location. A WAN refers to the connection made between two LANs. For example, when a company in New York decides to connect the computers in their office together, they form a LAN. When they decide to connect their New York network to the network of another company in Florida, they are now a WAN. A WAN and a LAN are implemented independently of the operating systems installed on the computers in a network. Therefore, the fact that a network contains Microsoft and/or Novell NetWare's computers has no bearing on the network being a LAN or a WAN.

For more information, see Chapter 2 of *Network+ Exam Cram*.

Question 9

Answer b is correct. A router is the most common connectivity device used to connect two LANs together to form a WAN. A router looks similar to a hub, but unlike a hub, it can "route" network traffic, identify packets by network address, and filter out unnecessary packets. A hub and a repeater are commonly used to connect computers together in a LAN. Token ring is a network topology that features the use of an MAU to connect computers together and is not used in an Ethernet 10BaseT network.

For more information, see Chapter 2 of *Network+ Exam Cram*.

Question 10

Answer a is correct. Full-duplex transmission allows data to travel in two directions simultaneously. When you are talking on a telephone, you are utilizing full-duplex transmission (both parties can speak at one time). Half-duplex transmission only allows data to travel in one direction at a time. When you use a walkie-talkie, you are utilizing half-duplex transmission (only one party can speak at one time). Full- and half-duplex are not specific to WANs or LANs.

For more information, see Chapter 6 of *Network+ Exam Cram*.

Question 11

Answers a, b, and d are correct. Microsoft's Windows NT, Novell's NetWare, and OS/2 are all network operating systems; DOS is not considered a network operating system. Novell NetWare is a popular network operating system that uses NetWare Directory Service (NDS). NDS is an object-oriented database that organizes network resources into a tree-like structure. From this NDS tree, users can access the resources on a NetWare network. NDS is based on a standard known as X.500, a standard developed by the Open Systems Interconnection (OSI) for file and directory services in networking. Windows 95, NT Server, and NT Workstation are all Microsoft operating systems. Microsoft's NT Server is a popular network operating system that utilizes the concept of a "domain" to organize a network. A domain is a logical grouping of computers with centralized resources and security. The OS/2 is an IBM network operating system that can run DOS and Windows programs.

For more information, see Chapter 3 of *Network+ Exam Cram*.

Question 12

Answer a is correct. There are two common security models a network administrator can employ to control users' access to network resources: share-level security and user-level security. When using share-level security, passwords are assigned to "resources." An example of share-level security is sharing a printer and assigning a password to that printer. When users need to connect to the printer, they will have to enter the password set on the printer to access it. The share-level security model is considered a less secure method than user-level security, because users are more likely to tell others the password to access a resource than they are to give away their own username and password. In user-level security, permissions are assigned to "users." An example of user-level security is sharing a printer and assigning permissions to users to access this resource. For users to access this printer, their user account must have permission to access it. Remember: Share-level security assigns passwords to resources (printers, files, programs, and so on). User-level security assigns permissions to users. Answer d does not exist.

For more information, see Chapter 12 of *Network+ Exam Cram*.

Question 13

Answer b is correct. When NT Server is installed, it creates an administrator account with the username Administrator. This account has full privileges on the NT Server and is the primary account used by a network administrator when managing users and resources in an NT network. "Admin" is the account created by Novell NetWare during installation. "Supervisor" and "Manager" are not user accounts created by NT Server.

For more information, see Chapter 3 of *Network+ Exam Cram*.

Question 14

Answer c is correct. A Token Ring network is a proprietary IBM topology. In a token ring topology, all computers are connected to an MAU. Inside this MAU is a logical "ring" that contains a "token" used by computers to transmit data. A token ring topology uses token passing as an access method and provides equal access for all computers through the use of a "token." This token travels around the ring, roughly at the speed of light, and each computer acts as a repeater for it. To send data, a computer accesses the token and places data in it. Because only one token is on the cable at all times, there cannot be any collisions of packets on the cable. The Ethernet standard for bus and star topologies utilizes an access method known as Carrier Sense Multiple Access/ Collision Detection (CSMA/CD). When using CSMA/CD, computers must first check to see if the cable is free before sending data, and only one computer at a time can place data on the cable. For this reason, CSMA/CD is considered a "contention" method of access, meaning that computers must compete with one another for access to the network. If two computers sense the cable is free at the same time, they will both place data on the cable simultaneously, and a collision will occur. In the event of a collision with CSMA/CD, packets are retransmitted.

For more information, see Chapter 2 of *Network+ Exam Cram*.

Question 15

Answer a is correct. An interrupt request (IRQ) line is a "line" of communication that a hardware device uses to communicate with a processor. All devices in a computer require a unique IRQ. (There are some exceptions to this rule, but stick with the rule on your exam). If Jenny kicked the plug out of the hub, the entire network would have gone down, because in a 10BaseT topology, the hub handles termination. If the cable fell out of Jenny's computer a week ago, she would have been unable to connect to the network yesterday, as stated in the question.

For more information, see Chapter 14 of *Network+ Exam Cram*.

Question 16

Answer a is correct. A hub is commonly used to connect computers in Ethernet 10BaseT, 10Base5, and 10Base2 networks. A hub can be used to connect networks that use dissimilar media (like Thinnet coaxial and twisted-pair), but a hub cannot make decisions on how to send network traffic. A hub simply passes traffic out all ports. An MAU is used to connect computers in IBM Token Ring networks. An MAU contains a logical "ring" that contains a token that travels around the network and is used by computers to send data.

For more information, see Chapter 2 of *Network+ Exam Cram*.

Question 17

Answer d is correct. The OSI model defines standards for networking based on a seven-layer model. All of the components used in networking (hubs, bridges, routers, cables, protocols, and so on) conform to various layers of the OSI model by "residing" at one or more of these seven layers. A bridge operates at the Data Link layer of the OSI model and manages network traffic by reading the media access control (MAC), or hardware address, of the packets it receives. The ability of a bridge to read the address of a packet enables it to make decisions on where to send packets. A bridge will not pass a local packet to other segments, reducing network traffic and improving performance. A MAC address, sometimes referred to as the hardware or physical address, is the address permanently attached to a network adapter card by the manufacturer. This process is referred to as "burning" the address onto the card. The reason a bridge can read MAC addresses is because it "resides" on the same layer of the OSI model as the network card driver (the MAC sublayer of the Data Link layer).

For more information, see Chapter 8 of *Network+ Exam Cram*.

Question 18

Answers a and c are correct. The OSI model defines standards for networking based on a seven-layer model. All of the components used in networking (hubs, bridges, routers, cables, protocols, and so on) conform to various layers of the OSI model by "residing" at one or more of these seven layers. Project 802 modified the Data Link layer of the OSI model by dividing it into two sublayers: Logical Link Control (LLC) and MAC. Standards for Ethernet (CSMA/CD) networks are defined in 802.3. The CSMA/CD refers to the type of access method used by Ethernet 802.3 networks. The LLC as specified in 802.2 defines the use of service access points (SAPs) used to transfer information over a network. Standards for token ring networks are defined by 802.5 specifications.

For more information, see Chapter 8 of *Network+ Exam Cram*.

Question 19

Answer b is correct. The OSI model defines standards for networking based on a seven-layer model. All of the components used in networking (hubs, bridges, routers, cables, protocols, and so on) conform to various layers of the OSI model by "residing" at one or more of these seven layers. A router operates at the network layer of the OSI model and manages network traffic by reading the network, or IP address, of the packets it receives. The reason a router can read network or IP addresses is because it resides at the same layer of the OSI model as network protocols, like IP (part of the TCP/IP protocol suite). A brouter combines the features of a bridge and a router and operates at the network and Data Link layer of the OSI model. A brouter functions like a router with network layer protocols and can also act as a bridge for nonroutable protocols. Examples of nonroutable protocols are NetBEUI (a small, fast nonroutable protocol used in Microsoft networks) and Local Area Transport (LAT) from Digital Corp. Nonroutable protocols are only suitable for use in a LAN.

For more information, see Chapter 8 of *Network+ Exam Cram*.

Question 20

Answer d is correct. The OSI model defines standards for networking based on a seven-layer model. All of the components used in networking (hubs, bridges, routers, cables, protocols, and so on) conform to various layers of the OSI model by "residing" at one or more of these seven layers. A brouter combines the features of a bridge and operates at the network and Data Link layer of the OSI model. A brouter functions like a router with network layer protocols and can also act as a bridge for nonroutable protocols. Examples of nonroutable protocols are NetBEUI (a small, fast nonroutable protocol used in Microsoft networks), and LAT. Examples of network layer protocols are IP (part of the TCP/IP protocol suite, used by Unix, Microsoft, Novell Netware5, and the Internet), IPX (part of the IPX/SPX protocol suite, used by Novell NetWare), and NWLink (Microsoft's NT implementation of the IPX/SPX protocol).

For more information, see Chapter 8 of *Network+ Exam Cram.*

Question 21

Answers a and c are correct. A protocol is the "language" used by computers to communicate. In this example, routers are used to facilitate the connection, therefore, only routable protocols can be used. A routable protocol is one that resides at the network layer of the OSI model, and because of that, it can only recognize protocols that "reside" at that layer. Examples of network layer protocols are IP (part of the TCP/IP protocol suite used by Unix, Microsoft, Novell NetWare5, and the Internet), IPX (part of the IPX/SPX protocol suite used by Novell NetWare), and NWLink (Microsoft's NT implementation of the IPX/SPX protocol). Examples of nonroutable protocols are NetBEUI (a small, fast nonroutable protocol used in Microsoft networks) and LAT.

For more information, see Chapter 4 of *Network+ Exam Cram.*

Question 22

Answer d is correct. A mesh topology features multiple links that can provide alternate routes to a host in the event of a single-line failure. Because of these multiple links, the cost of implementing a mesh topology is greater than any other networking topology. A bus topology is the least expensive to implement because no hubs are required. The star (hub) and ring topologies are more expensive to implement than a bus because they both require connectivity devices in addition to cabling, but cost less than a mesh topology to implement.

For more information, see Chapter 2 of *Network+ Exam Cram.*

Question 23

Answer a is correct. Users of this network will require a unique IP address and a subnet mask. The TCP/IP protocol is a popular communication protocol used on the Internet and is supported in Microsoft, Unix, and NetWare 5 networks. The TCP/IP is a configurable protocol, and all computers wishing to utilize it must have the correct settings. All computers using TCP/IP must have a "unique" IP address and a subnet mask. The only time a default gateway is required is when communicating in a WAN. An IP address identifies a TCP/IP host on the network, and it contains two important elements: a network ID and a host ID. The network ID of an IP address identifies the network the host is on. (For example, all users in a single location are said to be on the same network and, therefore, will all have the same network ID in their IP address.) The host ID of an IP address identifies the host, or individual computer, on a TCP/IP network. It is the host ID portion of an IP address that is the unique part. Therefore, in a single TCP/IP network users will all have the "same" network ID and "different" (or unique) host IDs. Internet Protocol (IP) addressing is similar to the way houses are addressed on your block. Many people live on Maple Street (network ID), but only one person lives at 21 Maple Street (host ID). A subnet mask is a required parameter for all TCP/IP hosts. A subnet mask is used to distinguish the network ID in an IP address from the host ID. When a computer using TCP/IP needs to communicate with another TCP/IP host, it uses the subnet mask to determine if the destination computer is local (on my network) or remote (on a different network). If the subnet mask determines the destination host is local, it simply places the packet on the cable for delivery. If the subnet mask determines the host it needs to communicate with is remote (on another network), it sends it to its default gateway. A default gateway is only required to be configured on TCP/IP hosts that need to communicate outside of their local network or in a WAN. A default gateway is the IP address of the router used by the local network to connect to another network in the outside world, like the Internet or another branch office location. A default gateway is not a required parameter when using TCP/IP in a LAN, because all computers are on the same network and have the same network ID.

For more information, see Chapter 4 of *Network+ Exam Cram*.

Question 24

Answer b is correct. The proposed solution in this case meets the required result and only the first optional result. The required result is met by implementing Dynamic Host Configuration Protocol (DHCP) and is used to automatically configure TCP/IP configuration information on TCP/IP hosts. In large networks, it can be time-consuming to configure TCP/IP settings on each computer one at a time. In these instances, a DHCP server can be used to automatically provide the clients on the network with this information. The first optional result is met by implementing Domain Name System/Server

(DNS), which provides name resolution in a TCP/IP network by resolving a TCP/IP computer's IP address to its hostname. Address Resolution Protocol (ARP) is used to resolve, or map, a computer's IP address to its MAC address and therefore does not meet any of the required or optional results in this question. To meet the second optional result, Windows Internet Naming Service (WINS) could be used; Microsoft networks utilize it to provide name resolution of NetBIOS names to IP addresses. Microsoft networks utilize the NetBIOS application programming interface (API) when communicating and it is an API that provides the "base" that Microsoft networks are built on; WINS will resolve, or associate, a NetBIOS name to its IP address. There are many types of NetBIOS names used in Microsoft networking (computer name, user name, domain name, and so on). Novell NetWare supports the use of NetBIOS applications, which are programs that support the NetBIOS API.

For more information, see Chapter 4 of *Network+ Exam Cram*.

Question 25

Answer a is correct. WINS is used in Microsoft networks to provide name resolution of NetBIOS names to IP addresses. Microsoft networks utilize the NetBIOS API when communicating because it provides the "base" that Microsoft networks are built on. WINS will resolve, or associate, a NetBIOS name to its IP address. All computers running TCP/IP specify a hostname that is used to identify themselves on the network. When TCP/IP hosts communicate, their IP addresses are resolved, or associated, with their IP address. DNS performs this hostname-to-IP-address-name resolution. The main difference between the name resolution services of WINS and DNS are the type of names they resolve; WINS resolves NetBIOS names to IP addresses, while DNS resolves hostnames, or Fully Qualified Domain Names (FQDNs), to IP addresses. All Internet addresses (**www.anything.com**, or **g.net**, and so on) are examples of FQDNs. DHCP and ARP do not provide IP addresses to NetBIOS name resolution; DHCP is used to automatically configure TCP/IP configuration information on TCP/IP hosts; and ARP is used to resolve, or map, a computer's IP address to its MAC address.

For more information, see Chapter 4 of *Network+ Exam Cram*.

Question 26

Answer b is correct. All computers running TCP/IP specify a hostname that is used to identify themselves on the network. When TCP/IP hosts communicate, their IP addresses are resolved, or associated, with their IP address. This hostname-to-IP-address-name resolution can be performed by using either a HOSTS file or DNS. A HOSTS file is a local file on every TCP/IP computer that resolves hostnames or domain names to IP addresses. Entries in a HOSTS file must be made manually in the file on each user's computer. DNS and a HOSTS file perform the same type of name resolution: host or domain name-to-IP address. When HOSTS files are to be used, separate entries have to be made in every user's HOSTS file on the network. In such a small network as the one in this example, it is acceptable to utilize HOSTS files for name resolution instead of the DNS. WINS is not an acceptable solution to this question. Although it provides names resolution, WINS resolves NetBIOS names to IP addresses, not hostnames. The Unix computers in this example are using hostnames. DHCP is used to automatically assign IP configuration information to clients, not to perform name resolution. An LMHOSTS file is a local file used for name resolution, but an LMHOSTS file resolve NetBIOS names to IP addresses, not hostname-to-IP-address-name resolution.

For more information, see Chapter 4 of *Network+ Exam Cram*.

Question 27

Answer a is correct. TCP and User Datagram Protocol (UDP) are part of the TCP/IP protocol suite. TCP is a connection-oriented protocol that provides guaranteed delivery of packets between hosts. TCP also ensures that packets will be delivered to the destination host in the same order they were sent. UDP is a connectionless protocol that does not guarantee delivery of packets; it's primarily used by TCP/IP utilities for broadcasting packets in a TCP/IP network.

For more information, see Chapter 4 of *Network+ Exam Cram*.

Question 28

Answer a is correct. Post Office Protocol (POP3) and Simple Mail Transfer Protocol (SMTP) are common protocols used with Internet email. POP3 is used to retrieve Internet mail from a mail server; SMTP is used to send outgoing Internet mail to a mail server. This example is a typical one used to configure clients for Internet email. Both SMTP and POP3 are part of the TCP/IP protocol suite. The key points to remember about these protocols are:

➤ You send mail using SMTP.

➤ You receive mail using POP3.

➤ Your POP3 server is your incoming mail server.

➤ Your SMTP server is your outgoing mail server.

For more information, see Chapter 4 of *Network+ Exam Cram.*

Question 29

Answer c is correct. Simple Network Management Protocol (SNMP) is commonly used to monitor computers in a TCP/IP network. This protocol can report on the traffic and on components of a TCP/IP network and can provide administrators with statistical data. It is implemented using agents and managers of which these agents are programs installed on TCP/IP computers in the network. With these agents in place, SNMP management software, installed on a TCP/IP computer, can be used to gather information from these agents on the status of the network. The information an SNMP manager collects from an SNMP agent is stored in a Management Information Base (MIB). POP3 is a protocol used to retrieve incoming Internet mail; TCP is a connection-oriented protocol that provides guaranteed delivery of packets. SMTP is a protocol used to send outgoing Internet mail.

For more information, see Chapter 4 of *Network+ Exam Cram.*

Question 30

Answer c is correct. SNMP is commonly used to monitor a TCP/IP network; it can report on the traffic and on components of a TCP/IP network, and it can provide administrators with statistical data. It is implemented using agents and managers; agents are programs installed on TCP/IP computers in the network, and with these agents in place, SNMP management software, installed on a TCP/IP computer, can be used to gather information from these agents on the status of the network. The information an SNMP manager collects from an SNMP agent is stored in an MIB. POP3 is a protocol used to retrieve incoming Internet mail. TCP is a connection-oriented protocol that provides guaranteed delivery of packets; SMTP is a protocol used to send outgoing Internet mail.

For more information, see Chapter 4 of *Network+ Exam Cram.*

Question 31

Answer c is correct. File Transfer Protocol (FTP) is used to transfer files between remote hosts on a TCP/IP network. It is commonly used on the Internet to upload and download files. SNMP is used to monitor a TCP/IP network, and it can report on the traffic and on components of that network and provide administrators with statistical data. POP3 is a protocol used to retrieve incoming Internet mail, whereas SMTP is a protocol used to send outgoing Internet mail.

For more information, see Chapter 4 of *Network+ Exam Cram.*

Question 32

Answer c is correct. Fault tolerance refers to the ability of a system to recover from a single hard disk failure, and standards for implementing fault tolerance are defined by RAID. A stripe set with parity, or RAID 5, is created by combining equal areas of free space on 3 to 32 disks to form one logical drive. Data is then written evenly across all members of the set, and the writing of data contains "parity" information that can be used to restore data in the event of a single-disk failure. If one member of a stripe set with parity fails, the failed member can be "regenerated" using the parity information that is stored on the remaining members of the set. The minimum number of disks required to implement a stripe set with parity is three. NT Server supports stripe sets with parity (RAID 5), as well as disk mirroring (RAID 1). The **DISKPERF—Y** command is used in NT to turn on disk counters for monitoring purposes and has nothing to do with fault tolerance. A stripe set with parity can be implemented across 1GB disks.

For more information, see Chapter 5 of *Network+ Exam Cram.*

Question 33

Answer d is correct. TCP/IP is an industry-standard, routable protocol that is widely supported, and all Microsoft operating systems support it (NT Server, NT Workstation, Windows 95/98, and so on). Unix also supports TCP/IP (TCP/IP was born in the Unix environment) as does Novell NetWare Version 5. It is also the protocol used on the Internet.

For more information, see Chapter 4 of *Network+ Exam Cram.*

Question 34

Answer c is correct. TCP/IP addresses are divided into three main classes: Class A, Class B, and Class C. The address range for each address class is as follows:

➤ **Class A** IP addresses that *begin* with numbers from 1 to 126.

➤ **Class B** IP addresses that *begin* with numbers from 128 to 191 (note that 127 is not used in IP addressing; it is reserved for localhost and is used for loopback diagnostic testing).

➤ **Class C** IP addresses that *begin* with numbers from 192 to 223.

When looking at any IP address, it is the number in the *first* octet that determines the address class of that address. For example, The 3.100.32.7 is a Class A address because it *begins* with 3, a number between 1 and 126. The 145.100.32.7 is a Class B address because it *begins* with 145, a number between 128 and 191. The 210.100.32.7 is a Class C address because it *begins* with 210, a number between 192 and 223.

For more information, see Chapter 4 of *Network+ Exam Cram*.

Question 35

Answer b is correct. All computers using TCP/IP must have a *unique* IP address, a subnet mask, and if used in a WAN, a default gateway. An IP address identifies a TCP/IP host on the network and contains two important elements: a network ID and a host ID. The network ID of an IP address identifies the network the host is on. (For example, all users in a single location are said to be on the same network and, therefore, will all have the same network ID in their IP address.) The host ID of an IP address identifies the host, or individual computer, on a TCP/IP network. It is the host ID portion of an IP address that is the unique part. Therefore, in a single TCP/IP network, users will all have the *same* network ID and *different* (or unique) host IDs. The subnet mask is used to "mask" the network portion of an IP address, with the number 255, so the IP can determine if the destination host is local or remote. A default subnet mask refers to the subnet mask that is used by a particular TCP/IP address class in a single subnet environment, like a LAN. Because each address class uses a different number of octets for the network ID and because the subnet mask "masks" the network portion of an IP address, the default subnet mask will be different for each class of IP addresses. The number 255 is the number reserved in TCP/IP for use by the default subnet mask, which will use 255s over the network portion of an IP address and 0s over the host portion of an IP address.

IP address Class A:

➤ Address range is from 1 to 126. For example, 2.45.65.8 is a Class A address. It begins with 2—a number *between* 1 and 126.

➤ Uses the first octet for the network ID, and the last 3 octets for the host ID. For example, the network ID of IP address 2.45.65.8 is 2, because it is a Class A address, and Class A uses the first octet for the network ID. The host ID is 45.65.8.

➤ Default subnet mask is 255.0.0.0 A default subnet mask uses 255 to mask the network portion of an IP address, and 0 to mask the host portion of an IP address.

IP address Class B:

➤ Address range is from 128 to 191. For example, 162.45.65.8 is a Class B address. It begins with 162—a number between 128 and 191.

➤ Uses the first two octets for the network ID and the last two octets for the host ID. For example, the network ID of IP address 162.45.65.8 is 162.45 because it is a Class B address, and Class B uses the first two octets for the network ID. The host ID is 65.8.

➤ Default subnet mask is 255.255.0.0. A default subnet mask uses 255 to mask the network portion of an IP address, and 0 to mask the host portion of an IP address

IP address Class C:

➤ Address range is from 192 to 223. For example, 202.85.65.8 is a Class C address. It begins with 202—a number between 192 and 223.

➤ Uses the first three octets for the network ID and the last octet for the host ID. For example, the network ID of IP address 202.85.65.8 is 202.85.65 because it is a Class C address, and Class C uses the first three octets for the network ID. The host ID is 8.

➤ Default subnet mask is 255.255.255.0. A default subnet mask uses 255 to mask the network portion of an IP address, and 0 to mask the host portion of an IP address.

For more information, see Chapter 4 of *Network+ Exam Cram.*

Question 36

Answer a is correct. The IP address in this question is a Class B address, and therefore uses a subnet mask of 255.255.0.0. All computers using TCP/IP must have a *unique* IP address, a subnet mask, and if used in a WAN, a default gateway. An IP address identifies a TCP/IP host on the network and contains two important elements: a network ID and a host ID. The network ID of an IP address identifies the network the host is on. The host ID of an IP address identifies the host, or individual computer, on a TCP/IP network. Therefore, in a single TCP/IP network, users will all have the *same* network ID and *differ-*

ent (or unique) host IDs. The subnet mask is used to "mask" the network portion of an IP address, with the number 255, so the IP can determine if the destination host is local or remote. A default subnet mask refers to the subnet mask that is used by a particular TCP/IP address class in a single subnet environment, like a LAN. Because each address class uses a different number of octets for the network ID and because the subnet mask "masks" the network portion of an IP address, the default subnet mask will be different for each class of IP addresses. The number 255 is the number reserved in TCP/IP for use by the default subnet mask. A default subnet mask will use 255s over the network portion of an IP address and 0s over the host portion of an IP address. See the explanation of Question 35 for more complete TCP/IP addressing information.

For more information, see Chapter 4 of *Network+ Exam Cram*.

Question 37

Answer a is correct. A port number is one of the items specified by TCP/IP hosts to establish a connection. Port numbers for common TCP/IP utilities are said to have well-known port numbers. A well-known port number is the port number that will be used when no port number is specifically designated. The most important port numbers to know are :

➤ **HTTP** Hypertext Transfer Protocol, the protocol used by the Web, uses port 80.

➤ **FTP** File Transfer Protocol, used to transfer files (upload/download), uses port 21.

➤ **SMTP** Simple Mail Transfer Protocol, used to send outgoing Internet mail, uses port 25.

➤ **POP3** Post Office Protocol, used to retrieve incoming Internet mail, uses port 110.

When using any of these well-known protocols, the port number does not need to be specified, so it is assumed the default will be used. Windows Sockets is an example of the use of a port number and is a "session" established between two TCP/IP computers. The "socket" created between hosts is used for reliable communication. To create a socket, hosts specify an IP address, the type of service (TCP or UDP), and a port number. If a different port number is to be used, other than the well-known number, it must be specifically designated, and it must be a number over 1024. (The number 1024 and numbers under it are used for well-known protocols.)

For more information, see Chapter 4 of *Network+ Exam Cram*.

Question 38

Answer b is correct. See the explanation of Question 37 for details.

For more information, see Chapter 4 of *Network+ Exam Cram*.

Question 39

Answer c is correct. A Token Ring is a proprietary IBM network topology that provides equal access for all computers through the use of a "token." This token travels around the ring roughly at the speed of light, and each computer acts as a repeater for it. To send data, a computer accesses the token and places data in it. The Ethernet standard for bus and star topologies utilizes the CSMA/CD access method. When using CSMA/CD, the computer must first check to see that the cable is free before sending, and only one computer at a time can place data on the cable. For this reason, CSMA/CD is considered a "contention" method of access, meaning that computers must compete with one another for access to the network.

For more information, see Chapter 2 of *Network+ Exam Cram*.

Question 40

Answer c is correct. An IP proxy, or proxy server, is ideal for providing security and increased performance to a local network accessing the Internet.

An IP proxy, or proxy server (they are the same thing), serves two main purposes:

➤ Firewall protection to protect users on the local network from the intrusion of the Internet.

➤ Improved Internet performance by increasing the speed that users on the local network retrieve Web pages.

An IP proxy can provide firewall security to protect users on the local network from the intrusion of the Internet. (A firewall is defined as any configuration, hardware or software, that protects users on a local network from the intrusion of the Internet.) When an IP proxy is used as a firewall, it typically will be a dedicated server that is configured with two network adapter cards. One network card will be used for an Internet connection, known as the external network adapter, and the other will be used for the connection to the local network, known as the internal network adapter. In this firewall configuration, the only computer connected to the Internet is the proxy server, through this dedicated external network card. For clients to access the Internet, they must configure their Web browsers to send all Internet requests to the IP proxy. When a client requests an Internet address, the request goes to the proxy server, and the proxy server retrieves the information from the Web site on behalf of the client. The proxy server "acts" like the client when retrieving this information, so the only IP address used in making all requests is the proxy server's external network adapter address. All internal IP addresses will not be seen by any Internet networks. For additional security, Proxy Server can be configured to deny access to Web sites or protocols for both incoming and outgoing requests.

Proxy Server also provides improved Internet performance. Because an IP proxy retrieves Web pages on behalf of all users in a local network, it places all these pages in its local cache (memory). This way, if a user requests an Internet address that was previously retrieved by a proxy server, the proxy server will give the user the page contained in its local cache. The process of providing users with cached Web pages is much faster than the standard means of requesting/retrieving the information from the Web site on the Internet.

A DHCP server is used to automatically assign IP addresses to clients in a TCP/IP network. POP3 is used to retrieve incoming Internet mail. A WINS server is used to provide name resolution of NetBIOS names to IP addresses.

For more information, see Chapter 7 of *Network+ Exam Cram*.

Question 41

Answer d is correct. DHCP is used to automatically configure TCP/IP configuration information on TCP/IP hosts. A DHCP server can provide clients with a unique IP address, a subnet mask, a default gateway, and many other TCP/IP parameters automatically. Examples of additional TCP/IP parameters that a DHCP can provide clients are the IP address of a WINS server and the IP address of a DNS server. In order for DHCP to assign unique IP addresses to hosts, it must be configured with a scope. A DHCP scope is the range of IP addresses it uses to distribute to hosts requesting an IP address. The configure a DHCP scope, two parameters must be specified: the "From" address and the "To" address. It is the addresses within this range, or scope, that a DHCP server will assign to clients.

For more information, see Chapter 4 of *Network+ Exam Cram*.

Question 42

Answer d is correct. A bus topology is known as a "passive" topology in which all computers "listen" for a signal and are not relied on to pass network traffic.

Therefore, as long as a bus topology maintains a continuos line of cable that is terminated at both ends, the network will still function even if a computer crashes or is turned off. Remember, a bus topology requires continuous links and termination to function properly and does not rely on computers being turned on to function.

For more information, see Chapter 2 of *Network+ Exam Cram.*

Question 43

Answer d is correct. See the explanation of Question 37 for details.

For more information, see Chapter 4 of *Network+ Exam Cram.*

Question 44

Answer a is correct. TCP/IP contains various command-line utilities used for troubleshooting/diagnosing a TCP/IP network. The key commands to know are **ARP, NBTSTAT, TRACERT**, and **NETSTAT**.

➤ **ARP** Address Resolution Protocol resolves, or associates, an IP address to a MAC address. A MAC address, also known as a hardware address, is the permanent address "burned" into every network adapter card by the manufacturer. The TCP/IP command **arp -a** will display the local computer's ARP cache, which is a list of all the IP addresses that have been resolved by ARP, along with the corresponding MAC address.

➤ **NETSTAT** A TCP/IP command-line utility used to display protocol statistics about the current TCP/IP connection. NETSTAT can be used to display information about the port number (80 for HTTP, 21 for FTP, and so on) and protocol (UDP, TCP) used in a given TCP/IP connection.

➤ **NBTSTAT** A TCP/IP command-line utility that displays the current TCP/IP NetBIOS name information. Microsoft networks commonly use NetBIOS names when communicating. To communicate using TCP/IP, NetBIOS names must be resolved or associated with their IP address. This name resolution can take place via WINS, broadcast, or LMHOSTS files. The **NBTSTAT** command can be used to display the NetBIOS names used by the local computer, **NBTSTAT –n**, as well as to provide a list of how NetBIOS name resolution is taking place, **NBTSTAT –r**, whether by WINS or broadcast.

➤ **TRACERT** A TCP/IP command used to trace a route to a remote host. TRACERT is used to determine the route a packet travels on the way to the destination computer. Typing "TRACERT" and the destination IP address will trace the path the packet travels to its destination.

For more information, see Chapter 4 of *Network+ Exam Cram*.

Question 45

Answer a is correct. All routers contain routing tables. The routing table in a router contains the information it uses to send, or "route," network traffic. A routing table can be either static or dynamic. With static routing, all information in the routing table must be entered manually. Dynamic routing, as the name implies, allows a router to automatically update its routing table. It does this by "talking" to other routers, checking various paths, counting distances between routes, and so on. Routing Information Protocol for Internet Protocol (RIP for IP) and Routing Information Protocol for Internetwork Packet Exchange (RIP for IPX) are some examples of the types of methods that can be used when employing dynamic routing. Automatic mid-distance vectoring and NY-to-FL link states do not exist.

For more information, see Chapter 8 of *Network+ Exam Cram*.

Question 46

Answer c is correct. See the explanation of Question 44 for details.

For more information, see Chapter 4 of *Network+ Exam Cram*.

Question 47

Answer b is correct. Although IPCONFIG and WINIPCFG are both used to display TCP/IP configuration information, NT Server and NT Workstation utilize IPCONFIG, not WINIPCFG. Windows 95 and Windows 98 support the **WINIPCFG** command to display TCP/IP configuration information. (Windows 98 actually supports both IPCONFIG and WINIPCFG). The IPCONFIG utility will display the IP address, subnet mask, and default gateway parameters. Typing "IPCONFIG/ALL" at a command prompt will display additional TCP/IP parameters, such as the IP address of the DNS, WINS, and DHCP servers being used by the client. WINIPCFG will display the IP address, subnet mask, and default gateway parameters, and also DNS, WINS, and DHCP information when clicking on the More Info button.

For more information, see Chapter 4 of *Network+ Exam Cram*.

Question 48

Answer a is correct. The IPX/SPX protocol is commonly used in Novell NetWare networks. IPX/SPX addresses are comprised of two elements: an external network address and an internal address. The external network address, also known as a network number, used in IPX/SPX identifies the network a computer is part of, similar to the network ID used by TCP/IP. For example, all users in a single location using IPX/SPX will all have the same external network address, because they are all on the same network. The external network address is specified by the system administrator. The internal address, also known as a node address, is used by IPX/SPX to uniquely identify an individual computer, similar to the host ID used in TCP/IP. The internal address must be unique to each computer and for this reason is usually the MAC address of the computer that is running IPX/SPX. (The MAC address is the hardware address that is "burned" on every network adapter card by the manufacturer.) The internal address is generated automatically by IPX/SPX when it is installed. A network ID and a subnet mask are TCP/IP parameters and are not used in IPX/SPX addressing.

For more information, see Chapter 4 of *Network+ Exam Cram*.

Question 49

Answer c is correct. The PING utility is a very useful tool when troubleshooting a TCP/IP network. PING is used to test for connectivity between hosts on a TCP/IP network. The syntax for the **PING** command is simple: Type "PING" and the IP address of the computer you want to connect to, then press Enter. PING will then attempt a connection to this host. If PING is successful, this verifies that the TCP/IP connection between these computers is valid. If PING is unsuccessful, this verifies that there is no communication between these hosts using TCP/IP. The **IPCONFIG** (NT Server and Workstation) and **WINIPCFG** (Windows 95) commands are used to display IP configuration information.

For more information, see Chapter 4 of *Network+ Exam Cram*.

Question 50

Answer d is correct. Telnet, or Telecommunications Network, is a terminal emulation program used in TCP/IP networks. Telnet allows users to connect their PC to a remote server. Once logged in, a Telnet user can enter commands through the Telnet program, and they will be executed the same as if they were entered directly on the server. PING is used to test for connectivity between hosts on a TCP/IP network. The IPCONFIG (NT Server and Workstation) command is used to display IP configuration information. TRACERT is a utility used to trace the route to a remote host.

For more information, see Chapter 4 of *Network+ Exam Cram*.

Question 51

Answer d is correct. The **NETSTAT** command was used in this example. NETSTAT is a TCP/IP command-line utility used to display protocol statistics about the current TCP/IP connection. NETSTAT can be used to display information about the port number (80 for HTTP, 21 for FTP, and so on) and protocol (UDP, TCP) used in a given TCP/IP connection. Notice it displays "active connections," and in the "Proto" column the protocol (TCP or UDP) is displayed. Also note in the Local Address column the port number used appears after the IP address. This output was produced using NETSTAT with the –n switch. See the explanation of Question 44 for further details.

For more information, see Chapter 4 of *Network+ Exam Cram*.

Question 52

Answer c is correct. Both Point-to-Point Protocol (PPP) and Serial Line Internet Protocol (SLIP) are used as dial-up protocols when using a modem to connect to a remote network or the Internet. PPP is a newer, more efficient dial-up protocol than SLIP. PPP automatically obtains configuration parameters with the remote server on connection. This simplifies the configurations required when making a remote connection; SLIP must be configured manually with these parameters. Another key difference between PPP and SLIP is the number of protocols supported. PPP supports IPX/SPX, AppleTalk, TCP/IP, and NetBEUI. SLIP only supports the use of the TCP/IP protocol.

For more information, see Chapter 6 of *Network+ Exam Cram*.

Question 53

Answer c is correct. In a token ring topology, all computers are connected to an MAU. Inside this MAU is a logical "ring" that contains a "token" used by computers to transmit data. A token ring topology uses token passing as an access method. With token passing, all computers act as repeaters and are counted on to "boost" the token around the network. Therefore, if one computer in a token ring network fails, it will miss its turn to boost the token, decreasing network performance. To return the network back to normal performance, the failed computer must be dropped from the ring by the MAU. To accomplish this, all other computers will start *beaconing*, or signaling, the MAU that they are still active. This allows the MAU to identify the failed computer and drop it from the ring. The bus, star, and mesh topologies are all known as passive topologies, meaning that computers are not relied on to boost a signal, so the failure of a single computer will not affect the network.

For more information, see Chapter 2 of *Network+ Exam Cram.*

Question 54

Answer c is correct. Point-to-Point Tunneling Protocol (PPTP) is used to create virtual private networks (VPN). A VPN is a private network that uses the Internet to make a connection. Users from each private network establish an Internet connection locally and use the network capabilities of the Internet to connect to each other. Because the Internet is a public network, connecting two private networks together in this manner does pose some security risks. To provide security for VPNs over the Internet, PPTP is used. With PPTP enabled, the only packets that will be allowed into members of the VPN are PPTP packets. Both PPP and SLIP are used as dial-up protocols when using a modem to connect to a remote network or the Internet. WINS is used to resolve NetBIOS names to IP addresses.

For more information, see Chapter 6 of *Network+ Exam Cram.*

Question 55

Answers a, b, and c are correct. In this example, all users will require a unique IP address, a subnet mask, and a default gateway. The TCP/IP protocol is a popular communication protocol used on the Internet and supported in Microsoft, Unix, and NetWare 5 networks. TCP/IP is a configurable protocol, and all computers wishing to utilize it must have the correct settings. All computers using TCP/IP must have a *unique* IP address and a subnet mask. The only time a default gateway is required is when communicating in a WAN. An IP address identifies a TCP/IP host on the network and contains two important elements: a network ID and a host ID. The network ID of an IP address identifies the network the host is on. (For example, all users in a single location are said to be on the same network and, therefore, will all have the same network ID in their IP address.) The host ID of an IP address identifies the host, or individual computer on a TCP/IP network. It is the host ID portion of an IP address that is the unique part. Therefore, in a single TCP/IP network, users will all have the *same* network ID and *different* (or unique) host IDs. IP addressing is similar to the way houses are addressed on your block. Many people live on Maple Street (network ID), but only one person lives at 21 Maple Street (host ID). A subnet mask is a required parameter for all TCP/IP hosts. A subnet mask is used to distinguish the network ID in an IP address from the host ID. When a computer using TCP/IP needs to communicate with another TCP/IP host, it uses the subnet mask to determine if the destination computer is local (on my network) or remote (on a different network). If the subnet mask determines the destination host is local, it simply places the packet on the cable for delivery. If the subnet mask determines the host it needs to communicate with is remote (on another network), it sends it to its default gateway. A default gateway is only required to be configured on TCP/IP hosts that need to communicate outside of their local network or in a WAN. A default gateway is the IP address of the router used by the local network to connect to another network in the outside world, like the Internet or another branch office location. A default gateway is not a required parameter when using TCP/IP in a LAN, because all computers are on the same network and have the same network ID.

For more information, see Chapter 4 of *Network+ Exam Cram*.

Question 56

Answer a is correct. Integrated Services Digital Network (ISDN) is a digital dial-up service that can send voice and data signals at 128Kbps (128,000 bits per second). ISDN uses two 64K channels, called "B" channels, when transmitting. ISDN uses a terminal adapter (TA) to connect to a computer in place of a modem. This is because the transmission is digital over ISDN and does not have to be "modulated," or converted, to analog as is the case with regular phone line. Public Switched Telephone Network (PSTN), also known as Plain Old Telephone Service (POTS), is the standard dial-up analog phone line used to send voice and data. PSTN can transmit data up to 28,800Bps. (The new 56Kbps standard achieves faster transmission speeds over 28.8Kbps by using a technique known as data compression.) PSTN uses a modem (modulate/demodulate) to connect to a computer. A modem converts, or modulates, a computer's digital signal to analog for transmission over PSTN, and the receiving computer's modem will demodulate that signal, or convert it, from analog to a digital signal.

For more information, see Chapter 6 of *Network+ Exam Cram*.

Question 57

Answers a and c are correct. There are two common security models a network administrator can employ to control users' access to network resources: share-level security and user-level security. When using share-level security, passwords are assigned to *resources*. An example of share-level security is sharing a printer and assigning a password to that printer. When users need to connect to the printer, they will have to enter the password set on the printer to access it. The share-level security model is considered a less secure method than user-level security because users are more likely to tell others the password to access a resource than they are to give away their own username and password. In user-level security, permissions are assigned to *users*. An example of user-level security is sharing a printer and assigning permissions to users to access this resource. In order for users to access this printer, their user account must have permission to access it. Remember: share-level security assigns passwords to *resources*, (printers, files, programs, and so on); user-level security assigns permissions to *users*.

For more information, see Chapter 7 of *Network+ Exam Cram*.

Question 58

Answer c is correct. Data encryption is the process of making data unreadable during transmission over network media. Encrypted data cannot be understandable to hackers who attempt to capture network traffic from a cable. When encryption is used, a "key" is required to decrypt the data into a readable form. Encryption is commonly used when transmitting sensitive information. An example of a data encryption method is Secure Sockets Layer (SSL). SSL can be used to provide data encryption between a Web browser and an Internet server and is frequently used when conducting financial transactions over the Internet, like transmitting your credit card information to a Web server to make a purchase. In this scenario, user-level and share-level security will not help if someone is "tapping" into your network cable and reading data.

For more information, see Chapter 7 of *Network+ Exam Cram*.

Question 59

Answer b is correct. Data encryption is the process of making data unreadable during transmission over network media. Encrypted data cannot be understandable to hackers who attempt to capture network traffic from a cable. When encryption is used, a "key" is required to decrypt the data into a readable form.

Encryption is commonly used when transmitting sensitive information. An example of a data encryption method is SSL. SSL can be used to provide data encryption between a Web browser and an Internet server and is frequently used when conducting financial transactions over the Internet, like transmitting your credit card information to a Web server to make a purchase. In this scenario, user-level and share-level security will not help if someone is "tapping" into your network cable and reading data. Data encryption is implemented separately than user-level or share-level security. Data Eletro Propagation (DEP) does not exist.

For more information, see Chapter 7 of *Network+ Exam Cram*.

Question 60

Answer b is correct. The OSI model defines standards for networking based on a seven-layer model. All of the components used in networking (hubs, bridges, routers, cables, protocols, and so on) conform to various layers of the OSI model by "residing" at one or more of these seven layers. A bridge operates at the Data Link layer of the OSI model and can be used in place of a hub to improve overall network performance. A bridge can read a MAC address; a MAC address, also referred to as the "hardware address," is the permanent address that is "burned" on every network card by the manufacturer. The ability to read MAC addresses allows a bridge to make decisions on where to send packets, making it a more efficient connectivity device than a hub. A bridge will not pass a local packet to other segments, reducing network traffic and improving performance. The reason a bridge can read MAC addresses is because they both "reside" on the same layer of the OSI model, the Data Link layer. A hub, which resides at the Physical layer of the OSI model, cannot read any packet information and therefore just passes the packets it receives out all ports. A router operates at the Network layer of the OSI model. Routers are the most common connectivity device used to connect two LANs together to form a WAN. A router manages network traffic by reading the "network" of the packets it receives. The reason a router can read network or IP addresses is because it resides at the same layer of the OSI model as network protocols, like IP (TCP/IP).

A gateway is commonly used as a "translator" to connect dissimilar networks. A gateway functions at the Application layer of the OSI model and can utilize all seven layers to perform packet translation.

For more information, see Chapter 8 of *Network+ Exam Cram*.

Question 61

Answer d is correct. Generally speaking, computers like temperature conditions similar to the ones people like. Room temperature should not be extreme, and the ideal temperature should be on the cool side. Humidity should be kept at approximately 50 to 70 percent. If humidity is too low, the instances of electrostatic discharge (ESD) will be increased because of the "dryness" of the particles in the air. An ESD shock can cause a computer to fail intermittently or cause more serious damage. High humidity produces excessive moisture in the air that could cause condensation to develop on the electrical components inside a computer and cause a short.

For more information, see Chapter 12 of *Network+ Exam Cram*.

Question 62

Answer c is correct. DHCP is used to automatically configure TCP/IP configuration information on TCP/IP hosts. All computers using TCP/IP must have a *unique* IP address, a subnet mask, and if used in a WAN, a default gateway. In large networks, it can be time-consuming to configure these settings on each computer one at a time. In these instances, a DHCP server can be used to automatically provide the clients on the network with this information. A DHCP server can provide clients with a unique IP address, a subnet mask, a default gateway, and many other TCP/IP parameters automatically. In order for DHCP to assign unique IP addresses to hosts, it must be configured with a scope. A DHCP scope is the "from " and "to" range of IP addresses assigned to hosts requesting an IP address. Name resolution services in TCP/IP are provided by WINS and DNS. ARP is used to resolve, or map, a computer's IP address to its MAC address. A computer's MAC address is the hardware address "burned" on the network card by the manufacturer.

For more information, see Chapter 4 of *Network+ Exam Cram*.

Question 63

Answer d is correct. Small Computer System Interface (SCSI) is a parallel interface standard for attaching peripheral devices to a computer. There are many variations of SCSI. In general, SCSI supports the use of Centronics 50, 68 HP, and DB-25 connectors when attaching an external SCSI device to a PC.

For more information, see Chapter 10 of *Network+ Exam Cram*.

Question 64

Answer d is correct. A peripheral is any external device that attaches to a computer. A printer, keyboard, mouse, external modem, monitor, and scanner are all examples of peripherals. The word "peripheral" means "surrounding, or around." These external devices are called peripherals because they "surround" a PC.

For more information, see Chapter 11 of *Network+ Exam Cram.*

Question 65

Answer d is correct. The maximum single-segment length of Thinnet coaxial cable is 185 meters (607 feet). To extend a length of Thinnet coaxial cable, a repeater must be used. A repeater is used to "boost" the signal back to its original strength so it can continue a longer distance. Patch cable is used when a length of coaxial cable is not long enough to reach a desired point. However, if patch cable is connected to a length of Thinnet without a repeater, it contributes to the total length of the cable and is not considered a separate segment.

For more information, see Chapter 2 of *Network+ Exam Cram.*

Question 66

Answer c is correct. A full backup and incremental backup will clear, or reset, the archive bit of files.

The attribute of a file used to determine its backup status is known as the archive bit. The archive bit attribute of a file can be one of two values: "set" or "cleared" (reset). When a full or incremental backup is performed, the backup program *clears*, or resets, the archive bit. When files that have been backed up are changed, the program that modifies the file will "set" the archive bit. The process of "setting" the archive bit of modified files allows the backup program to determine if a file has changed since the last time a backup was performed. There are three important backup methods to be aware of: differential, incremental, and full backup.

➤ **Differential** A differential backup will back up files that have their archive bit "set" but does not clear the archive bit. Performing daily backups get progressively slower each day. Restoring data from a differential backup only requires two tapes: the original full backup and the last differential backup

➤ **Incremental** An incremental backup will back up files that have their archive bit "set" and then clears the archive bit. Performing daily backups are faster than differential. Restoring data from an incremental backup requires many tapes: the original full backup tape and all incremental backups performed since the full backup.

➤ **Full backup** Backs up all files regardless of the archive bit attribute and clears the archive bit. Periodic full backups are recommended in addition to either incremental or differential backups.

For more information, see Chapter 5 of *Network+ Exam Cram*.

Question 67

Answers a and d are correct. A switch is a connectivity device that provides for full bandwidth utilization by passing packets only to the destination port. A hub will pass packets out of all ports. Switches can improve network performance considerably. The OSI model defines standards for networking based on a seven-layer model. All of the components used in networking (hubs, bridges, routers, cables, protocols, and so on) conform to various layers of the OSI model by "residing" at one or more of these seven layers. A switch resides at the Data Link layer of the OSI model and can read the MAC address of a packet. A hub resides at the Physical layer of the OSI model and cannot read any packet information and, therefore, cannot make any decisions on how to send network traffic.

For more information, see Chapter 8 of *Network+ Exam Cram*.

Question 68

Answer a is correct. See the explanation of Question 66 for details.

For more information, see Chapter 5 of *Network+ Exam Cram*.

Question 69

Answer a is correct. A Universal Naming Convention (UNC) name is a standard for connecting to shared resources on a network. A UNC is comprised of two key elements: a *computer name* and a *share name*. All computers in a network must have a computer name to identify themselves. When sharing a resource (a printer, files, CD-ROM, and so on), the shared resource must also be assigned a name, known as a share name. Connecting to a shared resource using a UNC simply involves specifying these two parameters, in the format

"\\computer name\share name". For example, to connect to a printer that has been assigned the share name PRINTER1 on the computer named USER1, the UNC to connect to this resource would be \\USER1\PRINTER1. DOS is an older operating system that does not understand the use of UNCs to connect to network resources. For this reason, DOS-based programs need to "capture" a virtual drive or port to a UNC when connecting to a network resource. The mapping of a virtual drive or port is done to "fool" DOS into thinking the resource it is connecting to is attached to the local computer. For example, in order for a DOS-based program to connect to a network printer with the share name PRINTER1 on a computer named USER1, the UNC \\USER1\PRINTER1 will have to be "captured" to a virtual port, like LPT3. In this example, LPT3 is considered a "virtual" port because it doesn't physically exist on the local computer. However, DOS will think there is an LPT3 port on the local computer and will now be able to print to this network resource.

For more information, see Chapter 12 of *Network+ Exam Cram*.

Question 70

Answer d is correct. Rights are the permissions given to users to access network resources and perform certain network tasks. To upgrade an NT Server operating system, as well as perform other administrative tasks, you must have administrative rights assigned to your user account. Rights can be assigned to either a user account or a group. In this question, the administrator could give your account administrative rights by simply adding your user account to the administrators group on the NT Server. Groups are primarily used by a network administrator to simplify administration of the users in a network. An administrator can assign rights to groups, then simply add users to the group, and they will inherit all the rights given to that group. You cannot be given any rights on an NT Server computer unless you have a valid user account first.

For more information, see Chapter 3 of *Network+ Exam Cram*.

Question 71

Answer c is correct. Both PPP and SLIP are used as dial-up protocols when using a modem to connect to a remote network or the Internet. PPP is a newer, more efficient dial-up protocol than SLIP. PPP automatically obtains configuration parameters with the remote server on connection. This simplifies the configurations required when making a remote connection; SLIP must be configured manually with these parameters. Another key difference between PPP and SLIP is the number of communication protocols supported. PPP supports IPX/SPX, AppleTalk, TCP/IP, and NetBEUI. SLIP only supports the use of the TCP/IP protocol.

For more information, see Chapter 6 of *Network+ Exam Cram*.

Question 72

Answer d is correct. Tape backup is the most common form of offline data storage. A good rule for backup is to back up everything you cannot afford to lose. The common items of importance that should be a part of all backups are user account information, the operating system, and important data files.

For more information, see Chapter 5 of *Network+ Exam Cram*.

Question 73

Answer a is correct. Rights are the permissions given to users to access network resources and perform certain network tasks. Permissions can be assigned to user accounts or to groups. User profiles are used to preserve a user's personal settings, such as a screen saver and shortcuts. A login script is used to execute a series of commands when a user logs into a server. Rights to access resources are assigned independently of user profiles and can be used with or without them.

For more information, see Chapter 3 of *Network+ Exam Cram*.

Question 74

Answer d is correct. A virus is a program that is written to cause varying degrees of damage to the files of the computer it is installed on. A virus ends up on a hard disk without the user's knowledge by "hiding" inside another program or file that is being transferred onto the hard drive. An antivirus program is a program that contains a list of "known" viruses. When an antivirus program scans a disk for a virus, it compares its "known virus" list to the programs on a disk. If an antivirus program finds a match between a program on a disk and its database, it detects the virus and attempts to remove it from the computer. New viruses are created frequently, so it is important to keep an antivirus program updated with a current list of known viruses. Antivirus software should be installed on all client and server computers and should be updated frequently. The best time to install antivirus programs is before a computer is infected, not after. The **FDISK** command is used to format a hard disk.

For more information, see Chapter 13 of *Network+ Exam Cram*.

Question 75

Answer c is correct. A crossover cable is used to connect two (and only two) 10BaseT computers together without the use of a hub. A crossover cable is made from twisted-pair cable with RJ-45 connectors at each end. The send and receive wires are "crossed" to allow the cable to act as a hub. A crossover cable can only be used to connect two computers, and both computers must have a 10BaseT network adapter card.

For more information, see Chapter 13 of *Network+ Exam Cram.*

Network+
Practice Test #2

Question 1

As part of a new network security plan, you are required to install antivirus software on all computers in the network. How often should you consider upgrading this newly installed antivirus software?

○ a. Upgrade the software when the manufacturer announces a new version number at least two numbers higher than your current version.

○ b. Upgrade the software frequently as new virus programs are created every day.

○ c. There is no need to upgrade antivirus software. It is good forever right out of the box.

○ d. There is no need to upgrade antivirus software if you purchased the full version of the product.

Question 2

Your network consists of ten Microsoft Windows 95 computers and one Novell NetWare server. All of the Windows 95 computers need to access file and printer resources on the NetWare server. Which of the following redirectors could you install on the Windows 95 computers to allow them to access the resources of this Novell NetWare server?

- ○ a. Install the Microsoft redirector on all the Windows 95 computers (Client for NetWare Networks).
- ○ b. Install the Novell NetWare redirector on all the Windows 95 computers (Client32).
- ○ c. Either a or b.
- ○ d. None of the above.

Question 3

Which of the following backup strategies will clear (reset) the archive bit of files?

- ○ a. Both incremental and differential
- ○ b. Both differential and full backup
- ○ c. Full backup, incremental, and differential
- ○ d. Both full backup and incremental

Question 4

Which of the following is the correct UNC command to access a network printer with the share name PRINTER1 that is located on a computer named USER1?

- ○ a. \\PRINTER1\USER1
- ○ b. \\USER1\PRINTER1
- ○ c. \PRINTER1\\USER1
- ○ d. \USER1\\PRINTER1

Question 5

What additional configuration do DOS-based programs require in order for them to connect to a network resource using a UNC?

- ○ a. In addition to a UNC, DOS-based programs require an upgrade to Windows 98 to connect to network resources.

- ○ b. In addition to a UNC, DOS-based programs require an increase in expanded memory to connect to network resources.

- ○ c. DOS-based programs require a virtual port to be "captured" to a UNC. This "fools" DOS into thinking the resource is on the local computer.

- ○ d. DOS-based programs cannot use remote network resources.

Question 6

You have just transferred from the Los Angeles location of your company to its New York office. You will be working as the network administrator in New York. You already have a user account on the server in New York that you used when you accessed the network from Los Angeles. However, this account did not give you full administrative privileges. What changes to your user account must you make to upgrade your privileges to the administrative level?

- ○ a. You need to change your password.

- ○ b. You need to have the rights assigned to your user account changed to administrative rights.

- ○ c   You need to rename your user account to "master" and keep the same password.

- ○ d. You need to rename your user account to "master" and change your password.

Question 7

Which of the following best describes a backbone?

- ○ a. A backbone is only used for backup purposes in a network.
- ○ b. A backbone features a single, high-speed cable run across servers in a network.
- ○ c. A backbone refers to the type of token ring wiring that is being used (ring-in to ring-out).
- ○ d. A backbone is only used in networks that rely on the demand priority access method.

Question 8

Vera, a user on your network, is experiencing problems with her computer. Her computer works fine the first few hours of the day, but around lunchtime it starts to fail intermittently. You inspect her work area and notice a space heater on the floor next to the CPU. The thermostat on the heater reads 85 degrees Fahrenheit. What observations can you make about the environment Vera's computer is in?

- ○ a. The space heater is probably causing the problem. It is too hot for the computer to function properly.
- ○ b. The space heater has nothing to do with the problem. You'll have to troubleshoot the PC first.
- ○ c. The space heater is probably improving the CPU's performance by warming it up. The problem must exist elsewhere.
- ○ d. The space heater is probably causing the problem because it is increasing the humidity level around the computer.

Question 9

Which of the following statements is true of external SCSI connectors?

- ○ a. SCSI supports the use of Centronics 50 connectors and Centronics 68 HP connectors, but not DB-25 connectors.
- ○ b. SCSI supports the use of Centronics 50 connectors and DB-25 connectors, but not Centronics 68 HP connectors.
- ○ c. SCSI supports the use of DB-25 connectors and Centronics 68 HP connectors, but not Centronics 50 connectors.
- ○ d. SCSI supports the use of Centronics 50, 68 HP, and DB-25 connectors.

Question 10

You are the network administrator for your company. The network consists of 25 computers wired in a 10Base2 topology. You need to add another computer to the network. The computer is located 200 meters away from the nearest hub. You run a single length of Thinnet coaxial cable to a distance of 185 meters. To make up for the remaining 15 meters, you use a 20-meter length of patch cable. You splice the patch cable to the 185 meter length cable by cutting both cable ends and twisting the copper cores together and complete the connection. Which of the following statements is true about the connection you just made?

- ○ a. The network will function properly; you did not exceed the single-segment length of Thinnet coaxial.

- ○ b. The network will not function properly, because to extend the maximum single-segment length of Thinnet coaxial cable, a repeater must be used to join the segments. A patch cable used in this manner simply contributes to the overall single cable length.

- ○ c. The network will function properly as long as the copper wires from each cable are touching each other.

- ○ d. Both a and c.

Question 11

You are the newly hired network administrator for a bank. The company wants to increase security and asks you to implement a new password scheme for all of your users. This new password scheme must be very secure. Which of the following password schemes provides the most security?

- ○ a. Require users to make their passwords at least four characters long.

- ○ b. Require users to make their passwords contain letters, numbers, and special characters.

- ○ c. Require users to make their passwords contain upper- and lowercase letters and numbers.

- ○ d. Require users to make their passwords contain upper- and lowercase letters, numbers, and special characters.

Question 12

You are the network administrator for your company. Users need access to a printer on the network. You share the printer and assign the password "swordfish" to the printer. When users need to access this printer, they are prompted to enter a password. All users must enter the password "swordfish" to access this printer. Based on this information, what security model are you using in your network?

- ○ a. Share-level security
- ○ b. User-level security
- ○ c. Semiuser-level security
- ○ d. Both a and c

Question 13

Which of the following statements are true of PPP and SLIP? [Choose the three best answers]

- ❑ a. Both PPP and SLIP can be used as dial-up protocols when using a modem to connect to the Internet.
- ❑ b. SLIP is used as a dial-up protocol to the internet; PPP is not.
- ❑ c. PPP supports the use of more communication protocols than SLIP.
- ❑ d. PPP is a newer, more efficient dial-up protocol than SLIP.

Question 14

What protocol of the TCP/IP protocol suite is used to provide for secure communications for Virtual Private Networks (VPNs)?

- ○ a. PPTP
- ○ b. SLIP
- ○ c. PPP
- ○ d. WINS

Question 15

The users on your network need to access the Internet. You are deciding on a connection method to use. You want a digital connection that is capable of transmission speeds of *more* than 56Kbps. You have the choice of either ISDN or POTS. Which of these can you choose to meet your requirement?

○ a. ISDN

○ b. PSTN

○ c. Both ISDN and POTS meet the requirement

○ d. Both ISDN and PSTN meet the requirement

Question 16

You are troubleshooting a computer on your network. The computer is using TCP/IP as the only protocol. You need to find out if this computer is using TCP or UDP when it connects to your server. What TCP/IP command-line utility can give you this information?

○ a. ARP

○ b. TRACERT

○ c. NBTSTAT

○ d. NETSTAT

Question 17

You are troubleshooting a computer on your network. The computer is using TCP/IP as the only protocol. You need information about how this computer is resolving NetBIOS names to IP addresses, either by WINS or by broadcast. What TCP/IP command-line utility can give you this information?

○ a. ARP

○ b. TRACERT

○ c. NBTSTAT

○ d. NETSTAT

Question 18

You are discussing the various data storage methods with your colleagues. Bill says that the most common form of offline data storage is a stripe set with parity. Carol disagrees and says that disk mirroring is. What can you interject into this conversation?

○ a. Tell them that they are both right, because a stripe set with parity and a mirror set are both forms of RAID.

○ b. Tell them that they are both wrong; the most common offline data storage method is tape backup.

○ c. Tell them that Bill is right, because only a stripe set with parity provides offline data storage.

○ d. Tell them they need to find other hobbies and that you are tired of always talking about computers.

Question 19

You are troubleshooting a Windows 95 computer on your network. The computer is using TCP/IP as the only protocol. You need to display the IP address, subnet mask, and default gateway parameters that this computer is using. You also need to know the IP address of the WINS and DNS servers that this computer is using. What TCP/IP command-line utility can give you this information?

○ a. WINIPCFG, then select the More Info button

○ b. IPCONFIG /ALL

○ c IPCONFIG

○ d. Both a and c

Question 20

You are troubleshooting a computer on your network. The computer is using TCP/IP as the only protocol. You need to verify that connectivity between this computer and your server is valid using TCP/IP. What TCP/IP command-line utility can give you this information?

○ a. PING

○ b. IPCONFIG

○ c. WINIPCFG

○ d. ARP

Question 21

You need to connect to a server on the Internet from your computer at home. What TCP/IP program could you use to do this?

- ○ a. Telnet
- ○ b. IPCONFIG
- ○ c. TRACERT
- ○ d. PING

Question 22

You are asked to look at the following that is displayed on the screen of a user's TCP/IP computer:

```
NetBIOS Names Resolution and Registration
      Statistics
--------------------------
Resolved by broadcast = 0
Resolved by name server = 3
Registered by broadcast = 0
Registered by name server = 8
```

What TCP/IP utility was used to produce this information?

- ○ a. ARP
- ○ b. TRACERT
- ○ c. NBTSTAT
- ○ d. NETSTAT

Question 23

You are configuring the settings for TCP/IP on your New York-based network. Users need to use TCP/IP to communicate with each other in the
local network and also to a branch office location in Florida. Your network
connects to the Florida location through a router in your office. What TCP/
IP parameters must you configure on each computer in this scenario?

○ a. All users require an IP address and a subnet mask only.

○ b. All users require an IP address, a subnet mask, and a default
      gateway.

○ c. All users require an IP address and a default gateway only.

○ d. No configuration is necessary; this is a wide area network,
      and TCP/IP only requires configuring in a local area network.

Question 24

What network topology is characterized by the use of a hub or hubs?

○ a. Bus

○ b. Star

○ c. Token ring

○ d. Token bus

Question 25

Which TCP/IP configuration parameter specifies the IP address of a router?

○ a. Subnet mask

○ b. Default gateway

○ c. IP address

○ d. This is not possible; TCP/IP cannot be used to connect to a
      router.

Question 26

You are the network administrator for a large law firm. Your network consists of 620 computers. You need to implement the TCP/IP protocol. Nancy, your assistant, insists it will take an entire weekend configuring TCP/IP manually on each computer, so you'd better get started right away. You tell Nancy to relax; you have a solution that will configure TCP/IP automatically on all client computers. What is your solution?

○ a. Use DHCP to configure TCP/IP information on all client computers.

○ b. Use WINS to configure TCP/IP information on all client computers.

○ c. Use DNS to configure TCP/IP information on all client computers.

○ d. Hire college apprentices to work over the weekend configuring TCP/IP manually on all computers.

Question 27

A TCP/IP network requires planning to be implemented correctly. TCP/IP provides a number of utilities to assist administrators with this task. Which of the following circumstances describe a good example of the use of a DNS server?

○ a. Use DNS when you need to provide a troubleshooting method.

○ b. Use DNS when you need to provide name resolution of hostnames or domain names.

○ c. Use DNS when you need to automatically assign IP configuration information to TCP/IP hosts.

○ d. None of the above.

Question 28

Your network consists of 67 Microsoft computers. You are using TCP/IP as the only communication protocol. You need to implement a name resolution solution that will resolve NetBIOS names to IP addresses. Which of the following resolves NeBIOS names to IP addresses?

○ a. DNS

○ b. WINS

○ c. HOSTS file

○ d. DHCP

Question 29

Which of the following statements are true regarding a HOSTS file and DNS?

○ a. HOSTS files manually assign IP addresses to clients; DNS automatically assigns IP addresses to clients.

○ b. HOSTS files resolve hostnames or domain names to IP addresses, DNS resolves NetBIOS names to IP addresses.

○ c. HOSTS files and DNS both resolve hostnames or domain names to IP addresses.

○ d. HOSTS files are used in WANs; DNS is used in LANs.

Question 30

Which component of the TCP/IP protocol stack guarantees packets will be received in the same order they were sent?

○ a. UDP

○ b. TCP

○ c. Both a and b

○ d. None of the above

Question 31

Which of the following protocols is used to send email?

○ a. POP3

○ b. SMTP

○ c. DHCP

○ d. WINS

Question 32

Which part of the TCP/IP protocol suite is used to monitor TCP/IP traffic
and components to gather statistical data?

○ a. SMTP

○ b   SNMP

○ c. POP3

○ d. TCP

Question 33

Which of the following components of the TCP/IP protocol suite is used to
upload and download files between two TCP/IP hosts?

○ a. TCP

○ b. SNMP

○ c. FTP

○ d. POP3

Question 34

What is the most common protocol used by the Web?

○ a. FTP

○ b. SNMP

○ c. HTTP

○ d. SMTP

Question 35

What is the address range for TCP/IP Class A addresses?

○ a   1 through 126

○ b. 128 through 191

○ c. 192 through 223

○ d. Both a and b

Question 36

What Class IP address is the address 200.200.200.17?

○ a. Class A

○ b. Class B

○ c. Class C

○ d. Class A and B

Question 37

What is the default subnet mask for a Class C IP address?

○ a. 255.0.0.0

○ b. 255.255.0.0

○ c. 255.255.255.0

○ d. 255.255.255.255

Question 38

Your network is a LAN of 130 computers in a single subnet and uses TCP/IP as the communication protocol. Your computer is configured with the IP address 1.5.250.72. What is the correct default subnet mask for this network?

○ a. 255.255.0.0

○ b. 255.0.0.0

○ c. 255.255.255.0

○ d. 255.255.255.255

Question 39

The SMTP protocol is part of the TCP/IP protocol suite. It is considered a well-known protocol. What port number does SMTP use?

- ○ a. 21
- ○ b. 25
- ○ c. 80
- ○ d. 110

Question 40

Which of the following best describes the function of an IP proxy (proxy server)? [Choose the two best answers]

- ❑ a. An IP proxy is used to automatically assign IP addresses to clients in a TCP/IP network.
- ❑ b. An IP proxy is used to increase the speed that users on the local network retrieve Web pages.
- ❑ c. An IP proxy is used as an Internet firewall to protect users on the local network from the intrusion of the Internet.
- ❑ d. Proxy server is used to resolve host names to IP addresses.

Question 41

The manner in which data flows on a network cable can be defined as either baseband or broadband. What is a key difference between baseband and broadband?

- ○ a. Baseband uses digital signaling; broadband uses analog signaling.
- ○ b. Broadband uses digital signaling; baseband uses analog signaling.
- ○ c. Baseband communicates unidirectionally; broadband communicates bidirectionally.
- ○ d. There is no difference between baseband and broadband.

Question 42

You are implementing the TCP/IP protocol on your network. The network consists of 25 Windows 95 computers and 1 NT Server computer. You configure the NT Server to be a DHCP server. This DHCP server will automatically assign TCP/IP addresses to all the Windows 95 computers. How must you configure your Windows 95 computers so they will get their IP address information from this DHCP server?

○ a. Install the TCP/IP protocol on all Windows 95 computers and configure them with the NetBIOS name of the DHCP server.

○ b. Install the TCP/IP protocol on all Windows 95 computers and configure them with the IP address of the DHCP server.

○ c. Install the TCP/IP protocol on all Windows 95 computers and configure them with the host name of the DHCP server.

○ d. Install the TCP/IP protocol on all Windows 95 computers and accept the default configuration of Obtain An IP Address Automatically.

Question 43

You are surfing the Web using your Web browser, Internet Explorer 4. You request the address **www.comptia.org**. When you connect to the site, you notice the HTTP protocol is being used, but you do not see any port number. You know that HTTP is a well-known protocol and has a port number. What port number is being used to make this connection?

○ a. 21

○ b. 25

○ c. 80

○ d. 110

Question 44

You are the network administrator for a large department store. Network performance has been poor, so you decide to segment the network using an NT Server configured to act as a router. The network uses TCP/IP as the only protocol. You configure your NT Server with three network adapter cards and enable routing by selecting the Enable IP Forwarding option in TCP/IP properties. What additional step could you perform to enable this NT Server to perform dynamic routing?

- ○ a. Install RIP for IP.
- ○ b. Install RIP for IPX.
- ○ c. Install POP3.
- ○ d. Do nothing. NT Server will automatically perform dynamic routing.

Question 45

On what layer of the OSI model does a router reside?

- ○ a. Transport
- ○ b. Network
- ○ c. Physical
- ○ d. Data Link

Question 46

Which of the following best describes the primary difference between a hub and a bridge?

- ○ a. A hub is used in Ethernet networks, and a bridge is used in token ring networks.
- ○ b. A hub resides at the Data Link layer of the OSI model, and a bridge resides at the Network layer of the OSI model.
- ○ c. A hub provides better performance than a bridge.
- ○ d. A hub resides at the Physical layer of the OSI model, and a bridge resides at the Data Link layer of the OSI model.

Question 47

What security model features the use of passwords assigned to resources on a network?

○ a. User-level security

○ b. No access share implemented resource distribution (NASIRD)

○ c. Password-protected, share-level security

○ d. Share-level security

Question 48

You are configuring a newly purchased Windows 98 computer that will be added to your network. You install and configure the devices as follows:

- **NIC card** IRQ 5
- **Modem** IRQ 10
- **Sound card** IRQ 5
- **Scanner** IRQ 7

Which of the following best describes this configuration?

○ a. It will work fine.

○ b. It will not work; there are too many devices.

○ c. It will not work; the network card has an IRQ conflict with the sound card.

○ d. There is no way to tell if there are any configuration conflicts unless it is attached to the network.

Question 49

The Institute of Electrical and Electronics Engineers, Inc. (IEEE) publishes standards used in networking. A subgroup of IEEE is Project 802, which defines network standards for the physical components of a network. Which of the following statements are true of Project 802 standards? [Choose the two best answers]

❑ a. Project 802.2 defines standards for token ring networks.

❑ b. Project 802.3 defines standards for CSMA/CD (Ethernet).

❑ c. Project 802.5 defines standards for CSMA/CD (Ethernet).

❑ d. Project 802.2 defines standards for the Logical Link Control (LLC).

Question 50

You need to access your company's database server from your home. You will be making this remote connection from your Windows 95 computer using a 56Kbps modem. The database server only supports the TCP/IP protocol for communication. Which of the following dial-up protocols could you use to make this connection?

◯ a. PPP

◯ b. SLIP

◯ c. Both a and b

◯ d. None of the above

Question 51

You need to extend a single-segment length of Thinnet coaxial cable. What connectivity device could you use? [Choose the two best answers]

□ a. Repeater

□ b. Hub

□ c. MAU

□ d. MOO

Question 52

Which of the following statements are true about the difference between ISDN and PSTN? [Choose the two best answers]

□ a. ISDN is a digital dial-up service; PSTN is an analog dial-up service.

□ b. ISDN provides faster transmission speeds than PSTN.

□ c. PSTN provides faster transmission speeds than ISDN.

□ d. ISDN can transmit voice and data; PSTN can only transmit data.

Question 53

You are administering a network of 30 computers connected in a bus topology that uses Thinnet coaxial cable. The network is spread out over two departments, Sales and Accounting. Olivia, a user in the Accounting department, accidentally kicks the cable out from the T-connector attached to the network card on her computer leaving one wire attached and one wire disconnected. What effect does this have on the network?

○ a. Only Olivia will not be able to communicate over the network.

○ b. Olivia and all the users in Accounting will not be able to communicate over the network, but the users in the Sales department will be able to communicate with each other.

○ c. Users in both departments will not be able to communicate.

○ d. All users will be able to communicate as long as the cable did not fall more than three meters away from the network card.

Question 54

You are hired as a consultant by a health care company that wishes to expand their current network. They are located on two floors of a large building, the first floor and the fiftieth floor. The first floor is the Executive department, and the fiftieth floor is the Accounting department. The floors are 400 meters apart. All users in the Executive department are networked together in a bus topology using Thinnet coaxial cable. All users in the Accounting department are networked together in a bus topology using Thinnet coaxial cable. The two departments are not currently connected to each other. You are asked to recommend a solution to connect users from both floors together. Your solution must provide for connectivity between all users and also minimize the costs associated with purchasing new cable. Which of the following is the best solution for this company?

○ a. Recommend that they keep their existing cabling and run a single segment of Thinnet coaxial cable between floors.

○ b. Recommend that they switch all of their cabling to twisted-pair and run a single segment of twisted-pair cable between floors.

○ c. Recommend they keep their existing cable and run a single segment of Thicknet cable to connect both segments together.

○ d. Recommend they replace all cable with fiber optic cable and run a single segment of fiber optic cable to connect both segments together.

Question 55

You are brought in as a consultant to assist in implementing TCP/IP for a large network. The network consists of 747 computers, who all require communication with each other as well as other offices through a router. The company asks you to configure TCP/IP configuration information on all clients. You wish to do this with the least amount of administrative effort. Which of the following TCP/IP utilities will you use?

○ a. WINS

○ b. DNS

○ c. ACP

○ d. None of the above

Question 56

You are administering a network of 30 computers connected in a star topology that uses twisted-pair cable. The network is spread out over two departments, Sales and Accounting. Patricia, a user in the Accounting department, accidentally kicks the cable out from the back of the network card on her computer. What effect does this have on the network?

○ a. Only Patricia will not be able to communicate over the network.

○ b. Patricia and all the users in Accounting will not be able to communicate over the network, but the users in the Sales department will be able to communicate with each other.

○ c. Users in both departments will not be able to communicate.

○ d. All users will be able to communicate as long as the cable did not fall more than three meters away from the network card.

Question 57

Which topology provides redundancy through the use of multiple links?

○ a. Star

○ b. Bus

○ c. Ring

○ d. Mesh

Question 58

What device is used to connect computers in an IBM Token Ring topology?

○ a. MAU

○ b. Hub

○ c. Router

○ d. Gateway

Question 59

You are the newly hired network administrator for a large latex manufacturing company. The company's network has 600 users and four servers:
a database server, a Web server, a print server, and a groupware server.
The network currently uses an Ethernet network in a star topology with
unshielded twisted-pair cable. All computers are connected to a single
patch panel that contains 30 hubs. Network performance is very poor,
especially during peak hours. You are asked to implement a solution to
improve network performance. The company is not concerned with cost
as much as it is with speeding up client access to the servers. Which of
the following solutions best meets this company's needs?

○ a. Replace the hubs with Multistation Access Units (MAUs).

○ b. Replace the twisted-pair cable with shielded twisted-pair
cable.

○ c. Implement a high-speed backbone across the servers with
routers controlling traffic across the backbone.

○ d. Implement an X-55 PAD assembly to uplink high-speed data
requests from the clients to the servers.

Question 60

What is the name of the tool used in NT Server to create and manage user
accounts?

○ a. NT administrator

○ b. User manager for domains

○ c. User administrator

○ d. NT user administrator

Question 61

Your network consists of five servers and 60 client computers. Because of recent problems with data loss, your company has decided to implement fault tolerance on all servers. Which of the following provide fault tolerance? [Choose the three best answers]

❑ a. Disk mirroring

❑ b. Disk striping with parity

❑ c. Disk duplexing

❑ d. Volume sets

Question 62

Air-Sea Travel has just moved to a new location and needs to build a new network. The company's network consists of 75 users, divided between two floors. The floors are 200 meters apart. Lillian, the network administrator, has decided to use Thinnet coaxial cable in a bus topology to connect all users. T-connectors attach the Thinnet to each network card, and the ends are terminated to a resistance of 50 ohms. There are no hubs or repeaters used in the network. After verifying all cables are plugged in correctly, Lillian discovers that the network is not functioning. What is the most likely reason for this?

○ a. T-connectors cannot be used to attach Thinnet cable to a network card.

○ b. The resistance required for Thinnet in a bus topology is 60 ohms.

○ c. Hubs are required for connecting networks in a bus topology.

○ d. Thinnet coaxial cable can only travel 185 meters in a single segment, and the distance between floors exceeds this limit.

Question 63

The Justel National Bank has retained your services as a network consultant. They need to join two of their branch offices together in a WAN. The offices are one kilometer apart. They will be wire transferring sensitive information, so security is imperative. They also require a fast data-transfer speed. They tell you money is no object, the most important criteria are speed and security. What media will you recommend?

○ a. Twisted-pair

○ b. Thicknet coaxial

○ c. Fiber optic

○ d. Thinnet coaxial

Question 64

Which of the following statements is true about the difference between 100BaseT and 100Base VG-AnyLAN?

○ a. 100BaseT supports category 5 UTP, and 100Base VG-AnyLAN does not.

○ b. 100BaseT transmits at 100Mbps; 100Base VG-AnyLAN does not.

○ c. 100BaseT uses CSMA/CD as an access method; 100Base VG-AnyLAN does not.

○ d. There is no difference between the two; the terms are interchangeable and refer to the same topologies.

Question 65

Which of the following statements best describes the function of a server?

○ a. A server is used to provide clients with access to resources and/or allow for central administration of a network.

○ b. A server is used to connect Unix clients together in a WAN.

○ c. A server is always used in a peer-to-peer network.

○ d. A server operating system is Windows 98.

Question 66

You are working phone support at the help desk of your company. A user calls from home complaining that she cannot retrieve her Internet email. The user has no problems sending Internet email messages, but cannot receive any. The user says everything was working fine until she altered the configuration settings in her email client. The user cannot remember if she changed her POP3 server information or her SMTP server information. Based on the information, what can you tell the user?

- ○ a. You probably changed your POP3 server information.
- ○ b. You probably changed your SMTP server information.
- ○ c. You probably changed both your SMTP and your POP3 server information.
- ○ d. You probably changed some other parameter; SMTP and POP3 have nothing to do with Internet email.

Question 67

Which type of data transmission is used by Ethernet 10BaseT, 10Base5, and 10Base2 networks?

- ○ a. Broadband
- ○ b. Baseband
- ○ c. Demand priority
- ○ d. Token passing

Question 68

Your friend Mario calls you on the phone to discuss data transmission methods. He insists that the conversation you are having with him on the phone is an example of a full-duplex transmission, because both of you can speak at the same time. You disagree and wager 50 bucks that the conversation is actually an example of half-duplex transmission. Who wins the bet and why?

○ a. Mario wins. Full-duplex transmission allows data to travel in two directions simultaneously.

○ b. You win. Half-duplex transmission allows data to travel in two directions simultaneously.

○ c. No one wins. Neither full- nor half-duplex transmission is used in a phone conversation.

○ d. You both are right, because full-duplex and half-duplex transmission are interchangeable terms for the same thing.

Question 69

What network operating system uses NDS and is based on X.500 standards?

○ a. NT Server

○ b. Novell NetWare

○ c. Windows 95

○ d. Windows NT Workstation

Question 70

You are the network administrator for a dental company. The network contains 40 users in a single location and uses TCP/IP as the only protocol. You need to provide all users with Internet access. You are concerned about security and want to implement a solution that will allow your entire location to only broadcast a single IP address when requesting Web pages. Which of the following solutions will allow you to do this?

○ a. An IP proxy server

○ b. A WINS server

○ c. A DNS server

○ d. This cannot be done

Question 71

Which of the following best describes a MAN?

- ○ a. A MAN is a Meteoric Ableing Nitrometer used for connecting wireless networks.

- ○ b. A MAN is a Motherboard Abacus Niche, used for math coprocessing in a CPU.

- ○ c. A MAN is a metropolitan area network, defining a network that covers an area the size of a city.

- ○ d. A MAN is a Metric Annotation Node used for internal CPU conversions.

Question 72

The network ID 127 is reserved by TCP/IP for a specific purpose. What is the reason that network ID 127 is reserved?

- ○ a. Network ID 127 is reserved so routers can use it to communicate with each other.

- ○ b. Network ID 127 is reserved so WANs can connect through this "special" network ID without conflict.

- ○ c. Network ID 127 is reserved for local host-loopback testing. You can PING 127.0.0.1 to verify TCP/IP is correctly installed on your computer.

- ○ d. Both a and b.

Question 73

As part of the configuration of the IPX/SPX protocol, a frame type is specified. Which of the following statements best describes a frame type?

- ○ a. A frame type identifies the type of junction box, or "frame," used in IPX/SPX networks.

- ○ b. In order for IPX/SPX computers to communicate, they must both support the same frame type.

- ○ c. In order for IPX/SPX computers to communicate, they must both support a different frame type.

- ○ d. A frame type is an optional configuration in IPX/SPX and is not required for communication.

Question 74

You are administering a Novell NetWare network of ten computers. There is one NetWare server and nine client computers running Novell NetWare client software. All ten computers connect to a single hub. You are using IPX/SPX as the only communication protocol. Which of the following statements is true about the IPX/SPX addresses that will be used in this network?

○ a. All computers will have a unique internal address and the same external network address.

○ b. All computers will have a unique host ID and the same subnet mask.

○ c. All computers will have a unique external network address and the same internal address.

○ d. All computers will have the same internal address and a unique default gateway.

Question 75

Which of the following best describes a crossover cable?

○ a. A crossover cable is used to "cross" a LAN "over" into a WAN.

○ b. A crossover cable is used to connect two 10BaseT computers together without the use of a hub.

○ c. A crossover cable is used to connect an MAU to a frame type.

○ d. Both a and c.

Network+
Answer Key #2

1. b	16. d	31. b	46. d	61. a, b, c
2. c	17. c	32. b	47. d	62. d
3. d	18. b	33. c	48. c	63. c
4. b	19. a	34. c	49. b, d	64. c
5. c	20. a	35. a	50. c	65. a
6. b	21. a	36. c	51. a, b	66. a
7. b	22. c	37. c	52. a, b	67. b
8. a	23. b	38. b	53. c	68. a
9. d	24. b	39. b	54. c	69. b
10. b	25. b	40. b, c	55. d	70. a
11. d	26. a	41. a	56. a	71. c
12. a	27. b	42. d	57. d	72. c
13. a, c, d	28. b	43. c	58. a	73. b
14. a	29. c	44. a	59. c	74. a
15. a	30. b	45. b	60. b	75. b

Question 1

Answer b is correct. Antivirus software should be installed on all computers and updated frequently, regardless of the version number or type of product purchased. A virus is a program that is written to cause varying degrees of damage to the files of the computer it is installed on. A virus ends up on a hard disk without the user's knowledge by "hiding" inside another program or file that is being transferred onto the hard drive. An antivirus program is a program that contains a list of known viruses. When an antivirus program scans a disk for a virus, it compares its known virus list to the programs on a disk. If an antivirus program finds a match between a program on a disk and its database, it detects the virus and attempts to remove it from the computer. The best time to install antivirus program is before a computer is infected, not after.

For more information, see Chapter 13 of *Network+ Exam Cram.*

Question 2

Answer c is correct. In order for a computer to access a network resource, it must have the appropriate redirector installed. A redirector is a Presentation layer component that takes a request made on the local computer and "redirects" it out onto the network. In this question, a NetWare client redirector must be installed on the Windows 95 computers to allow them to access file and printer resources on this NetWare Server. Both Microsoft and Novell NetWare offer a redirector that can be used for this purpose. The Microsoft redirector for connecting Windows 95 computers to NetWare servers is called Client for NetWare Networks and is included with Windows 95. Novell also provides a redirector for this purpose, called Client32. Installing either one of these redirectors on the Windows 95 computers will allow them to access resources on a NetWare server.

For more information, see Chapter 3 of *Network+ Exam Cram.*

Question 3

Answer d is correct. Full backup and incremental backup will clear, or reset, the archive bit of files.

The attribute of a file used to determine its backup status is known as the archive bit. The archive bit attribute of a file can be one of two values: "set" or "reset" (cleared). When a *full* or *incremental* backup is performed, the backup program *clears*, or resets, the archive bit. When files that have been backed up are changed, the program that modifies the file will "set" the archive bit. The process of "setting" the archive bit of modified files allows the backup program to determine if a file has changed since the last time a backup was performed. There are three important backup methods to be aware of: differential, incremental, and full backup.

➤ **Differential** A differential backup will back up files that have their archive bit "set" but does not clear the archive bit. Performing daily backups get progressively slower each day. Restoring data from a differential backup only requires two tapes: the original full backup and the last differential backup

➤ **Incremental** An incremental backup will back up files that have their archive bit "set," then clears the archive bit. Restoring data from an incremental backup requires many tapes: the original full backup tape and all incremental backups performed since the full backup.

➤ **Full backup** Backs up all files regardless of the archive bit attribute and clears the archive bit. Periodic full backups are recommended in addition to either incremental or differential backups.

For more information, see Chapter 15 of *Network+ Exam Cram.*

Question 4

Answer b is correct. A Universal Naming Convention (UNC) name is a standard for connecting to shared resources on a network. A UNC is comprised of two key elements: a computer name and a share name. All computers in a network must have a computer name to identify themselves. When sharing a resource (a printer, a directory or folder, a CD-ROM, and so on), the shared resource must also be assigned a name, known as a share name. Connecting to a shared resource using a UNC simply involves specifying these two parameters, in the format "\\computer name\share name". For example, to connect to a printer that has been assigned the share name PRINTER1 on the computer named USER1, the UNC to connect to this resource would be \\USER1\PRINTER1.

For more information, see Chapter 12 of *Network+ Exam Cram.*

Question 5

Answer c is correct. DOS-based programs require a virtual port to be mapped to a UNC. A UNC name is a standard for connecting to shared resources on a network. A UNC is comprised of two key elements: a computer name and a share name. All computers in a network must have a computer name to identify themselves. When sharing a resource (a printer, files, CD-ROM, and so on), the shared resource must also be assigned a name, known as a share name. Connecting to a shared resource using a UNC simply involves specifying these two parameters, in the format "\\computer name\share name". For example, to connect to a printer that has been assigned the share name PRINTER1 on the computer named USER1, the UNC to connect to this resource would be \\USER1\PRINTER1. DOS is an older operating system that does not understand the use of UNCs to connect to network resources. For this reason, DOS-based programs need to "map" a virtual drive or port to a UNC when connecting to a network resource. The mapping of a virtual drive or port is done to "fool" DOS into thinking the resource it is connecting to is attached to the local computer. For example, for a DOS-based program to connect to a network printer with the share name PRINTER1 on a computer named USER1, the UNC \\USER1\PRINTER1 will have to be "capture" to a virtual port, like LPT3. In this example, LPT3 is considered a "virtual" port because it doesn't physically exist on the local computer. However, DOS will think there is an LPT3 port on the local computer and will now be able to print to this network resource.

For more information, see Chapter 12 of *Network+ Exam Cram*.

Question 6

Answer b is correct. Rights are the permissions given to users to access network resources and perform certain network tasks. To perform administrative tasks, you must have administrative rights assigned to your user account. Rights can be assigned to either a user account or to a group. Simply changing your password has no effect on your rights in a network. Naming your account "master" will have no effect on your rights on the network.

For more information, see Chapter 12 of *Network+ Exam Cram*.

Question 7

Answer b is correct. A backbone is characterized by a single, high-speed cable run across servers and or routers. Implementing a backbone, along with routers, can improve network performance, especially in larger (250 users or more) networks. Demand priority is an access method used by 100VG-AnyLAN.

For more information, see Chapter 2 of *Network+ Exam Cram*.

Question 8

Answer a is correct. In this instance, the space heater is probably affecting the performance of the CPU, either by overloading the circuit or overheating. It probably takes a few hours for the consequences of the heat to take effect (from morning until lunchtime), but excessive heat can cause computers to malfunction. A space heater will lower the humidity in a room by drying the air, not increase it. Generally speaking, computers like the same temperature conditions that people do. Room temperature should not be extreme, and ideal temperature should be on the cool side. Humidity should be kept at approximately 50 to 70 percent. If humidity is too low, the instances of electrostatic discharge (ESD) will be increased because of the "dryness" of the particles in the air. An ESD shock can cause a computer to fail intermittently or cause more serious damage. High humidity produces excessive moisture in the air that could cause condensation to develop on the electrical components inside a computer and cause a short.

For more information, see Chapter 13 of *Network+ Exam Cram*.

Question 9

Answer d is correct. Small Computer System Interface (SCSI) is a parallel interface standard for attaching peripheral devices to a computer. There are many variations of SCSI. In general, SCSI supports the use of Centronics 50, 68 HP, and DB-25 connectors when attaching an external SCSI device to a PC.

For more information, see Chapter 10 of *Network+ Exam Cram*.

Question 10

Answer b is correct. The maximum single-segment length of Thinnet coaxial cable is 185 meters (607 feet). In order to extend a length of Thinnet coaxial cable, a repeater must be used. A repeater is used to "boost" the signal back to its original strength, so it can continue a longer distance. Patch cable is used when a length of coaxial cable is not long enough to reach a desired point. However, if patch cable is connected to a length of Thinnet without a repeater, it contributes to the total length of the cable and is not considered a separate segment.

For more information, see Chapter 2 of *Network+ Exam Cram*.

Question 11

Answer d is correct. The most secure type of password scheme is one that utilizes upper- and lowercase letters, numbers, and special characters, like "!@#$" and or using the Alt key with a number. Because all passwords are case sensitive, using a combination of upper- and lowercase letters can provide additional security against a potential hacker. All of the answers here are types of password schemes, but answer d is the most secure.

For more information, see Chapter 7 of *Network+ Exam Cram*.

Question 12

Answer a is correct. There are two common security models a network administrator can employ to control users' access to network resources: share-level security and user-level security. When using share-level security, passwords are assigned to *resources*. An example of share-level security is sharing a printer and assigning a password to that printer. When users need to connect to the printer, they will have to enter the password set on the printer in order to access it. The share-level security model is considered a less secure method than user-level security because users are more likely to tell others the password to access a resource than they are to give away their own username and password. In user-level security, permissions are assigned to *users*. An example of user-level security is sharing a printer and assigning permissions to user accounts or groups to access this resource. For users to access this printer, their user account must have permissions to access it. Remember: share-level security assigns passwords to *resources* (printers, files, programs, and so on). User-level security assigns permissions to *users*.

For more information, see Chapter 7 of *Network+ Exam Cram*.

Question 13

Answers a, c, and d are correct. Both Point-to-Point Protocol (PPP) and Serial Line Internet Protocol (SLIP) are used as dial-up protocols when using a modem to connect to a remote network or the Internet. PPP is a newer, more efficient dial-up protocol than SLIP. PPP automatically obtains configuration parameters with the remote server on connection. This simplifies the configurations required when making a remote connection. SLIP must be configured manually with these parameters. Another key difference between PPP and SLIP is the number of communication protocols supported. PPP supports IPX/SPX, AppleTalk, TCP/IP, and NetBEUI. SLIP only supports the use of the TCP/IP protocol.

For more information, see Chapter 6 of *Network+ Exam Cram*.

Question 14

Answer a is correct. Point-to-Point Tunneling Protocol (PPTP) is used to create Virtual Private Networks (VPNs). A VPN is a private network that uses the Internet to make a connection. Users from each private network establish an Internet connection locally and use the network capabilities of the Internet to connect to each other. Because the Internet is a public network, connecting two private networks together in this manner does pose some security risks. To provide security for VPNs over the Internet, the PPTP protocol is used. With PPTP enabled, the only packets that will be allowed into members of the VPN are PPTP packets. Both PPP and SLIP are used as dial-up protocols when using a modem to connect to a remote network or the Internet. Windows Internet Naming Service (WINS) is used to resolve NetBIOS names to IP addresses.

For more information, see Chapter 6 of *Network+ Exam Cram.*

Question 15

Answer a is correct. Integrated Services Digital Network (ISDN) is a digital dial-up service that can send voice and data signals at 128Kbps (128,000 bits per second). ISDN uses two 64K channels, called "B" channels, when transmitting. ISDN uses a terminal adapter (TA) to connect to a computer in place of a modem. This is because the transmission is digital over ISDN and does not have to be "modulated," or converted, to analog as is the case with regular phone line. Public Switched Telephone Network (PSTN), also known as Plain Old Telephone Service (POTS), is the standard dial-up analog phone line used to send voice and data. PSTN can transmit data up to 28,800Bps. (The new 56K standard achieves approximately 56Kbps transmission speeds by using a digital lines and data compression). PSTN uses a modem (modulate/demodulate) to connect to a computer. A modem converts, or modulates, a computer's digital signal to analog for transmission over PSTN, and the receiving computer's modem will demodulate that signal, or convert it, from analog to a digital signal.

For more information, see Chapter 6 of *Network+ Exam Cram.*

Question 16

Answer d is correct. TCP/IP contains various command-line utilities used for troubleshooting/diagnosing a TCP/IP network. The key commands to know are **ARP**, **NBTSTAT**, **TRACERT**, and **NETSTAT**.

➤ **ARP** Address Resolution Protocol resolves, or associates, an IP address to a media access control (MAC) address. A MAC address, also known as a hardware address, is the permanent address "burned" into every network adapter card by the manufacturer. The TCP/IP command **ARP** –a will display the local computer's ARP cache, which is a list of all the IP addresses that have been resolved by ARP, along with the corresponding MAC address.

➤ **NETSTAT** A TCP/IP command-line utility used to display protocol statistics about the current TCP/IP connection. **NETSTAT** can be used to display information about the port number (80 for HTTP, 21 for FTP, and so on) and protocol (User Datagram Protocol [UDP], Transmission Control Protocol [TCP]) used in a given TCP/IP connection.

➤ **NBTSTAT** A TCP/IP command-line utility that displays the current TCP/IP NetBIOS name information. Microsoft networks commonly use NetBIOS names when communicating. To communicate using TCP/IP, NetBIOS names must be resolved, or associated, with their IP address. This name resolution can take place via WINS, broadcast, or LMHOSTS files. The **NBTSTAT** command can be used to display the NetBIOS names used by the local computer, **NBTSTAT** –n, as well as to provide a list of how NetBIOS name resolution is taking place, NBTSTAT –r, whether by broadcast or WINS.

➤ **TRACERT** A TCP/IP command used to trace a route to a remote host. TRACERT is used to determine the route a packet travels on the way to the destination computer. Typing "TRACERT" and the destination IP address will trace the path the packet travels to its destination.

For more information, see Chapter 4 of *Network+ Exam Cram.*

Question 17

Answer c is correct. See explanation of Question 16 for details.

For more information, see Chapter 4 of *Network+ Exam Cram.*

Question 18

Answer b is correct. The most common method of storing data offline is tape backup. Redundant arrays of independent disks (RAID) is a form of fault tolerance, and though it does provide data storage, fault tolerance is not considered the most common form of offline data storage. No form of fault tolerance replaces regular tape backups.

For more information, see Chapter 5 of *Network+ Exam Cram.*

Question 19

Answer a is correct. Although IPCONFIG and WINIPCFG are both used to display TCP/IP configuration information, Windows 95 supports the **WINIPCFG** command to display TCP/IP configuration information. Windows 98 supports both the **WINIPCFG** and **IPCONFIG** commands. WINIPCFG will display the IP address, subnet mask, and default gateway parameters, and also Domain Names System (DNS), WINS, and Dynamic Host Configuration Protocol (DHCP) information when clicking on the More Info button.

NT Server and NT Workstation utilize IPCONFIG, not WINIPCFG. The IPCONFIG utility will display the IP address, subnet mask, and default gateway parameters. Typing "IPCONFIG /ALL" will display additional TCP/IP parameters, such as the IP address of the DNS, WINS, and DHCP servers being used by the client.

For more information, see Chapter 4 of *Network+ Exam Cram.*

Question 20

Answer a is correct. The PING utility is a very useful tool when troubleshooting a TCP/IP network. PING is used to test for connectivity between hosts on a TCP/IP network. The syntax for the **PING** command is simple: Type "PING" and the IP address of the computer you want to connect to, and press Enter. PING will then attempt a connection to this host. If PING is successful, this verifies that the TCP/IP connection between these computers is valid. If PING is unsuccessful, this verifies that there is no communication between these hosts using TCP/IP. The IPCONFIG (NT Server and Workstation) and WINIPCFG (Windows 95) commands are used to display IP configuration information. The TCP/IP command **ARP –a** will display the local computer's ARP cache, which is a list of all the IP addresses that have been resolved by ARP, along with the corresponding MAC address.

For more information, see Chapter 4 of *Network+ Exam Cram.*

Question 21

Answer a is correct. Telnet, or Telecommunications Network, is a terminal emulation program used in TCP/IP networks. Telnet allows users to connect their PC to a remote server. Once logged in, a Telnet user can enter commands through the Telnet program, and they will be executed the same as if they were entered directly on the server. **PING** is used to test for connectivity between hosts on a TCP/IP network. The **IPCONFIG** (NT Server and Workstation) and **WINIPCFG** (Windows 95) commands are used to display IP configuration information.

For more information, see Chapter 4 of *Network+ Exam Cram*.

Question 22

Answer c is correct. The NBTSTAT command was used in this example. Notice it displays "NetBIOS Names Resolution And Registration Statistics," which is one use for the NBTSTAT utility. This output was produced using NBTSTAT with the –r switch. TCP/IP contains various command-line utilities used for troubleshooting/diagnosing a TCP/IP network. The key commands to know are ARP, NBTSTAT, TRACERT, and NETSTAT:

➤ **ARP** Address Resolution Protocol resolves, or associates, an IP address to a MAC address. A MAC address, also known as a hardware address, is the permanent address "burned" into every network adapter card by the manufacturer. The TCP/IP command **ARP –a** will display the local computers ARP cache, which is a list of all the IP addresses that have been resolved by ARP, along with the corresponding MAC address.

➤ **NETSTAT** A TCP/IP command-line utility used to display protocol statistics about the current TCP/IP connection. **NETSTAT** can be used to display information about the port number (80 for HTTP, 21 for FTP, and so on) and protocol (UDP, TCP) used in a given TCP/IP connection.

➤ **NBTSTAT** A TCP/IP command-line utility that displays the current TCP/IP NetBIOS name information. Microsoft networks commonly use NetBIOS names when communicating. To communicate using TCP/IP, NetBIOS names must be resolved, or associated, with their IP address. This name resolution can take place via WINS, broadcast,or LMHOSTS files. The **NBTSTAT** command can be used to display the NetBIOS names used by the local computer, **NBTSTAT –n**, as well as to provide a list of how NetBIOS name resolution is taking place, **NBTSTAT –r**, either by broadcast or by WINS.

➤ **TRACERT** A TCP/IP command used to trace a route to a remote host. TRACERT is used to determine the route a packet travels on the way to the destination computer. Typing "TRACERT" and the destination IP address will trace the path the packet travels to its destination.

For more information, see Chapter 4 of *Network+ Exam Cram*.

Question 23

Answer b is correct. The TCP/IP protocol is a popular communication protocol used on the Internet and supported in Microsoft and NetWare 5 networks. TCP/IP is a configurable protocol, and all computers wishing to utilize it must have the correct settings. All computers using TCP/IP must have a *unique* IP address, a subnet mask, and if used in a wide area network (WAN), a default gateway. An IP address identifies a TCP/IP host on the network, and contains two important elements: a network ID and a host ID. The network ID of an IP address identifies the network the host is on. (For example, all users in a single location are said to be on the same network and, therefore, will all have the same network ID in their IP address). The host ID of an IP address identifies the host, or individual, computer on a TCP/IP network. It is the host ID portion of an IP address that is the unique part. Therefore, in a single TCP/IP network, users will all have the same network ID and different (unique) host IDs. IP addressing is similar to the way houses are addressed on your block. Many people live on Maple Street (network ID), but only one person lives at 21 Maple Street (host ID). A subnet mask is a required parameter for all TCP/IP hosts. A subnet mask is used to distinguish the network ID in an IP address from the host ID. When a computer using TCP/IP needs to communicate with another TCP/IP host, it uses the subnet mask to determine if the destination computer is local (on my network) or remote (on a different network). If the subnet mask determines the destination host is local, it simply places the packet on the cable for delivery. If the subnet mask determines the host it needs to communicate with is remote (on another network), it sends it to its default gateway. A default gateway is only required to be configured on TCP/IP hosts that need to communicate outside of their local network or in a WAN. A default gateway is the IP address of the router used by the local network to connect to another network in the outside world, like the Internet or another branch office location. A default gateway is not a required parameter when using TCP/IP in a local area network (LAN), because all computers are on the same network and have the same network ID.

For more information, see Chapter 4 of *Network+ Exam Cram.*

Question 24

Answer b is correct. In a star topology, each computer is connected to a hub. The hub handles termination and distributes packets to all segments. Hubs may be connected together, or "daisy chained," to expand a star topology. A bus topology features a single segment of computers in a continuous, single line, terminated at both ends. A token ring topology uses a device that looks similar to a hub, known as a multistation access unit (MAU), to connect computers together. There is no such thing as a token bus topology.

For more information, see Chapter 2 of *Network+ Exam Cram*.

Question 25

Answer b is correct. The TCP/IP protocol is a popular communication protocol used on the Internet and supported in Microsoft and NetWare 5 networks. TCP/IP is a configurable protocol, and all computers wishing to utilize it must have the correct settings. All computers using TCP/IP must have a *unique* IP address, a subnet mask, and if used in a WAN, a default gateway. An IP address identifies a TCP/IP host on the network and contains two important elements: a network ID and a host ID. The network ID of an IP address identifies the network the host is on. (For example, all users in a single location are said to be on the same network and, therefore, will all have the same network ID in their IP address.) The host ID of an IP address identifies the host, or individual, computer on a TCP/IP network. It is the host ID portion of an IP address that is the unique part. Therefore, in a single TCP/IP network, users will all have the *same* network ID and *different* (unique) host IDs. IP addressing is similar to the way houses are addressed on your block. Many people live on Maple Street (network ID), but only one person lives at 21 Maple Street (host ID). A subnet mask is a required parameter for all TCP/IP hosts. A subnet mask is used to distinguish the network ID in an IP address from the host ID. When a computer using TCP/IP needs to communicate with another TCP/IP host, it uses the subnet mask to determine if the destination computer is local (on my network) or remote (on a different network). If the subnet mask determines the destination host is local, it simply places the packet on the cable for delivery. If the subnet mask determines the host it needs to communicate with is remote (on another network), it sends it to its default gateway. A default gateway is only required to be configured on TCP/IP hosts that need to communicate outside of their local network or in a WAN. A default gateway is the IP address of the router used by the local network to connect to another network in the outside world, like the Internet or another branch office location. A default gateway is not a required parameter when using TCP/IP in a LAN, because all computers are on the same network and have the same network ID.

For more information, see Chapter 4 of *Network+ Exam Cram*.

Question 26

Answer a is correct. DHCP is used to automatically configure TCP/IP configuration information on TCP/IP hosts. All computers using TCP/IP must have a *unique* IP address, a subnet mask, and if used in a WAN, a default gateway. In large networks, it can be time-consuming to configure these settings on each computer one at a time. In these instances, a DHCP server can be used to automatically provide the clients on the network with this information. A DHCP server can provide clients with a unique IP address, a subnet mask, a default gateway, and many other TCP/IP parameters automatically. In order for DHCP to assign unique IP addresses to hosts, it must be configured with a scope. A DHCP scope is the range of IP addresses it uses to distribute to hosts requesting an IP address. The configure a DHCP scope, two parameters must be specified: the "From" address and the "To" address. It is the addresses within this range, or scope, that a DHCP server will assign to clients. WINS and DNS are used for name resolution in a TCP/IP network.

For more information, see Chapter 4 of *Network+ Exam Cram*.

Question 27

Answer b is correct. DNS (DNS stands for Domain Name Service) is used to provide name resolution of hostnames or Fully Qualified Domain Name (FQDN) to IP addresses in a TCP/IP network. All computers running TCP/IP specify a hostname that is used to identify themselves on the network. When TCP/IP hosts communicate, their IP addresses are resolved, or associated, with their IP address. DNS performs this hostname-to-IP-address-name resolution. An example of an FQDN would be an Internet address, like **www.anything. com**. DHCP is used to dynamically assign IP configuration information to TCP/IP hosts.

For more information, see Chapter 4 of *Network+ Exam Cram*.

Question 28

Answer b is correct. Although DNS, HOSTS files, and WINS are all used for name resolution, only WINS answers the question. WINS is used in Microsoft networks to provide name resolution of NetBIOS names to IP addresses. Microsoft networks utilize the NetBIOS application programming interface (API) when communicating. NetBIOS is an API that provides the "base" that Microsoft networks are built on. WINS will resolve, or associate, a NetBIOS name to its IP address. All computers running TCP/IP specify a hostname that is used to identify themselves on the network. When TCP/IP hosts communicate, their IP addresses are resolved, or associated, with their IP address. DNS performs this hostname-to-IP address name resolution. The main difference between the name resolution services of WINS and DNS are the types of names they resolve. WINS resolves NetBIOS names to IP addresses, while DNS resolves hostnames or FQDNs to IP addresses. All Internet addresses (www.anything.com, .org, .net, and so on) are examples of FQDN names. A HOSTS file is local file on a TCP/IP computer that resolves hostnames or FQDNs to IP addresses, similar to DNS. Entries in a HOSTS file must be made manually in the file on each user's computer. DHCP is used to automatically configure TCP/IP configuration information on TCP/IP hosts.

For more information, see Chapter 4 of *Network+ Exam Cram*.

Question 29

Answer c is correct. HOSTS files and DNS both resolve hostnames or FQDNs to IP addresses. All computers running TCP/IP specify a hostname that is used to identify themselves on the network. When TCP/IP hosts communicate, their IP addresses are resolved, or associated, with their IP address. DNS or HOSTS files can be used to perform this hostname-to-IP address name resolution. A HOSTS file is a local file on a TCP/IP computer that resolves hostnames or FQDNs to IP addresses. Entries in a HOSTS file must be made manually in the file on each user's computer. DNS resolves hostnames or FQDNs to IP addresses. When DNS is used for name resolution in place of HOSTS files, an entire network can utilize the services of a single DNS server, making administration easier. WINS or LMHOSTS files are used in Microsoft networks to provide name resolution of NetBIOS names to IP addresses. DHCP is used to automatically configure TCP/IP configuration information on TCP/IP hosts.

For more information, see Chapter 4 of *Network+ Exam Cram*.

Question 30

Answer b is correct. TCP and UDP are part of the TCP/IP protocol suite. TCP is a connection-oriented protocol that provides guaranteed delivery of packets between hosts. TCP also ensures that packets will be delivered to the destination host in the same order they were sent. UDP is a connectionless protocol that does not guarantee delivery of packets. UDP is primarily used by TCP/IP utilities and for broadcasting packets in a TCP/IP network.

For more information, see Chapter 4 of *Network+ Exam Cram*.

Question 31

Answer b is correct. Post Office Protocol (POP3) and Simple Mail Transfer Protocol (SMTP) are common protocols used with Internet email. POP3 is used to retrieve Internet mail from a mail server. SMTP is used to send outgoing Internet mail to a mail server, as well as move mail between mail servers. Both SMTP and POP3 are part of the TCP/IP protocol suite. DCHP and WINS have nothing to do with Internet email.

The key points to remember about these protocols are:

➤ You send mail using SMTP.

➤ You receive mail using POP3.

➤ Your POP3 server is your incoming mail server.

➤ Your SMTP server is your outgoing mail server.

For more information, see Chapter 4 of *Network+ Exam Cram*.

Question 32

Answer b is correct. Simple Network Management Protocol (SNMP) is commonly used to monitor a TCP/IP network. SNMP can report on the traffic and components of a TCP/IP network and provide administrators with statistical data. SNMP is implemented using agents and managers. SNMP agents are programs installed on TCP/IP computers in the network. With these agents in place, SNMP management software, installed on a TCP/IP computer, can be used to gather information from these agents on the status of the network. The information an SNMP manager collects from an SNMP agent is stored in a Management Information Base (MIB). The MIB is located on the device being managed and contains a database of information and settings that an SNMP manager uses to communicate with the device. POP3 is a protocol used to retrieve incoming Internet mail. TCP is a connection-oriented protocol that provides guaranteed delivery of packets. SMTP is a protocol used to send outgoing Internet mail.

For more information, see Chapter 4 of *Network+ Exam Cram*.

Question 33

Answer c is correct. File Transfer Protocol (FTP) is used to transfer files between remote hosts on a TCP/IP network. FTP is commonly used on the Internet to upload and download files between a Web browser and a Web server. SNMP is commonly used to monitor a TCP/IP network. SNMP can report on the traffic and components of a TCP/IP network and provide administrators with statistical data. POP3 is a protocol used to retrieve incoming Internet mail. TCP is a connection-oriented protocol that provides guaranteed delivery of packets. SMTP is a protocol used to send outgoing Internet mail.

For more information, see Chapter 4 of *Network+ Exam Cram*.

Question 34

Answer c is correct. Hypertext Transfer Protocol (HTTP) is the protocol used on the Web. When you request an internet address that begins with **www**, that signifies a location on the Web and also signifies the protocol to be used is HTTP. A common use for HTTP is the communication made between a Web browser, like Netscape Navigator or Internet Explorer, and a Web site (like **www.anything.com**). FTP is used to transfer files between remote hosts on a TCP/IP network. SNMP is commonly used to monitor a TCP/IP network. SMTP is a protocol used to send outgoing Internet mail.

For more information, see Chapter 4 of *Network+ Exam Cram*.

Question 35

Answer a is correct. TCP/IP addresses are divided into three main classes: Class A, Class B, and Class C. The address range for each address class is as follows:

➤ **Class A** IP addresses that *begin* with numbers from 1 to 126.

➤ **Class B** IP addresses that *begin* with numbers from 128 to 191 (note that 127 is not used in IP addressing; it is reserved for localhost).

➤ **Class C** IP addresses that *begin* with numbers from 192 to 223.

When looking at any IP address, it is the number in the *first* octet that determines the address class of that address. For example:

➤ The IP address 3.100.32.7 is a Class A address, because it *begins* with 3, a number between 1 and 126.

➤ The IP address 145.100.32.7 is a Class B address, because it *begins* with 145, a number between 128 and 191.

➤ The IP address 210.100.32.7 is a Class C address, because it *begins* with 210, a number between 192 and 223.

An IP address is made up of a network ID and a host ID. The network ID identifies the network a user is on, and the host ID identifies the user. An IP address is specified using four individual numbers separated by periods. Each one of these "sections" is known as an octet (because it contains eight bits). Each address class uses different combinations of octets to specify a network ID and host ID. The configuration is as follows:

➤ **Class A** Uses the *first* octet for the network ID, and the last three octets for the host ID. Example: IP address 2.3.45.9 is a Class A address because it begins with 2, a number between 1 and 126. The network ID of this IP address is 2, and the host ID is 3.45.9 because a Class A address uses the first octet for the network ID and the last three octets for the host ID.

➤ **Class B** Uses the *first two* octets for the network ID and the last two octets for the host ID. Example: IP address 167.211.32.5 is a Class B address because it begins with 167, a number between 128 and 191. The network ID of this IP address is 167.211, and the host ID is 32.5, because a Class B address uses the first two octets for the network ID and the last two octets for the host ID.

➤ **Class C** Uses the *first three* octets for the network ID and the last octet for the host ID. Example: IP address 200.3.11.75 is a Class C address, because it begins with 200, a number between 192 and 223. The network ID of this IP address is 200.3.11, and the host ID is 11, because a Class C address uses the first three octets for the network ID and the last octet for the host ID.

For more information, see Chapter 4 of *Network+ Exam Cram*.

Question 36

Answer c is correct. Please see the explanation of Question 35 for details.

For more information, see Chapter 4 of *Network+ Exam Cram*.

Question 37

Answer c is correct. All computers using TCP/IP must have a *unique* IP address, a subnet mask, and if used in a WAN, a default gateway. An IP address identifies a TCP/IP host on the network, and contains two important elements: a network ID and a host ID. The network ID of an IP address identifies the network the host is on. (For example, all users in a single location are said to be on the same network, and, therefore, will all have the same network ID in their IP address.) The host ID of an IP address identifies the host, or individual, computer on a TCP/IP network. It is the host ID portion of an IP address that is the unique part. Therefore, in a single TCP/IP network, users will all have the *same* network ID and *different* (unique) host IDs. The subnet mask is used to "mask" the network portion of an IP address, with the number 255, so IP can determine if the destination host is local or remote. A default subnet mask refers to the subnet mask that is used by a particular TCP/IP address class in a single subnet environment, like a LAN. Because each address class uses a different number of octets for the network ID, and the subnet mask "masks" the network portion of an IP address, the default subnet mask will be different for each class of IP addresses. The number 255 is the number reserved in TCP/IP for use by the default subnet mask. A default subnet mask will use 255s over the network portion of and IP address, and 0s over the host portion of an IP address.

IP address Class A:

➤ Address range is from 1 to 126. Example: 2.45.65.8 is a Class A address. It begins with 2—a number *between* 1 and 126.

➤ Uses the first octet for the network ID, and the last three octets for the host ID. Example: The network ID of IP address 2.45.65.8 is 2, because it is a Class A address, and Class A uses the first octet for the network ID. The host ID is 45.65.8.

➤ Default subnet mask is 255.0.0.0. A default subnet mask uses 255 to mask the network portion of an IP address and 0 to mask the host portion of an IP address.

IP address Class B:

➤ Address range is from 128 to 191. Example: 162.45.65.8 is a Class B address. It begins with 162—a number between 128 and 191.

➤ Uses the first two octets for the network ID and the last two octets for the host ID. Example: The network ID of IP address 162.45.65.8 is 162.45, because it is a Class B address, and Class B uses the first two octets for the network ID. The host ID is 65.8.

➤ Default subnet mask is 255.255.0.0. A default subnet mask uses 255 to mask the network portion of an IP address, and 0 to mask the host portion of an IP address.

IP address Class C:

➤ Address range is from 192 to 223. Example: 202.85.65.8 is a Class C address. It begins with 202—a number between 192 and 223.

➤ Uses the first three octets for the network ID and the last octet for the host ID. Example: The network ID of IP address 202.85.65.8 is 202.85.65, because it is a Class C address, and Class C uses the first three octets for the network ID. The host ID is 8.

➤ Default subnet mask is 255.255.255.0. A default subnet mask uses 255 to mask the network portion of an IP address, and 0 to mask the host portion of an IP address.

For more information, see Chapter 4 of *Network+ Exam Cram*.

Question 38

Answer b is correct. The IP address in this question is a Class B address, and therefore uses a subnet mask of 255.255.0.0. All computers using TCP/IP must have a *unique* IP address, a subnet mask, and if used in a WAN, a default gateway. An IP address identifies a TCP/IP host on the network and contains two important elements: a network ID and a host ID. The network ID of an IP address identifies the network the host is on. (For example, all users in a single location are said to be on the same network and, therefore, will all have the same network ID in their IP address.) The host ID of an IP address identifies the host, or individual, computer on a TCP/IP network. It is the host ID portion of an IP address that is the unique part. Therefore, in a single TCP/IP network, users will all have the *same* network ID and *different* (unique) host IDs. The subnet mask is used to "mask" the network portion of an IP address with the number 255, so IP can determine if the destination host is local or remote. A default subnet mask refers to the subnet mask that is used by a particular TCP/IP address class in a single subnet environment, like a LAN. Because each address class uses a different number of octets for the network ID, and the subnet mask "masks" the network portion of an IP address, the default subnet mask will be different for each class of IP addresses. The number 255 is the number reserved in TCP/IP for use by the default subnet mask. A default subnet mask will use 255s over the network portion of and IP address, and 0s over the host portion of an IP address. See the table in the previous question for more complete information on IP addressing.

For more information, see Chapter 4 of *Network+ Exam Cram*.

Question 39

Answer b is correct. A port number is one of the items specified by TCP/IP hosts to establish a connection. Port numbers for common TCP/IP utilities are said to have "well-known" port numbers. A well-known port number is the port number that will be used when no port number is specifically specified. The most important port numbers to know are:

➤ **HTTP** The protocol used by the Web; uses port 80.

➤ **FTP** Used to transfer files (upload/download); uses port 21.

➤ **SMTP** Used to send outgoing Internet mail; uses port 25.

➤ **POP3** Used to retrieve incoming Internet mail; uses port 110.

When using any of these well-known utilities, the port number does not need to be specified; it is assumed the default will be used. Windows Sockets is an example of the use of a port number. Windows Sockets is a "session" established between two TCP/IP computers. The "socket" created between hosts is used for reliable communication. To create a socket, hosts specify an IP address, the type of service (UDP or TCP), and a port number. If a different port number is to be used other than the well-known number, it must be specifically designated and must be a number over 1024. (The number 1024 and numbers below it are used for well-known programs.)

For more information, see Chapter 4 of *Network+ Exam Cram*.

Question 40

Answers b and c are correct. An IP proxy, or proxy server (same thing), serves two main purposes:

➤ Firewall protection to protect users on the local network from the intrusion of the Internet.

➤ Improved Internet performance by increasing the speed that users on the local network retrieve Web pages.

An IP proxy can provide firewall security to protect users on the local network from the intrusion of the Internet. (A firewall is defined as any configuration, hardware or software, that protects users on a local network from the intrusion of the Internet.) When an IP proxy is used as a firewall, it typically will be a dedicated server that is configured with two network adapter cards. One network card will be used for an Internet connection, known as the external network adapter, and the other will be used for the connection to the local network, known as the internal network adapter. In this firewall configuration, the only computer connected to the Internet is the proxy server, through this dedicated external network card. In order for clients to access the Internet, they must configure their Web browsers to send all Internet requests to the IP proxy. When a client requests an Internet address, the request goes to the proxy server, and the proxy server retrieves the information from the Web site on behalf of the client. The proxy server "acts" like the client when retrieving this information, so the only IP address used in making all requests is the proxy server's external network adapter address. All internal IP addresses will not be seen by any Internet networks. For additional security, the proxy server can be configured to deny access to Web sites or protocols for both incoming and outgoing requests.

The proxy server also provides improved Internet performance. Because an IP proxy retrieves Web pages on behalf of all users in a local network, it places all these pages in its local cache (memory). This way, if a user requests an Internet address that was previously retrieved by the proxy server, the proxy server will give the user the page contained in its local cache. The process of providing users with cached Web pages is much faster than the standard means of requesting/retrieving the information from the Web site on the Internet. DNS or HOSTS files are used to resolve hostnames to IP addresses. DHCP is used to automatically assign IP address information to clients.

For more information, see Chapter 7 of *Network+ Exam Cram*.

Question 41

Answer a is correct. The manner in which data flows on a network cable can be defined as either baseband or broadband. Baseband, as used by Ethernet 802.3, employs digital signaling over a single frequency. Baseband can send information bidirectionally and utilizes repeaters to boost a signal. Broadband uses analog signaling over a range of frequencies. Broadband sends information unidirectionally and uses amplifiers to boost a signal.

For more information, see Chapter 6 of *Network+ Exam Cram*.

Question 42

Answer d is correct. DHCP is used to automatically configure TCP/IP configuration information on TCP/IP hosts. A DHCP server can provide clients with a unique IP address, a subnet mask, a default gateway, and many other TCP/IP parameters automatically. In order for clients to receive their IP configuration from a DHCP server, the TCP/IP protocol must be installed on all client computers. In Windows 95 computers, the option Obtain An IP Address Automatically in TCP/IP properties must be checked, and when TCP/IP is installed, this option is enabled by default. Windows 95 DHCP client computers do not have to specify the IP address or computer name of the DHCP server. (In fact, this cannot be done.)

For more information, see Chapter 4 of *Network+ Exam Cram*.

Question 43

Answer c is correct. A port number is one of the items specified by TCP/IP hosts to establish a connection. Port numbers for common TCP/IP utilities are said to have well-known port numbers. A "well-known" port number is the port number that will be used when no port number is specifically specified. The most important port numbers to know are:

➤ **HTTP** The protocol used by the Web; uses port 80.

➤ **FTP** Used to transfer files (upload/download); uses port 21.

➤ **SMTP** Used to send outgoing Internet mail; uses port 25.

➤ **POP3** Used to retrieve incoming Internet mail; uses port 110.

When using any of these well-known utilities, the port number does not need to be specified; it is assumed the default will be used. Windows Sockets is an example of the use of a port number. Windows Sockets is a "session" established between two TCP/IP computers. The "socket" created between hosts is used for reliable communication. To create a socket, hosts specify an IP address, the type of service (UDP or TCP), and a port number. If a different port number is to be used other than the well-known number, it must be specifically designated and must be a number over 1024. (The number 1024 and the numbers below it are used for well-known programs.)

For more information, see Chapter 4 of *Network+ Exam Cram*.

Question 44

Answer a is correct. An NT Server computer can perform routing functions to segment a network. Installing and configuring multiple adapters and selecting the Enable IP Forwarding option in TCP/IP properties will allow NT Server to act as a router with a static routing table. A routing table can be either static or dynamic. With static routing, all information in the routing table must be entered manually. This can be done in NT Server using the **ROUTE ADD** command. Dynamic routing, as the name implies, allows a router to automatically update its routing table. Routing Information Protocol for Internet Protocol (RIP for IP) and Routing Information Protocol for Internetwork Packet Exchange (RIP for IPX) are some examples of the types of methods that can be used when employing dynamic routing. While both RIP for IP and RIP for IPX will allow NT Server to perform dynamic routing, in this example the only protocol used is TCP/IP, so only RIP for IP is required. POP3 is used to retrieve Internet mail and has nothing to do with routing tables.

For more information, see Chapter 4 of *Network+ Exam Cram*.

Question 45

Answer b is correct. A router operates at the network layer of the Open System Interconnection (OSI) model. The OSI model defines standards for networking based on a seven-layer model. All of the components used in networking (hubs, bridges, routers, cables, protocols, and so on) conform to various layers of the OSI model by "residing" at one or more of these seven layers. Routers are the most common connectivity device used to connect two LANs together to form a WAN. A router manages network traffic by reading the network addresses or IP address of the packets it receives. The reason a router can read network or IP addresses is because it resides at the same layer of the OSI model as network protocols, like IP (TCP/IP).

For more information, see Chapter 8 of *Network+ Exam Cram*.

Question 46

Answer d is correct. A bridge can be used in place of a hub to improve overall network performance. A bridge can read a MAC address. A MAC address, also referred to as the "hardware address," is the permanent address that is "burned" on every network card by the manufacturer. The ability to read MAC addresses allows a bridge to make decisions on where to send packets, making it a more efficient connectivity device than a hub. The OSI model defines standards for networking based on a seven-layer model. All of the components used in networking (hubs, bridges, routers, cables, protocols, and so on) conform to various layers of the OSI model by "residing" at one or more of these seven layers. A bridge resides at the Data Link layer of the OSI model. A hub, which resides at the physical layer of the OSI model, cannot read any packet information and, therefore, just passes the packets it receives out all ports. An MAU is the connectivity device used in token ring networks.

For more information, see Chapter 8 of *Network+ Exam Cram*.

Question 47

Answer d is correct. There are two common security models a network administrator can employ to control users access to network resources: Share-level security and user-level security. When using share-level security, passwords are assigned to *resources*. An example of share-level security is sharing a printer and assigning a password to that printer. When users need to connect to the printer, they will have to enter the password set on the printer to access it. The share-level security model is considered a less secure method than user-level security, because users are more likely to tell others the password to access a resource than they are to give away their own username and password. In user-level security, permissions are assigned to users. An example of user-level security is sharing a printer and assigning permissions to users to access this resource. In order for users to access this printer, their user account must have permissions to access it. Remember: share-level security assigns passwords to *resources*, (printers, files, programs, and so on). User-level security assigns permissions to *users*. Answer b does not exist.

For more information, see Chapter 7 of *Network+ Exam Cram*.

Question 48

Answer c is correct. An interrupt request (IRQ) line is a "line" of communication that a hardware device uses to communicate with a processor. All devices in a computer require a unique IRQ. (There are some exceptions to this rule, but stick with the rule on your exam.) The number of devices that can be added to a computer is dependent on the available ports/slots. The computer does not have to be connected to the network to see if there are internal device conflicts. Windows 98 includes a tool, Device Manager, that is used for this purpose.

For more information, see Chapter 14 of *Network+ Exam Cram*.

Question 49

Answers b and d are correct. The OSI model defines standards for networking based on a seven-layer model. All of the components used in networking (hubs, bridges, routers, cables, protocols, and so on) conform to various layers of the OSI model by "residing" at one or more of these seven layers. Project 802 modified the Data Link layer of the OSI model by dividing it into two sublayers: logical link control (LLC) and MAC. Standards for Ethernet (CSMA/CD) networks are defined in 802.3. CSMA/CD refers to the type of access method used by Ethernet 802.3 networks. The LLC, as specified in 802.2, defines the use of service access points (SAPs) used to transfer information over a network. Standards for token ring networks are defined by 802.5 specifications.

For more information, see Chapter 8 of *Network+ Exam Cram*.

Question 50

Answer c is correct. Both PPP and SLIP are used as dial-up protocols when using a modem to connect to a remote network or the Internet. PPP is a newer, more efficient dial-up protocol than SLIP. PPP automatically obtains configuration parameters with the remote server on connection. This simplifies the configurations required when making a remote connection. SLIP must be configured manually with these parameters. Another key difference between PPP and SLIP is the number of communication protocols supported. PPP supports IPX/SPX, AppleTalk, TCP/IP, and NetBEUI. SLIP only supports the use of the TCP/IP protocol.

For more information, see Chapter 6 of *Network+ Exam Cram*.

Question 51

Answers a and b are correct. A hub is commonly used to connect computers in 10BaseT, 10Base5, and 10Base2 networks. A hub can also be used to connect network cable to extend the length of a network. A repeater can also be used to connect Thinnet coaxial cable together and boost the signal. Most hubs can act as repeaters, boosting the signals they pass. An MAU is used to connect computers in IBM Token Ring networks. "MOO" is the sound a cow makes, not a connectivity device.

For more information, see Chapter 2 of *Network+ Exam Cram*.

Question 52

Answers a and b are correct. ISDN is a digital dial-up service that can send voice and data signals at 128Kbps (128,000 bits per second). ISDN uses two 64K channels, called "B" channels, when transmitting. ISDN uses a TA to connect to a computer in place of a modem. This is because the transmission is digital over ISDN and does not have to be "modulated" (converted to analog), as is the case with regular phone line. PSTN (Public Switched Telephone Network), also known as POTS (Plain Old Telephone Service), is the standard dial-up analog phone line used to send voice and data. PSTN can transmit data up to 28,800Bps. (The new 56Kbps standard achieves faster transmission speeds over 28.8Kbps by using a digital lines and data compression.) PSTN uses a modem (modulate/demodulate) to connect to a computer. A modem converts, or modulates, a computer's digital signal-to-analog for transmission over PSTN, and the receiving computer's modem will demodulate that signal, or convert it from analog to a digital signal.

For more information, see Chapter 6 of *Network+ Exam Cram*.

Question 53

Answer c is correct. A bus topology requires termination at both ends for it to function. When the cable disconnected from the T-connector on Olivia's computer, termination was lost on both sides of the network. Therefore, all users will be down until this is fixed. This is a major disadvantage of a bus topology, because in a large network, troubleshooting can be time-consuming, and the failure of the cable at any point will take the entire network down. The fact that that there are different departments here is irrelevant; it is the topology that will determine what action to take for troubleshooting.

For more information, see Chapter 2 of *Network+ Exam Cram*.

Question 54

Answer c is correct. Fiber-optic cable could be used in this scenario, but it does not meet the customer's requirement of keeping costs down. Fiber optic is very fast, goes very far, and provides great security, but it is very expensive. Thinnet coaxial meets the requirement of costs being kept to a minimum, but a single-segment length cannot be used for distances greater than 185 meters. Thicknet coaxial is commonly used in this type of scenario for long cable runs and can travel up to 500 meters in a single segment. Shielded twisted-pair is limited to 100 meters per single segment.

For more information, see Chapter 2 of *Network+ Exam Cram*.

Question 55

Answer d is correct. The correct utility to use in this case would be DHCP. DHCP is used to automatically configure TCP/IP configuration information on TCP/IP hosts. All computers using TCP/IP must have a *unique* IP address, a subnet mask, and if used in a WAN, a default gateway. In large networks, it can be time-consuming to configure these settings on each computer one at a time. In these instances, a DHCP server can be used to automatically provide the clients on the network with this information. A DHCP server can provide clients with a unique IP address, a subnet mask, a default gateway, and many other TCP/IP parameters automatically. In order for DHCP to assign unique IP addresses to hosts, it must be configured with a scope. A DHCP scope is the range of IP addresses it uses to distribute to hosts requesting an IP address. The configure a DHCP scope, two parameters must be specified: the "From" address and the "To" address. It is the addresses within this range, or scope, that a DHCP server will assign addresses to clients. WINS and DNS are used for name resolution in a TCP/IP network. There is no such thing as ACP.

For more information, see Chapter 4 of *Network+ Exam Cram*.

Question 56

Answer a is correct. In a star topology, all computers are directly connected to a hub, and the hub handles termination. Therefore, when a cable is removed from a network card, only that computer is affected. If this was a bus topology, all computers would be down, because termination would have been lost. Ease of troubleshooting is a big advantage of a star topology over a bus topology.

For more information, see Chapter 2 of *Network+ Exam Cram*.

Question 57

Answer d is correct. A mesh topology features multiple links that can provide alternate routes to a host in the event of a single line failure. A mesh topology is the most expensive of all the networking topologies and can be confusing to implement. A bus topology is configured by connecting nodes together with a continuous line of cable that is terminated at both ends. The cable used in a bus topology must be continuous and terminated at both ends or the entire network will fail. In a star topology, computers connect directly to a hub, and the hub handles termination. In a token ring topology, computers connect to an MAU, which provides equal access for all computers by circulating a "token" across the network.

For more information, see Chapter 2 of *Network+ Exam Cram*.

Question 58

Answer a is correct. An MAU looks similar to a hub, but is different in that it contains a logical "ring" that is used for token passing, the access method used in a ring topology. A router is used to connect networks in different locations together. A gateway is used to connect networks together that use dissimilar protocols.

For more information, see Chapter 2 of *Network+ Exam Cram*.

Question 59

Answer c is correct. A high-speed backbone is a good choice for large networks of 250 or more users. A backbone features a "trunk" segment that is run across all servers that provides high-speed data access to clients. Routers receive client requests and manage network traffic. An MAU is used in token ring networks, not Ethernet networks. Shielded twisted-pair cable provides more resistance to crosstalk than unshielded twisted-pair, but it does not transfer data any faster. There is no such thing as an X-55 PAD.

For more information, see Chapter 2 of *Network+ Exam Cram*.

Question 60

Answer b is correct. NT Server is a server operating system made by Microsoft. The tool used to manage users' accounts in NT Server is called User Manager for Domains. With User Manager for Domains, an administrator can create and manage user accounts on an NT Server. The other answers are not valid.

For more information, see Chapter 3 of *Network+ Exam Cram*.

Question 61

Answers a, b, and c are correct. Fault tolerance refers to the ability of a system to recover from a single hard disk failure. Standards for implementing fault tolerance are defined by RAID. A volume set is created by combining areas of free space from one or more hard disks into one logical drive. Volume sets do not provide fault tolerance. In fact, if one member of a volume set fails, all data is lost. A mirror set, or RAID 1, is created using two disks, with one disk acting as a "mirror" of the other, providing redundancy. In the event of a single disk failure in a mirror set, the other disk may be used. Disk duplexing is a physical form of RAID 1 mirroring, and requires two physical disks and two disk controllers to be implemented. A stripe set with parity, or RAID 5, is created by combining equal areas of free space on 3 to 32 disks to form one logical drive. If one member of a stripe set with parity fails, the failed member can be "regenerated" using the parity information that is stored on the remaining members of the set.

For more information, see Chapter 5 of *Network+ Exam Cram*.

Question 62

Answer d is correct. Thinnet coaxial cable can travel 185 meters (or 607 feet) per segment by specification. Exceeding this limit can cause the network to malfunction. To properly extend the single-segment length of Thinnet coaxial, a repeater must be used to boost the signal back to its original strength. A hub can also act as a repeater. T-connectors are used to connect Thinnet coaxial to a network adapter card. The correct resistance in a bus network that uses Thinnet coaxial cable is 50 ohms (a tolerance of +/- 2 is acceptable). Hubs are not required in a bus topology.

For more information, see Chapter 2 of *Network+ Exam Cram*.

Question 63

Answer c is correct. Fiber optic is an extremely fast, secure media that can transport a signal for miles. Fiber optic sends a signal as a pulse of light, so it is impervious to electrical interference. Data traveling through a fiber-optic cable cannot be tapped and read. Fiber optic is typically used in situations like this, in which speed and security are the utmost concerns. Thicknet (500 meters), Thinnet (185 meters), and twisted-pair (100 meters) have limited distances, and all can be tapped and the data read.

For more information, see Chapter 2 of *Network+ Exam Cram*.

Question 64

Answer c is correct. 100BaseT and 100Base VG-AnyLAN are two totally different topologies. 100BaseT is an Ethernet standard that supports categories 3, 4, and 5 twisted-pair cable. (Although categories 3 and 4 are supported, category 5 is required for 100Mbps transmission.) 100BaseT uses CSMA/CD as an access method. An access method is a standard that defines how a packet is placed on a network cable. With CSMA/CD, computers "listen" to the cable, and when they sense it is free, a packet is sent. 100Base VG-AnyLAN is know by several names: VG, AnyLAN, 100VG-AnyLAN, 100BaseVG. It supports categories 3, 4, and 5 twisted-pair cable and requires special hubs and network cards to be implemented. The access method used by 100Base VG-AnyLAN is known as demand priority. The demand priority access method relies on these special hubs to control access to the network cable.

For more information, see Chapter 2 of *Network+ Exam Cram*.

Question 65

Answer a is correct. A server is a computer that has a server operating system installed on it. Popular server operating systems are Novell's NetWare and Microsoft's NT Server. A server is typically used to provide clients or workstations with access to resources. Additionally, a server-based network features a server that is used to centrally manage the clients in a network. A peer-to-peer network is comprised of computers that are all running client operating systems, such as Windows 9X or NT Workstation. Because all computers in a peer-to-peer network utilize a client operating system, they are all considered to be equal, or "peers" of one another.

For more information, see Chapter 3 of *Network+ Exam Cram*.

Question 66

Answer a is correct. Based on the fact that the user can send mail but not retrieve it, she probably changed her POP3 server information. If the user had changed both her POP3 and SMTP settings, she would not be able to send or receive mail. POP3 and SMTP are common protocols used with Internet email. POP3 is used to retrieve Internet mail from a mail server. SMTP is used to send outgoing Internet mail to a mail server. Both SMTP and POP3 are part of the TCP/IP protocol suite. The key points to remember about these protocols are:

➤ You receive mail using POP3.

➤ You send mail using SMTP.

➤ Your POP3 server is your incoming mail server.

➤ Your SMTP server is your outgoing mail server.

For more information, see Chapter 4 of *Network+ Exam Cram*.

Question 67

Answer b is correct. The manner in which data flows on a network cable can be defined as either baseband or broadband. Baseband, as used by Ethernet 802.3, uses digital signaling over a single frequency. Baseband can send information bidirectionally and utilizes repeaters to boost a signal. Broadband uses analog signaling over a range of frequencies. Broadband sends information unidirectionally and uses amplifiers to boost a signal. Demand priority is an access method used by 100Base VG-AnyLAN. The demand priority access method relies on special hubs to control access to the network cable. Token passing is an access method used in IBM Token Ring networks.

For more information, see Chapter 6 of *Network+ Exam Cram*.

Question 68

Answer a is correct. Full-duplex transmission allows data to travel in two directions simultaneously. When you are talking on a telephone, you are utilizing full-duplex transmission (both parties can speak at one time). Half-duplex transmission only allows data to travel in one direction at a time. When you use a walkie-talkie, you are utilizing half-duplex transmission (only one party can speak at one time).

For more information, see Chapter 2 of *Network+ Exam Cram*.

Question 69

Answer b is correct. Novell NetWare is a popular network operating system that uses NetWare Directory Services (NDS). NDS is an object-oriented database that organizes network resources into a hierarchical tree-like structure. From this NDS tree, users can access the resources on a NetWare network. NDS is based on a standard known as X.500. X.500 is a standard developed by the OSI for file and directory services in networking. Windows 95, NT Server, and NT Workstation are all Microsoft operating systems.

Microsoft's NT Server is a popular network operating system that utilizes the concept of a "domain" to organize a network. A domain is a logical grouping of computers with centralized resources and security. Windows 95 and Windows NT Workstation are Microsoft desktop operating systems designed to run on client computers. These client computers can be members of an NT Server "domain."

For more information, see Chapter 3 of *Network+ Exam Cram*.

Question 70

Answer a is correct. An IP proxy, or proxy server, is ideal for providing security and increased performance to a local network accessing the Internet.

An IP proxy, or proxy server (same thing), serves two main purposes:

➤ Firewall protection to protect users on the local network from the intrusion of the Internet.

➤ Improved Internet performance by increasing the speed that users on the local network retrieve Web pages.

An IP proxy can provide firewall security to protect users on the local network from the intrusion of the Internet. (A firewall is defined as any configuration, hardware or software, that protects users on a local network from the intrusion of the Internet.) When an IP proxy is used as a firewall, it typically will be a dedicated server that is configured with two network adapter cards. One network card will be used for an Internet connection, known as the external network adapter and the other will be used for the connection to the local network, known as the internal network adapter. In this firewall configuration, the only computer connected to the Internet is the proxy server, through this dedicated external network card. In order for clients to access the Internet, they must configure their Web browsers to send all Internet requests to the IP proxy. When a client requests an Internet address, the request goes to the proxy server, and the proxy server retrieves the information from the Web site on behalf of the client. The proxy server "acts" like the client when retrieving this information, so the only IP address used in making all requests is the proxy server's external network adapter address. All internal IP addresses will not be seen by any Internet networks. For additional security, the proxy server can be configured to deny access to Web sites or protocols for both incoming and outgoing requests.

The proxy server also provides improved Internet performance. Because an IP proxy retrieves Web pages on behalf of all users in a local network, it places all those pages in its local cache (memory). This way, if a user requests an Internet address that was previously retrieved by the proxy server, the proxy server will give the user the page contained in its local cache. The process of providing users with cached Web pages is much faster than the standard means of requesting/retrieving the information from the Web site on the Internet.

Both WINS and DNS provide name resolution services, not security services.

For more information, see Chapter 7 of *Network+ Exam Cram*.

Question 71

Answer c is correct. A metropolitan area network (MAN) defines a network that covers an area approximately the size of a city or town (approximately 62 miles). A MAN is a WAN that covers a limited distance, but larger than a LAN. The other answers do not exist.

For more information, see Chapter 2 of *Network+ Exam Cram*.

Question 72

Answer c is correct. The network ID 127 is reserved by TCP/IP for loopback testing. Every computer running TCP/IP has an entry "127.0.0.1" in its local HOSTS file that is resolved to the name "localhost". When troubleshooting TCP/IP, a loopback test can be performed on the local computer using the command **PING 127.0.0.1**. If the **PING** of 127.0.0.1 is successful, this verifies that TCP/IP is correctly installed on the computer. A loopback test can also be performed using **PING localhost**, instead of 127.0.0.1.

For more information, see Chapter 4 of *Network+ Exam Cram*.

Question 73

Answer b is correct. The Internetwork Packet Exchange/Sequenced Packet Exchange (IPX/SPX) protocol is commonly used in Novell NetWare networks. As part of IPX/SPX configuration, a frame type must be specified. The frame type identifies the type of packet supported. In order for computers running IPX/SPX to communicate, they must support the same frame type. Different versions of Novell NetWare support different frame types. For example, Novell NetWare 3.11 uses the frame type Ethernet 802.3, and Novell NetWare 4.1 uses frame type Ethernet 802.2. IPX/SPX can be configured to support multiple frame types to allow for communication between different versions of NetWare.

For more information, see Chapter 4 of *Network+ Exam Cram*.

Question 74

Answer a is correct. The IPX/SPX protocol is commonly used in Novell NetWare networks. IPX/SPX addresses are comprised of two elements: an external network address and an internal address. The external network address used in IPX/SPX identifies the network a computer is part of, similar to the network ID used by TCP/IP. For example, all users in a single location using IPX/SPX will have the same external network address because they are all on the same network. The external network address is specified by the system administrator. The internal address is used by IPX/SPX to uniquely identify an individual computer, similar to the host ID used in TCP/IP. The internal address must be unique to each compute, and for this reason is usually the MAC address of the computer that is running IPX/SPX. (The MAC address is the hardware address that is "burned" on every network adapter card by the manufacturer.) The internal address is generated automatically by IPX/SPX when it is installed. A network ID, default gateway, and a subnet mask are TCP/IP parameters and are not used in IXP/SPX addressing.

For more information, see Chapter 4 of *Network+ Exam Cram*.

Question 75

Answer b is correct. A crossover cable is used to connect two (and only two) 10BaseT computers together without the use of a hub. A crossover cable is made from twisted-pair cable with RJ-45 connectors at each end. The send and receive wires are "crossed" to allow the cable to act as a hub. A crossover cable can only be used to connect two computers, and both computers must have a 10BaseT network adapter card.

For more information, see Chapter 14 of *Network+ Exam Cram*.

Network+
Practice Test #3

Question 1

You administer a server-based network of 20 computers. All servers are located in a small utility room. Lately, network performance has become erratic, and the servers are intermittently failing. You go into the utility room and observe the room temperature to be 55 degrees Fahrenheit, and the humidity level is 50 percent. What observations can you make about the room conditions these servers are in?

○ a. These conditions are suitable for computers. The problem is not caused by room conditions.

○ b. These conditions are not suitable for computers. The room is too cold.

○ c. These conditions are not suitable for computers. The room is too hot.

○ d. These conditions are not suitable for computers. The humidity is too high.

Question 2

You need to attach an external SCSI device to your PC. The only available external connectors on your PC are a dual RJ-11 connector and a DB-25 parallel connector. Which of the following connectors can you use to connect this external SCSI device?

- O a. You can use either the DB-25 connector or the dual RJ-11 connector.
- O b. You can only use the dual RJ-11 connector.
- O c. You can probably use the DB-25 parallel connector.
- O d. You cannot use any of these connectors to attached your external SCSI device.

Question 3

Your 10BaseT network consists of 25 computers as follows:

- 10 Windows 98
- 10 Windows NT Workstation
- 3 Unix computers
- 1 Novell NetWare Server
- 1 Windows NT Server

All computers have 10BaseT network cards installed and are connected to a single hub. How many of these computers have MAC addresses?

- O a. The Microsoft (Windows 98, NT Workstation, and NT Server) computers have MAC addresses. The others do not.
- O b. The Unix computers and the Microsoft computers (Windows 98, NT Workstation, and NT Server) have MAC addresses. The NetWare computer does not.
- O c. All the computers have MAC addresses because it is "burned" on each network card.
- O d. It is impossible to tell what computers have MAC addresses. Not enough information is given.

Question 4

Which of the following is true about the use of patch cables with Thinnet coaxial cable?

- ○ a. A patch cable can be use to extend the length of coaxial cable, but if not used with a repeater, will contribute to the overall length of the cable.

- ○ b. A patch cable can be used to extend the length of coaxial cable and can be spliced into coaxial cable without the use of a repeater, without contributing to the overall length of the cable.

- ○ c. A patch cable is only used in fiber optic networks.

- ○ d. None of the above.

Question 5

Which of the following backup strategies will *not* clear (reset) the archive bit of files?

- ○ a. Incremental

- ○ b. Differential

- ○ c. Full backup

- ○ d. All of the above

Question 6

Which of the following is the correct UNC command to access a network printer with the share name DOCS that is located on a computer named ACCOUNTING?

- ○ a. \\ACCOUNTING\DOCS

- ○ b. \ACCOUNTING\\DOCS

- ○ c. \\DOCS\\ACCOUNTING

- ○ d. \DOCS\\ACCOUNTING

Question 7

You are the network administrator for your company. Emily, a user on your network, complains that she cannot access a directory called Database on the network. She says when she attempts to connect to this resource, she receives an "access denied" message. She says that she has no trouble accessing any other network resources. You check her permissions and discover that Emily is a member of the Database Users group. This group has full control permission to the Database directory. What is a possible reason Emily cannot access this resource even though she belongs to a group that has sufficient permissions?

- ○ a. Emily is logging onto the network with the incorrect password.
- ○ b. Emily is not logged onto the network.
- ○ c Emily has permissions assigned to her user account that override her group permissions.
- ○ d Emily's account has expired.

Question 8

When is the best time to install antivirus software?

- ○ a. Antivirus software should be installed after a computer has been infected with a virus.
- ○ b. Antivirus software should be installed before a computer has been infected with a virus.
- ○ c. It does not matter when antivirus software is installed on a computer.
- ○ d. On a server, install antivirus software before infection; on a client, install antivirus software after infection.

Question 9

What TCP/IP command is used to perform a localhost loopback test?

- ○ a. **NBTSTAT**
- ○ b. **TRACERT**
- ○ c. **PING 127.0.0.1**
- ○ d. **NETSTAT**

Question 10

Novell NetWare networks make use of the IPX/SPX protocol for communication. A configuration parameter of IPX/SPX is a frame type. Which of the following best describes what will happen if two computers running IPX/SPX do not have the same frame type?

○ a. If two computers running IPX/SPX have different frame types, communication is limited to the local network (LAN).

○ b. If two computers running IPX/SPX have different frame types, communication is limited to a WAN.

○ c. If two computers running IPX/SPX have different frame types, communication will not take place.

○ d. If two computers running IPX/SPX have different frame types, communication will take place just fine.

Question 11

What is the default account created by Novell NetWare 4 upon installation of a server?

○ a. ADMIN

○ b. ADMINISTRATOR

○ c. BOSS

○ d. Computer_Name_SUP

Question 12

TCP/IP is an industry-standard protocol that requires configuration to perform properly. Which of the following correctly states what will happen if two users on the same TCP/IP network have identical IP addresses?

- ○ a. If two users in a single TCP/IP network have identical IP addresses, neither one of them will be able to communicate on the network.

- ○ b. If two users in a single TCP/IP network have identical IP addresses, the first person to initialize his or her IP address will be able to communicate. The other person will then receive an error message when attempting to initialize.

- ○ c. If two users in a single TCP/IP network have identical IP addresses, both will be able to communicate. This is normal for TCP/IP configuration.

- ○ d. If two users in a single TCP/IP network have identical IP addresses, both will be able to communicate on the LAN, but not the WAN.

Question 13

You administer a server-based network of 20 computers. All servers are located in a small utility room. Lately, network performance has become erratic, and the servers are failing intermittently. You go into the utility room and observe the room temperature to be 60 degrees Fahrenheit, and the humidity level is three percent. What observations can you make about the room conditions these servers are in?

- ○ a. These conditions are suitable for computers.

- ○ b. These conditions are not suitable for computers. The room is too cold.

- ○ c. These conditions are not suitable for computers. The room is too hot.

- ○ d. These conditions are not suitable for computers. The humidity is too low.

Question 14

What type of cable is commonly used in backbones or for making long cable runs over 200 meters between floors?

○ a. Thinnet coaxial

○ b. Thicknet coaxial

○ c. Twisted-pair

○ d. Shielded twisted-pair

Question 15

What type of connector is used to attach twisted-pair cable to a network adapter card?

○ a. RJ-45 connector

○ b. RJ-11 connector

○ c. Drop cable with a vampire tap into the Thicknet and a 15-pin AUI connector to the network adapter card

○ d. BNC barrel connector

Question 16

A server on your network is configured with five hard disks; each is 2GB in size. Three of these disks are configured in a stripe set without parity. A very important database is stored on this server and resides on the stripe set without parity. Suddenly, one of the disks in the stripe set without parity fails. How do you get the database information back?

○ a. The only way to get the information back is to restore it from tape backup.

○ b. Replace the failed disk, and the stripe set without parity will regenerate the missing data.

○ c. No action is necessary, the other members of the stripe set without parity have the entire database information.

○ d. Replace the failed disk, reboot the computer with a fault tolerance boot disk, and select Regenerate.

Question 17

You are managing a network for a midsize sales company. Your network consists of 23 Unix computers, 58 Windows NT Workstation computers, and three NT Server computers. Users need to communicate with each other and also require access to the Internet. At the very least, how many communication protocols are needed for communication between all computers on this network, and what are they?

○ a. At least two protocols are required: TCP/IP and IPX/SPX.

○ b. At least two protocols are required: IPX/SPX and NetBEUI.

○ c. At least three protocols are required: IPX/SPX, NetBEUI, and TCP/IP.

○ d. Only one protocol is required: TCP/IP.

Question 18

Julia wants to add a newly purchased computer to her existing 10BaseT network. There are 10 available ports in the existing hub. What must Julia do to physically connect this computer to the network?

○ a. Attach a length of twisted-pair cable from the hub to an available serial port on the new computer.

○ b. Attach a length of coaxial cable from the hub to an available parallel port on the new computer.

○ c Attach a length of twisted-pair cable from the hub to the RJ-11 connection on the 10BaseT network cards of the new computer.

○ d. Attach a length of twisted-pair cable from the hub to the RJ-45 connection on the 10BaseT network card of the new computer.

Question 19

You are discussing the TCP/IP protocol with your colleagues. Don says TCP/IP is used on the Internet. Scott says TCP/IP is supported by all Microsoft operating systems. Stuart says Novell's NetWare 5 supports TCP/IP. Annie says Unix supports TCP/IP. They ask your opinion. What will you say?

- ○ a. Everyone is right except Stuart. Novell's NetWare version 5 does not support TCP/IP.

- ○ b. Everyone is right except Don. The Internet does not support TCP/IP.

- ○ c. Everyone is right except Annie. Unix does not support TCP/IP.

- ○ d. Everyone is right. TCP/IP is supported by the Internet, Microsoft, Unix, and Novell NetWare 5.

Question 20

Which of the following connectivity devices can act as a "translator" between a PC-based network and an IBM mainframe network?

- ○ a. Router
- ○ b. Repeater
- ○ c. Gateway
- ○ d. Hub

Question 21

TCP/IP is a configurable protocol. One of the configurations is a subnet mask. Which of the following is true about a subnet mask?

- ○ a. A subnet mask is used to distinguish the network ID from the host ID in an IP address.

- ○ b. A subnet mask is used only in TCP/IP when connecting to a WAN.

- ○ c. A subnet mask is used only in TCP/IP when connecting in a LAN.

- ○ d. A subnet mask is not a required configuration for TCP/IP; it is optional to use one.

Question 22

You are asked to implement a network topology for a beverage company. The office is on one floor and contains 87 users. The company would like to use the existing category 5 twisted-pair cable that has been preinstalled in the office. They require a data transmission speed of 100Mbps. The maximum distance between any user and the IT department is 50 meters. Which of the following is the best solution for this customer?

○ a. Implement a 10Base2 network.

○ b. Implement a 100BaseT network.

○ c. Implement a 10BaseT network.

○ d. This cannot be done because no network topologies support the use of category 5 twisted-pair cable.

Question 23

What type of connector is used to connect Thinnet coaxial cable to a network card in a bus topology?

○ a. RJ-45

○ b. RJ-11

○ c. T-connector (BNC)

○ d. AUI

Question 24

You are administering a network of 30 computers connected in a star topology that uses twisted-pair cable. The network is spread out over two departments: Sales and Accounting. Each department contains one hub that connects all users in that department, and the hubs are connected together with a single twisted-pair cable. While performing a routine check on the network, you accidentally kick the power plug out from the hub that connects the Accounting department. What effect does this have on the network?

- ○ a. The network will not be affected as long as the RJ-45 cables are still plugged into the ports on the hub.

- ○ b. All the users in Accounting will not be able to communicate over the network, but the users in the Sales department will be able to communicate with each other.

- ○ c. Users in both departments will not be able to communicate until the hub is plugged back in.

- ○ d. All users will be able to communicate as long as the cable did not fall more than three meters away from the network card.

Question 25

You have just been hired as a network administrator for a network of 300 computers. The network is spread out over two locations: New York and Florida. Each location contains two routers that connect both locations with separate T1 lines. Users in New York and Florida can communicate with each other over either one of the T1 lines. If one of the T1 lines fails, the other can still be used for communication. The routers can also choose from multiple paths from which to connect to each other. What type of network is this, and what type of topology is most likely being used between the routers?

- ○ a. The network is a WAN, and the routers are using a mesh topology.

- ○ b. The network is a LAN, and the routers are using a mesh topology.

- ○ c. The network is a MAN, and the routers are using a link-state topology.

- ○ d. The network is a WAN, and the routers are using a bus topology.

Question 26

You have been hired as a consultant to expand the network of an insurance company. The company is presently using a token ring topology with 15 users connected to a single MAU. The company is now adding an additional 15 users who all require access to the network. There are no more available client connections in the present MAU, so you decide to add a second MAU. Which of the following is the correct method for connecting these two MAUs together?

○ a. Each MAU has a ring-out and a ring-in port. The ring-in port from one MAU should be connected to the ring-out port in the other MAU.

○ b. Each MAU has an inlink and a downlink port. The inlink from one MAU should be connected to the downlink in the other MAU.

○ c. The connectors on a MAU are all the same. Simply connect one free port in one MAU to a free port in the other MAU.

○ d. This cannot be done, because in a token ring network only one MAU is allowed. Explain to the customer that she will have to purchase a new MAU with more available client ports.

Question 27

The Susquehanna Hat Company has hired you as a network consultant. It currently has a 200-user, 10BaseT network spread over two floors—one and two—with 100 users on each floor. All users on the first floor are connected to a patch panel that contains 10 hubs. All users on the second floor are connected to a patch panel that contains 10 hubs. The patch panels on each floor are connected together. Network performance has been very slow, especially during peak hours, and you are asked to implement a solution. Mr. Costello, the manager, informs you that he doesn't mind spending money on this project, but he wants to keep costs down if possible. Which of the following is the best solution for this customer?

○ a. Change the cable to fiber optic and implement a wireless network.

○ b. Change hubs to MAUs.

○ c. Implement a bridge or bridges to segment the network.

○ d. Implement a multiplex-line feeder ring to segment the network.

Question 28

Which of the following fault tolerance strategies requires two physical disks and two disk controllers?

- ○ a. Mirror set
- ○ b. Stripe set without parity
- ○ c. Stripe set with parity
- ○ d. Disk duplexing

Question 29

Performing regular tape backups are an important part of data protection. Common backup strategies are differential, incremental, and full. Which of the following statements is true about these backup methods?

- ○ a. Incremental and differential backup will not clear, or reset, the archive bit of files.
- ○ b. Incremental and full backups will clear, or reset, the archive bit of files.
- ○ c. Full backup and differential backup will not clear, or reset, the archive bit of files.
- ○ d. Incremental, differential, and full backups will clear, or reset, the archive bit of files.

Question 30

You are the recently hired network administrator for a small computer manufacturer. To provide Internet access to all users, you have just installed an IP proxy. Which of the following configurations could you make on each of the client computers in order for them to connect to this IP proxy for Internet access?

- ○ a. Specify the IP address of the IP proxy in each user's C:\Proxyroot folder.
- ○ b. Specify the IP address of the IP proxy in each user's DHCP file.
- ○ c Specify the IP address of the IP proxy in each user's CERN-compliant Web browser.
- ○ d. None. IP proxy cannot be used to provide users with Internet access.

Question 31

You are the network administrator for a large coffee importer. Your boss tells you he has been hearing a lot about VPNs and the Internet. He asks you to explain what a VPN is and what it has to do with the Internet. Which of the following statements best describes what you would tell your boss?

○ a. A VPN is a Very Personal Network, which refers to the free personal Web space offered by some ISPs.

○ b. A VPN is a Virtual Private Network, which is a private network that uses the Internet to make a connection.

○ c. A VPN is a Virtual Private Network, which is a network that uses invisible, or "virtual," cables to connect.

○ d. A VPN is a Vector Privacy Node, which refers to the main Internet computers that route Internet traffic.

Question 32

You are asked to upgrade your 10BaseT network to the 100BaseT standard. The network consists of 40 users and uses category 3 twisted-pair cable. Each computer has a 10BaseT network card. One 10BaseT hub connects all users. The maximum distance from the hub for all computers is 90 meters. You replace the current hub with a 100BaseT hub, and the current network cards with 100BaseT network cards. Will performing these actions produce a network that transmits at 100Mbps?

○ a. No, because 100BaseT has a maximum length of 75 meters.

○ b. No, because category 3 twisted-pair only supports transmission speeds up to 10Mbps.

○ c. No, because 100BaseT only supports transmission speeds up to 75Mbps.

○ d. Yes, this will produce 100Mbps transmission.

Question 33

Which of the following statements are true about twisted-pair cable? [Choose the three best answers]

❑ a. Twisted-pair can be shielded (STP) or unshielded (UTP).

❑ b. Twisted-pair is available in categories 3, 4, and 5.

❑ c. Twisted-pair uses RJ-45 connectors at its cable ends.

❑ d. Twisted-pair uses BNC at its cable ends.

Question 34

You are implementing a network design for the Bowlaire Lanes Bowling Alley. Computers will be located across the entire length of the building. Cable will have to be run over a total length of 900 meters. You decide to implement a 10Base2 network. Which of the following best describes your solution?

- ○ a. 10Base2 will work fine in this scenario, because the total length of a 10Base2 network can be up to 925 meters.

- ○ b. 10Base2 is not a good choice for this network, because it is limited to a total length of 185 meters.

- ○ c. 10Base2 will work fine in this scenario, because there is no limit to the total length of the network.

- ○ d. 10Base2 will not work in this scenario, because it is not suitable for indoor use.

Question 35

You are the newly hired network administrator for a professional football team. You are asked to implement a network topology. You estimate the network will span a distance of 1,000 meters. You suggest implementing a 10Base5 topology as follows: Run three lengths of 400-meter Thicknet cable connected by three repeaters (hubs). Attach computers to this segment using drop cables with a vampire tap into the Thicknet and an RJ-45 connector to the network adapter card. Coach Bill tells you this will not work, and if you can't fix the problem, you will be released. What is wrong with your suggestion?

- ○ a. Thicknet coaxial cable is not used in a 10Base5 topology.

- ○ b. Thicknet coaxial cable cannot travel more than 185 meters in a single segment.

- ○ c. RJ-45 connectors are not used with drop cables. You need AUI connectors at the end of the drop cable.

- ○ d. The distance of 1,000 meters exceeds the limit of 10Base5.

Question 36

You are the network administrator for your company. Users need access to a printer on the network. You share the printer and assign permissions to user accounts to access this resource. The only users that can access this printer are the user accounts that you have given permission to do so. Based on this information, what security model are you using in your network?

○ a. Share-level security

○ b. User-level security

○ c. Semiuser-level security

○ d. It is impossible to tell what security model is being used

Question 37

Helena's Flowers has a network of 30 computers. Twenty of these computers are running Windows 98, nine are running NT Workstation, and one computer is running Windows 95. All users are responsible for administering their own computer. Which of the following best describes the type of network Helena has employed?

○ a. This is a server-based network.

○ b. This is a peer-to-peer network.

○ c. This is a token ring network.

○ d. It is impossible to tell what type of network this is. There is not enough information given.

Question 38

Which of the following statements is true regarding the "Base" in 10BaseT, 10Base2, and 10Base5?

○ a. The "Base" refers to baseband, which refers to the manner in which data flows on the network cable.

○ b. The "Base" refers to Base 2, the binary numbering system used by computers.

○ c. The "Base" refers to the Ethernet standard this topology is "based" on.

○ d. The "Base" refers to the low frequency rate of transmission used by the topology. (Base is low.)

Question 39

You are the network administrator for an air freight forwarder. The network uses PCs and is server based. The client computers are running Windows 98, and there is one NT Server computer. Your company decides to add an IBM mainframe computer that all users will need to access. What device is best suited to connect your PC-based network to this IBM mainframe?

O a. Router

O b. Repeater

O c. Gateway

O d. Hub

Question 40

Which of the following devices can be used to connect an Ethernet network that uses both twisted-pair and coaxial cable?

O a. MAU

O b. Hub

O c. Multiplexer

O d. Both a and c

Question 41

The IEEE (Institute of Electrical and Electronics Engineers, Inc.) publishes standards used in networking. A subgroup of IEEE is Project 802, which defines network standards for the physical components of a network. Which of the following statements are true of Project 802 standards? [Choose the two best answers]

❑ a. Project 802.2 defines standards for the LLC (Logical Link Control).

❑ b. Project 802.3 defines standards for CSMA/CD (Ethernet).

❑ c. Project 802.2 defines standards for CSMA/CD (Ethernet).

❑ d. Project 802.3 defines standards for the LLC (Logical Link Control).

Question 42

You have just been promoted to network administrator for your company. One of your first objectives is to determine the current performance level of the network. What is the purpose of establishing this baseline of system performance?

- ○ a. A baseline of system performance is useful in providing a reference point against which abnormal system performance can be compared.
- ○ b. A baseline of system performance can assist an administrator in determining what device or devices on the network are causing poor performance.
- ○ c. A baseline of system performance is used to check the "baseband" of a "linefeeder."
- ○ d. Both a and b.

Question 43

On what layer of the OSI model does routing occur?

- ○ a. Application
- ○ b. Session
- ○ c. Data Link
- ○ d. Network

Question 44

You are the network administrator for your company in New York. Your office is connected to another office located in Florida. Routers are used to connect the two locations. When you installed the router at your location, you had to manually add all the routing information into the routing table. In addition, as routes change, you must also manually update the routing table. What type of routing table is your router using?

- ○ a. Dynamic
- ○ b. RIP for IP
- ○ c. Static
- ○ d. RIP for IPX

Question 45

Which of the following is the correct UNC command to access a network directory with the share name DATAFILES that is located on a computer named SALES?

○ a. \\DATAFILES\SALES

○ b. \\SALES\DATAFILES

○ c. \DATAFILES\\SALES

○ d. \SALES\\DATAFILES

Question 46

Gina's Lawn Furniture contracts your services to help expand its network. It currently has 35 computers connected together in one location. The network uses TCP/IP as the only protocol. It wants to connect to the Internet and also to its main supplier's factory, located in another state. You suggest the company add a router to provide the connection outside of the office. What TCP/IP configuration parameter will specify the IP address of the newly added router?

○ a. Subnet mask

○ b. Default gateway

○ c. IP address

○ d. This is not possible; TCP/IP cannot be used to connect to the Internet.

Question 47

Which TCP/IP configuration parameter must be unique for all users on the local network?

○ a. Subnet mask

○ b. Default gateway

○ c. IP address

○ d. All of the above

Question 48

Which of the following is true about a DHCP scope?

- ○ a. A DHCP scope is used to "scope" out clients on a TCP/IP network when troubleshooting.
- ○ b. A DHCP scope is not a required parameter when configuring DHCP.
- ○ c. A DHCP scope is the range of IP addresses that will be given out by a DHCP server.
- ○ d. There is no such thing as a DHCP scope.

Question 49

Which of the following statements is true regarding the difference between WINS and DNS?

- ○ a. WINS manually assigns IP addresses to clients; DNS automatically assigns IP addresses to clients.
- ○ b. WINS resolves hostnames or domain names to IP addresses; DNS resolves NetBIOS names to IP addresses.
- ○ c. DNS is used in LANs; WINS is used in WANs.
- ○ d. WINS resolves NetBIOS names to IP addresses; DNS resolves hostnames or domain names to IP addresses.

Question 50

Your TCP/IP network is using only HOSTS files for name resolution. What type of names can be resolved using these HOSTS files? [Choose the two best answers]

- ❑ a. Hostnames
- ❑ b. NetBIOS names
- ❑ c. Domain names
- ❑ d. A HOSTS file is not used for name resolution; it is used for troubleshooting.

Question 51

Which component of the TCP/IP protocol stack does not guarantee packets will be delivered and is primarily used for broadcasting messages in a TCP/IP network?

○ a. UDP

○ b. TCP

○ c. Both a and b

○ d. None of the above

Question 52

Which of the following protocols is used to retrieve Internet email?

○ a. POP3

○ b. SMTP

○ c. DHCP

○ d. WINS

Question 53

You are the network administrator of a large TCP/IP network. You suspect network performance is slow and decide to gather statistical data about how your TCP/IP network is performing. Which of the following could you use to monitor TCP/IP traffic and gather statistical data?

○ a. SNMP

○ b. SMTP

○ c. POP3

○ d. TCP

Question 54

You are the network administrator for a small advertising company. The network uses TCP/IP as the only protocol. You need to set up an intranet so users can download files from your main server. What TCP/IP protocol could you use to allow users to download files from your server?

○ a. TCP

○ b. SNMP

○ c. FTP

○ d. POP3

Question 55

TCP/IP is a widely used industry-standard routable protocol. TCP/IP is made up of an entire suite of protocols. What component of the TCP/IP protocol suite adds a network address to a packet?

○ a. UDP

○ b. TCP

○ c. IP

○ d. SMTP

Question 56

Which of the following external connectors can be used by SCSI? [Choose the three best answers]

❑ a. Centronics 50

❑ b. Centronics 68 HP

❑ c. DB-25

❑ d. Dual RJ-11

Question 57

What is the address range for TCP/IP Class B addresses?

○ a. 1 through 126

○ b. 128 through 191

○ c. 192 through 223

○ d. Both b and c

Question 58

A router contains a routing table that it uses to locate other routers and to send network packets. Which of the following statements is true about routing tables?

○ a. A dynamic routing table requires more administration than a static routing table.

○ b. A dynamic routing table requires less administration than a static routing table.

○ c. A static routing table requires the same amount of administration as a dynamic routing table.

○ d. None of the above.

Question 59

What is the default subnet mask for a Class A IP address?

○ a. 255.0.0.0

○ b. 255.255.0.0

○ c. 255.255.255.0

○ d. 255.255.255.255

Question 60

The HTTP protocol is part of the TCP/IP protocol suite. It is considered a well-known protocol. What port number does HTTP (Hypertext Transfer Protocol) use?

- ○ a. 21
- ○ b. 25
- ○ c. 80
- ○ d. 110

Question 61

You are the network administrator for a midsized company. Your network consists of 70 users, who all require access to the Internet. You want to provide these users with Internet access, but your boss is concerned about the security risks posed by exposing your network to the Internet. She says that she saw a television commercial about a company that had their internal network destroyed by an Internet hacker. What can you tell your boss to persuade her to change her mind?

- ○ a. Tell your boss you will install a DHCP server that will protect your internal network from potential Internet attacks.
- ○ b. Tell your boss you will install an IP proxy server that will protect your internal network from potential Internet attacks.
- ○ c. Tell your boss you will install a POP3 server that will protect your internal network from potential Internet attacks.
- ○ d. Tell your boss that Internet attacks are impossible, and that she shouldn't believe everything she sees on television.

Question 62

What layer of the OSI model does a redirector reside?

- ○ a. Application
- ○ b. Presentation
- ○ c. Transport
- ○ d. Network

Question 63

Which of the following best describes an LMHOSTS file?

○ a. An LMHOSTS file is a local file in a computer that resolves NetBIOS names to IP addresses.

○ b. An LMHOSTS file is a local file in a computer that resolves hostnames to IP addresses.

○ c   An LMHOSTS file is a local file in a computer that resolves Internet names to IP addresses.

○ d. An LMHOSTS file is a local file in a computer that resolves FQDN (Fully Qualified Domain Names) to IP addresses.

Question 64

When using the TCP/IP protocol, all clients are required to have a unique IP address. What component of the TCP/IP protocol suite adds an IP address to a packet?

○ a. UDP

○ b. TCP

○ c. IP

○ d. SMTP

Question 65

You are troubleshooting a computer on your network. The computer is using TCP/IP as the only protocol. You need to find out what port number this computer is using when it connects to your server. What TCP/IP command-line utility can give you this information?

○ a. ARP

○ b. TRACERT

○ c   NBTSTAT

○ d. NETSTAT

Question 66

You are troubleshooting a computer on your network. The computer is using TCP/IP as the only protocol. You need to trace the path an IP packet is taking to get to a remote host. What TCP/IP command-line utility can give you this information?

○ a. ARP

○ b. TRACERT

○ c. NBTSTAT

○ d. NETSTAT

Question 67

What type of cable/connector is used to attach Thicknet coaxial cable to a network adapter card?

○ a. Twisted-pair cable with an RJ-45 connector

○ b. Shielded twisted-pair with and RJ-11 connector

○ c. Drop cable with a vampire tap into the Thicknet, and a 15-pin AUI connector to the network adapter card

○ d. Fiber optic cable with an RG-58 /U connector to the network adapter card

Question 68

You are troubleshooting your TCP/IP network. Mary's computer cannot connect to Debra's computer using TCP/IP. Debra has no problem connecting to other users on the network. You record their IP information as follows:

Mary: IP address 200.200.200.5; subnet mask 255.255.255.0

Debra: IP address 200.200.200.10; subnet mask 255.255.255.0

You want to check for TCP/IP connectivity between these two computers. What TCP/IP utility could you use, and what is the correct way to enter the command?

- ○ a. Use the IPCONFIG utility. Type "IPCONFIG 200.200.200.10" while seated at Mary's computer.

- ○ b. Use the WINIPCFG utility. Type "WINIPCFG 200.200.200.5" while seated at Mary's computer.

- ○ c. Use the PING utility. Type "PING 200.200.200.10" while seated at Mary's computer.

- ○ d. Use the ARP utility. Type "ARP 200.200.200.5" while seated at Debra's computer.

Question 69

You are asked to look at the following that is displayed on the screen of a user's TCP/IP computer:

```
Interface: 208.100.50.109 on Interface
        0x1000002Internet Address
        Physical Address      Type208.100.50.1
        00-a0-c9-2b-82-b6     dynamic
```

What TCP/IP utility was used to produce this information?

- ○ a. ARP

- ○ b. TRACERT

- ○ c. NBTSTAT

- ○ d. NETSTAT

Question 70

You are asked to look at the following table displayed on the screen of a user's TCP/IP computer:

```
Node IP address: [208.100.50.109] Scope ID:

NetBIOS Local Name Table
Name                Type            Status
BOBTECH<00>         UNIQUE          Registered
JETS <00>           GROUP           Registered
BOBTECH<03>         UNIQUE          Registered
BOBTECH<20>         UNIQUE          Registered
JETS<1E>            GROUP           Registered
JETS<1D>            UNIQUE          Registered
MSBROWSE__<01>      GROUP           Registered
BOB<03>             UNIQUE          Registered
```

What TCP/IP utility was used to produce this information?

- ○ a. ARP
- ○ b. TRACERT
- ○ c. NBTSTAT
- ○ d. NETSTAT

Question 71

Your boss, Homer, asks you to install server software on your network's brand-new server. Your boss also wants you to implement a fault tolerance strategy on the server. The server has two physical disks, each with a single 2GB partition. The server will be used only to authenticate users and will not have data stored on it. Currently no software is installed on the server. Which of the following is the best solution in this scenario?

- ○ a   Install NT Server software on the server, and implement RAID 1.
- ○ b. Install Novell NetWare software on the server, and implement RAID 0.
- ○ c. Install NT Server software on the server, and implement RAID 0.
- ○ d. Install Windows 95 on the server and implement RAID 0.

Question 72

You need to access your company's database server from your home. You will be making this remote connection from your Windows 95 computer using a 56Kbps modem. The database server only supports the IPX/SPX protocol for communication. Which of the following dial-up protocols could you use to make this connection?

- ○ a. PPP
- ○ b. SLIP
- ○ c. Both a and b
- ○ d. None of the above

Question 73

Which of the following statements is true about PPTP?

- ○ a   PPTP is used to provide secure communication between VPNs (Virtual Private Networks) over the Internet.
- ○ b. PPTP is a dial-up protocol that is much more efficient than its predecessor, SLIP.
- ○ c. PPTP is used to test for connectivity between TCP/IP hosts.
- ○ d. PPTP is used to PinPoint (PP) the TimePeriod (TP) elapsed during a datagram transmission.

Question 74

You use your computer at home to connect to the Internet. You are presently using a 56Kbps modem to connect over a regular phone line. You want to improve the speed of your Internet access. Which of the following connection services offer faster connection speeds than your present configuration?

- ○ a. PSTN
- ○ b. POTS
- ○ c. PSTN and POTS
- ○ d. ISDN

Question 75

What security model features the use of permissions given to user accounts to access resources on a network?

- ○ a. User-level security
- ○ b. Share-level security
- ○ c. Password-protected, share-level security
- ○ d. No access share implemented resource distribution (NASIRD)

Network+
Answer Key #3

1. a	16. a	31. b	46. b	61. b
2. c	17. d	32. b	47. c	62. b
3. c	18. d	33. a, b, c	48. c	63. a
4. a	19. d	34. a	49. d	64. c
5. b	20. c	35. c	50. a, c	65. d
6. a	21. a	36. b	51. a	66. b
7. c	22. b	37. b	52. a	67. c
8. b	23. c	38. a	53. a	68. c
9. c	24. b	39. c	54. c	69. a
10. c	25. a	40. b	55. c	70. c
11. a	26. a	41. a, b	56. a, b, c	71. a
12. b	27. c	42. d	57. b	72. a
13. d	28. d	43. d	58. b	73. a
14. b	29. b	44. c	59. a	74. d
15. a	30. c	45. b	60. c	75. a

Question 1

Answer a is correct. Generally speaking, computers like temperature conditions similar to people. Room temperature should not be extreme, and ideal temperature should be on the cool side. Humidity should be kept at approximately 50 to 70 percent. If humidity is too low, the instances of electrostatic discharge (ESD) will be increased, due to the "dryness" of the particles in the air. An ESD shock can cause a computer to intermittently fail or cause more serious damage. High humidity produces excessive moisture in the air that could cause condensation to develop on the electrical components inside a computer, and cause a short.

For more information, see Chapter 12 of *Network+ Exam Cram*.

Question 2

Answer c is correct. Small Computer System Interface (SCSI) is a parallel interface standard for attaching peripheral devices to a computer. There are many variations of SCSI. In general, SCSI supports the use of Centronics 50, 68 HP, and DB-25 connectors when attaching an external SCSI device to a PC. Dual RJ-11 connectors are used to connect telephone line to a modem card.

For more information, see Chapter 10 of *Network+ Exam Cram*.

Question 3

Answer c is correct. In an Ethernet network, such as 10BaseT, all computers that have network adapter cards will have a MAC address, regardless of the operating system installed on the computer. The MAC address, also referred to as the "hardware address," is the permanent address that is "burned" on every network card by the manufacturer. Burning this unique address into every network card guarantees that each computer on a network will have a unique identifier associated with it. Having this type of unique identifier function separately from an operating system is one reason why networks that contain different types of computers, like the one in this example, can communicate with each other.

For more information, see Chapter 8 of *Network+ Exam Cram*.

Question 4

Answer a is correct. The maximum single-segment length of Thinnet coaxial cable is 185 meters (607 feet). To extend a length of Thinnet coaxial cable, a repeater must be used. A repeater is used to "boost" the signal back to its original strength, so it can continue a longer distance. Patch cable is used when a length of coaxial cable is not long enough to reach a desired point. However, if patch cable is connected to a length of Thinnet without a repeater, it contributes to the total length of the cable and is not considered a separate segment.

For more information, see Chapter 2 of *Network+ Exam Cram*.

Question 5

Answer b is correct. A differential backup will not clear the archive bit of a file. Full backup and incremental backup will clear, or reset, the archive bit of files. The attribute of a file used to determine its backup status is known as the archive bit. The archive bit attribute of a file can be one of two values: set or reset (cleared). When a full or incremental backup is performed, the backup program clears, or resets, the archive bit. When files that have been backed up are changed, the program that modifies the file will set the archive bit. The process of setting the archive bit of modified files allows the backup program to determine if a file has changed since the last time a backup was performed. There are three important backup methods to be aware of: differential, incremental, and full backup.

➤ **Differential** A differential backup will back up files that have their archive bit "set," but does not clear the archive bit. Performing daily backups get progressively slower each day. Restoring data from a differential backup only requires two tapes: the original full backup and the last differential backup.

➤ **Incremental** An incremental backup will back up files that have their archive bit "set" and then clears the archive bit. Restoring data from an incremental backup requires many tapes: the original full backup tape and all incremental backups performed since the full backup.

➤ **Full backup** Backs up all files regardless of the archive bit attribute, and clears the archive bit. Periodic full backups are recommended in addition to either incremental or differential backups.

For more information, see Chapter 5 of *Network+ Exam Cram*.

Question 6

Answer a is correct. A Universal Naming Convention (UNC) name is a standard for connecting to shared resources on a network. A UNC is comprised of two key elements: a computer name and a share name. All computers in a network must have a computer name to identify themselves. When sharing a resource (a printer, files, CD-ROM, and so on), the shared resource must also be assigned a name, known as a "share" name. Connecting to a shared resource using a UNC simply involves specifying these two parameters, in the format "\\computer name\share name". For example, to connect to a directory that has been assigned the share name DATAFILES on the computer named SALES, the UNC to connect to this resource would be \\SALES\DATAFILES.

For more information, see Chapter 12 of *Network+ Exam Cram*.

Question 7

Answer c is correct. Rights are the permissions given to users to access network resources and perform certain network tasks. Permissions can be assigned to user accounts or to groups. Groups are primarily used by a network administrator to simplify administration of the users in a network. With groups, an administrator can assign rights to groups, then simply add user accounts to the group, and the user inherits all the rights given to that group. Because permissions can be assigned to user accounts and groups, it is possible to have user and group permissions to the same resource. In a situation like this, a user's effective permission to access this resource becomes a combination of both her user and group permissions. If Emily had been assigned the "No Access" permission to this resource on her user account, that permission would override the "full control" permission assigned to the group she belongs to. If Emily had entered the wrong password, if her account expired, or if she did not log onto the network, she would not be able to access any network resources.

For more information, see Chapter 12 of *Network+ Exam Cram*.

Question 8

Answer b is correct. Antivirus software should be installed on all computers, regardless of their operating system, and updated frequently. A virus is a program that is written to cause varying degrees of damage to the files of the computer it is installed on. A virus ends up on a hard disk without the user's knowledge by "hiding" inside another program or file that is being transferred onto the hard drive. An antivirus program is a program that contains a list of "known" viruses. When an antivirus program scans a disk for a virus, it compares its "known virus" list to the programs on a disk. If an antivirus program finds a match between a program on a disk and its database, it detects the virus and attempts to remove it from the computer The best time to install antivirus program is before a computer is infected, not after. The **FORMAT** command is used to format a hard disk.

For more information, see Chapter 13 of *Network+ Exam Cram*.

Question 9

Answer c is correct. The network ID 127 is reserved by TCP/IP for loopback testing. Every computer running TCP/IP has an entry "127.0.0.1" in its local HOSTS file that is resolved to the name "localhost". When troubleshooting TCP/IP, a loopback test can be performed on the local computer using the command **PING 127.0.0.1**. If the PING of 127.0.0.1 is successful, this verifies that TCP/IP is correctly installed on the computer. NBTSTAT is used to display NetBIOS over TCP/IP naming information. NETSTAT is used to display protocol statistics of a TCP/IP session. TRACERT is used to verify the path to a remote host using TCP/IP.

For more information, see Chapter 4 of *Network+ Exam Cram*.

Question 10

Answer c is correct. The Internetwork Packet Exchange/Sequenced Packet Exchange (IPX/SPX) protocol is commonly used in Novell NetWare networks. As part of IPX/SPX configuration, a frame type must be specified. The frame type identifies the type of packet supported. In order for computers running IPX/SPX to communicate, they must support the same frame type. Different versions of Novell NetWare support different frame types. For example, Novell NetWare version 3.11 uses the frame type Ethernet 802.3, and Novell NetWare 4.1 uses frame type Ethernet 802.2. IPX/SPX can be configured to support multiple frame types to allow for communication between different versions of NetWare.

For more information, see Chapter 4 of *Network+ Exam Cram*.

Question 11

Answer a is correct. The ADMIN account is created by NetWare 4 on installation and is given supervisor rights to the server. The ADMINISTRATOR account is create during installations of Microsoft's NT. Answers c and d are invalid.

For more information, see Chapter 3 of *Network+ Exam Cram*.

Question 12

Answer b is correct. When using TCP/IP, each user must be configured with a unique IP address. If two users both have the same IP address, then the first user to attempt to communicate using TCP/IP will be able to access the network, but the second user will receive an error message stating that a duplicate IP address has been detected.

For more information, see Chapter 4 of *Network+ Exam Cram*.

Question 13

Answer d is correct. Generally speaking, computers like similar temperature conditions as people do. Room temperature should not be extreme, and ideal temperature should be on the cool side. Humidity should be kept at approximately 50 to 70 percent. If humidity is too low, the instances of ESD will be increased, due to the "dryness" of the particles in the air. Low humidity can also increase static which can cause paper to "stick" together and jam a printer for no apparent reason An ESD shock can cause a computer to fail intermittently or cause more serious damage. High humidity produces excessive moisture in the air that could cause condensation to develop on the electrical components inside a computer and cause a short.

For more information, see Chapter 12 of *Network+ Exam Cram*.

Question 14

Answer b is correct. Although Thinnet and twisted-pair can be used for cable runs and backbones, Thicknet is specifically designed for this purpose and is the most common type of cable used in these type of installations. Thicknet coaxial cable is 1/2 inch in diameter and is not very flexible, but it can be used for distances of up to 500 meters in a single segment. Thicknet attaches to a network adapter card by using a vampire tap into the Thicknet and a drop cable to the network card. The connector at the end of a drop cable is an Attachment Unit Interface (AUI) 15-pin connector. An AUI is also called a DIX connector, named after the companies that developed it: Digital, Intel, and Xerox. None of the other cables listed can travel over 200 meters in a single-segment length. Twisted-pair equals 100 meters, Thinnet coaxial equals 185 meters. Shielded twisted-pair is commonly used in IBM Token Ring networks.

For more information, see Chapter 2 of *Network+ Exam Cram*.

Question 15

Answer a is correct. Twisted-pair is the most common, least expensive type of network cable in use today and is connected to a network adapter card using an RJ-45 connector. An RJ-11 connector connects twisted-pair to analog phone lines. (The handset cord on your telephone uses an RJ-11 connector.) Thicknet coaxial cable attaches to a network by using a vampire tap into the Thicknet and a drop cable to the network card. The connector at the end of a drop cable is an AUI or DIX (Digital, Intel, and Xerox) 15-pin connector. A barrel-type BNC is used to extend a length of coaxial cable.

For more information, see Chapter 2 of *Network+ Exam Cram*.

Question 16

Answer a is correct. In a stripe set without parity (RAID 0), data is written evenly across all members in the set. This can improve performance because disks can be read simultaneously. A severe drawback to stripe sets without parity is that they do not provide fault tolerance. If any one member of the set fails, all data is lost and cannot be re-created. In this instance, the only way to get information back is to revert to the last tape backup. A failed stripe set without parity cannot be regenerated.

For more information, see Chapter 5 of *Network+ Exam Cram*.

Question 17

Answer d is correct. TCP/IP is a widely used communication protocol that is supported by major operating systems and the Internet. Unix and *all* Microsoft operating systems support the TCP/IP protocol. TCP/IP is the protocol used on the Internet. IPX/SPX is the communication protocol commonly used in Novell NetWare networks. Microsoft's implementation of IPX/SPX is NWLink. NetBEUI is a small, fast, nonroutable protocol used in Microsoft networks.

For more information, see Chapter 4 of *Network+ Exam Cram*.

Question 18

Answer d is correct. In a 10BaseT topology, computers connect to a hub using twisted-pair cable with RJ-45 connectors at each end. All computers in a network must have a network interface card (NIC), or network adapter card, installed that supports the topology being used on the network. You cannot attach an RJ-45 connector to a serial port.

For more information, see Chapter 2 of *Network+ Exam Cram*.

Question 19

Answer d is correct. TCP/IP is an industry-standard routable protocol that is widely supported. All Microsoft operating systems support TCP/IP (NT Server, NT Workstation, DOS, Windows 95/98, and so on). Unix also supports TCP/IP. (In fact TCP/IP was born in the Unix environment.) Novell NetWare 5 also supports the use of TCP/IP. TCP/IP is also the protocol used on the Internet.

For more information, see Chapter 4 of *Network+ Exam Cram.*

Question 20

Answer c is correct. A gateway is commonly used as a "translator" to connect dissimilar networks. Because a PC-based network uses a different data structure than an IBM mainframe, a "translator" or gateway is needed for communication. A gateway converts packets from one network into a recognizable format that the underlying network will understand. In this example, Microsoft's SNA Server could be used as a gateway to connect these networks together. A gateway functions at the Application layer of the OSI model and can utilize all seven layers to perform packet translation. The term "gateway," as it is used in this example, is different than a "default gateway" that is specified as a configuration parameter when using the TCP/IP protocol. A default gateway is the IP address of the router to which TCP/IP clients send remote packets. A repeater and a hub simply boost a signal's strength.

For more information, see Chapter 8 of *Network+ Exam Cram.*

Question 21

Answer a is correct. All computers using TCP/IP must have a *unique* IP address, a subnet mask, and if used in a WAN, a default gateway. An IP address identifies a TCP/IP host on the network and contains two important elements: a network ID and a host ID. The network ID of an IP address identifies the network the host is on. (For example, all users in a single location are said to be on the same network and therefore will all have the same network ID in their IP address.) The host ID of an IP address identifies the host, or individual computer, on a TCP/IP network. It is the host ID portion of an IP address that is the unique part. Therefore, in a single TCP/IP network, users will all have the *same* network ID and *different* (unique) host IDs. The subnet mask is used to "mask" the network portion of an IP address, so IP can determine of the destination host is local or remote. When a computer using TCP/IP needs to communicate with another TCP/IP host, it uses the subnet mask to determine if the destination computer is local (on my network) or remote (on a different network). If the subnet mask determines the destination host is local, it simply places the packet on the cable for delivery. If the subnet mask determines the host it needs to communicate with is remote (on another network), it sends it to its default gateway. The number 255 is the number reserved in TCP/IP for use by the default subnet mask. A default subnet mask will use 255s over the network portion of an IP address and 0s over the host portion of an IP address.

For more information, see Chapter 4 of *Network+ Exam Cram*.

Question 22

Answer b is correct. A 100BaseT network is the best solution in this scenario. 100BaseT is wired in a star topology, supports category 5 twisted-pair cable, and transmits data at 100Mbps. The maximum distance from computer to hub in a 100BaseT network is 100 meters. A 100BaseT network can support up to 1,024 users. Ethernet 10Base2 is not a good solution for this customer because it uses Thinnet coaxial cable, not twisted-pair. 10Base2 transmits at 10Mbps, and single segment can travel 185 meters. The total number of users in a 10Base2 network is 1,024. Ethernet 10BaseT uses twisted-pair cable, but only transmits at 10Mbps.

For more information, see Chapter 2 of *Network+ Exam Cram*.

Question 23

Answer c is correct. Thinnet coaxial cable is attached to a network card in a bus topology with a T-connector. Termination is required at both ends in a bus topology, and this is provided by a 50-ohm terminator. An RJ-45 connector is used to connect twisted-pair cable to a node. RJ-11 is used to connect twisted-pair cable to a phone line. The connector at the end of a drop cable is an AUI 15-pin connector. An AUI or DIX connector is used to connect a drop cable from Thicknet coaxial to a network adapter card. An AUI is also called a DIX connector, named after the companies that developed it (Digital, Intel, and Xerox).

For more information, see Chapter 2 of *Network+ Exam Cram*.

Question 24

Answer b is correct. In a star topology, the hub handles termination, so when the power was taken away from the Accounting department's hub, they lost termination and, therefore, connectivity. The users in Sales have their own hub, which is still functioning and therefore still providing termination for all the computers that are connected to it. A key point to understand here is that in a star topology, if a hub fails, the entire group of users connected to it will fail, but other hubs that are connected to it will still be able to provide connectivity to the users connected to it.

For more information, see Chapter 2 of *Network+ Exam Cram*.

Question 25

Answer a is correct. A mesh topology features multiple links that can provide alternate routes to a host in the event of a single-line failure. A wide area network (WAN) is categorized by multiple locations connected through routers. A local area network (LAN) is a local network that does not contain any type of connectivity device, like a router. A metropolitan area network (MAN) is limited to a distance of 60 miles.

For more information, see Chapter 2 of *Network+ Exam Cram*.

Question 26

Answer a is correct. A token ring network uses a multistation access unit (MAU) to connect computers together. By specification, up to 12 MAUs may be connected together in a single token ring network. The proper way to connect MAUs together is by linking the "ring out" port from one MAU to the "ring in" port in the other MAU.

For more information, see Chapter 8 of *Network+ Exam Cram*.

Question 27

Answer c is correct. A bridge is a connectivity device that looks similar to a hub but can be used to segment a network. Dividing a network into segments can significantly improve performance. Because a bridge can read the MAC, or hardware address, of a computer, it can manage network traffic more efficiently than a hub. (A hub cannot read anything about network traffic and simply passes everything that comes to it.) With bridges in place, a good amount of unnecessary network traffic will be eliminated, freeing the network cable and improving performance. A token ring network uses an MAU and would not work in a 10BaseT network. Answer d does not exist.

For more information, see Chapter 8 of *Network+ Exam Cram*.

Question 28

Answer d is correct. Fault tolerance is the ability to recover from a single hard disk failure. A standard created for implementing fault tolerant strategies is known as Redundant Array of Independent Disks (RAID). A mirror set, or RAID 1, is created using two disks, with one disk acting as a "mirror" of the other, providing redundancy. In the event of a single-disk failure in a mirror set, the other disk may be used. Disk duplexing is a physical form of RAID 1 mirroring and requires two physical disks and two disk controllers to be implemented. A stripe set with parity, or RAID 5, is created by combining equal areas of free space on 3 to 32 disks to form one logical drive. If one member of a stripe set with parity fails, the failed member can be "regenerated" using the parity information that is stored on the remaining members of the set. A stripe set without parity, or RAID 0, is created by combining equal areas of free space on 2 to 32 disks to form one logical drive. Stripe sets without parity do not provide fault tolerance.

For more information, see Chapter 5 of *Network+ Exam Cram*.

Question 29

Answer b is correct. A differential backup will not clear the archive bit of a file. Full backup and incremental backup will clear, or reset, the archive bit of files.

The attribute of a file used to determine its backup status is known as the archive bit. The archive bit attribute of a file can be one of two values: set or reset (cleared). When a full or incremental backup is performed, the backup program clears, or resets, the archive bit. When files that have been backed up are changed, the program that modifies the file will set the archive bit. The process of setting the archive bit of modified files allows the backup program to determine if a file has changed since the last time a backup was performed. There are three important backup methods to be aware of: differential, incremental, and full backup.

➤ **Differential** A differential backup will back up files that have their archive bit set, but does not clear the archive bit. Restoring data from a differential backup only requires two tapes: the original full backup and the last differential backup.

➤ **Incremental** An incremental backup will back up files that have their archive bit set and then clear the archive bit. Restoring data from an incremental backup requires many tapes: the original full backup tape and all incremental backups performed since the full backup.

➤ **Full backup** This one backs up all files regardless of the archive bit attribute and clears the archive bit. Periodic full backups are recommended in addition to either incremental or differential backups.

For more information, see Chapter 5 of *Network+ Exam Cram*.

Question 30

Answer c is correct. A common method for allowing users to access a proxy server is configuring their Web browsers with the IP address (or computer name) of the IP proxy. Answers a and b do not exist. An IP proxy, or proxy server (same thing), serves two main purposes:

➤ Firewall protection to protect users on the local network from the intrusion of the Internet.

➤ Improved Internet performance by increasing the speed that users on the local network retrieve Web pages.

An IP proxy can provide firewall security to protect users on the local network from the intrusion of the Internet. (A firewall is defined as any configuration, hardware or software, that protects users on a local network from the intrusion of the Internet.) When an IP proxy is used as a firewall, it typically will be a dedicated server that is configured with two network adapter cards. One network card will be used for an Internet connection, known as the external network adapter, and the other will be used for the connection to the local network, known as the internal network adapter. In this firewall configuration, the only computer connected to the Internet is the proxy server through this dedicated external network card. In order for clients to access the Internet, they must configure their Web browsers to send all Internet requests to the IP proxy. When a client requests an Internet address, the request goes to the proxy server, and the proxy server retrieves the information from the Web site on behalf of the client. The proxy server acts like the client when retrieving this information, so the only IP address used in making all requests is the proxy server's external network adapter address. All internal IP addresses will not be seen by any Internet networks. For additional security, the proxy server can be configured to deny access to Web sites or protocols for both incoming and outgoing requests.

A proxy server also provides improved Internet performance. Because an IP proxy retrieves Web pages on behalf of all users in a local network; it places all these pages in its local cache (memory). This way, if a user requests an Internet address that was previously retrieved by the proxy server, the proxy server will give the user the page contained in its local cache. The process of providing users with cached Web pages is much faster than the standard means of re-questing/retrieving the information from the Web site on the Internet.

For more information, see Chapter 6 of *Network+ Exam Cram.*

Question 31

Answer b is correct. A VPN is a private network that uses the Internet to make a connection. Users from each private network establish an Internet connection locally and use the network capabilities of the Internet to connect to each other. Because the Internet is a public network, connecting two private networks together in this manner does pose some security risks. To provide security for VPNs over the Internet, the Point-to-Point Tunneling Protocol (PPTP) is used. With PPTP enabled, the only packets that will be allowed into members of the VPN are PPTP packets. This provides an extra measure of security against potential hackers. The other choices do not exist.

For more information, see Chapter 6 of *Network+ Exam Cram.*

Question 32

Answer b is correct. The 100BaseT standard supports transmission speeds up to 100Mbps. It requires category 5 twisted-pair cable to transmit at 100Mbps. Category 3 twisted-pair supports data transmission up to 10Mbps. In order for a 100BaseT network to function at 100Mbps, the hub(s) must be 100BaseT, the network cards must be 100BaseT, and cable must be Category 5 twisted-pair. The maximum single segment length for twisted-pair is 100 meters, or 328 feet.

For more information, see Chapter 2 of *Network+ Exam Cram.*

Question 33

Answers a, b, and c are correct. Twisted-pair is the most widely used, least expensive network cable in use today. Shielded twisted-pair contains more insulation than unshielded twisted-pair and is more resistant to electrical interference. The different categories of twisted-pair represent different levels of transmission speed supported: category 3 equals 10Mbps, category 4 equals 16Mbps, and category 5 equals 100Mbps. (Mbps is million bits per second.) A BNC (British Naval Connector) is used with coaxial cable.

For more information, see Chapter 2 of *Network+ Exam Cram.*

Question 34

Answer a is correct. The total length of a 10Base2 network can be up to 925 meters, according to a specification known as the 5-4-3 rule. The 5-4-3 rule states that up to five segments of cable can be connected together using four repeaters (hubs), but only three segments can have computers connected. Since a single segment length of Thinnet coaxial cable can travel 185 meters, the total length by specification (5-4-3 rule) is 925 meters. 10Base2 is commonly used indoors. Ethernet 10Base2 uses Thinnet coaxial cable in a bus topology. 10Base2 transmits at 10Mbps. The total number of users supported in a 10Base2 network is 1,024.

For more information, see Chapter 2 of *Network+ Exam Cram*.

Question 35

Answer c is correct. In order to keep your job on the team, you'll need to use AUI connectors instead of RJ-45 connectors. Ethernet 10Base5 uses Thicknet coaxial cable, transmits at 10Mbps, and a single-segment length can travel up to 500 meters. The total length of a 10Base5 network can be up to 2,500 meters, according to a specification known as the 5-4-3 rule. The 5-4-3 rule states that up to five segments of cable can be connected together using four repeaters (hubs), but only three segments can have computers connected. Since a single segment length of thicknet coaxial cable can travel 500 meters, the total length by specification (5-4-3 rule) is 2,500 meters. Computers attach to Thicknet through the use of a drop cable. The drop cable is crimped into the Thicknet using a vampire tap and attached to the network card using a DIX or AUI 15-pin male connector. An AUI is also called a DIX connector, named after the companies that developed it (Digital, Intel, and Xerox).

For more information, see Chapter 2 of *Network+ Exam Cram*.

Question 36

Answer b is correct. There are two common security models a network administrator can employ to control users' access to network resources: share-level security and user-level security. When using share-level security, passwords are assigned to *resources*. An example of share-level security is sharing a printer and assigning a password to that printer. When users need to connect to the printer, they will have to enter the password set on the printer in order to access it. The share-level security model is considered a less secure method than user-level security, because users are more likely to tell others the password to access a resource than they are to give away their own username and password. In user-level security, permissions are assigned to *users*. An example of user-level security is sharing a printer and assigning permissions to users to access this resource. For users to access this printer, their user account must have permissions to access it. Remember: share-level security assigns passwords to resources, (printers, files, programs, and so on). User-level security assigns permissions to users. Semiuser-level security does not exist.

For more information, see Chapter 7 of *Network+ Exam Cram.*

Question 37

Answer b is correct. A peer-to-peer network is comprised of computers that are all running client operating systems, such as Windows 9X or NT Workstation. Because all computers in a peer-to-peer network utilize a client operating system, they are all considered to be equal, or "peers" of one another. In a peer-to-peer network, all users are considered to be administrators of their own computers. A peer-to peer network is usually not suitable for networks larger than 10 because of this decentralized administration. A server-based network features a server that is used to centrally manage the clients in a network. Popular server operating systems are Novell NetWare and Microsoft NT Server.

For more information, see Chapter 9 of *Network+ Exam Cram.*

Question 38

Answer a is correct. The manner in which data flows on a network cable can be defined as either baseband or broadband. Baseband, as used by Ethernet 802.3, uses digital signaling over a single frequency. Baseband can send information bidirectionally and utilizes repeaters to boost a signal. Broadband uses analog signaling over a range of frequencies. Broadband sends information unidirectionally on each frequency and uses amplifiers to boost a signal.

For more information, see Chapter 2 of *Network+ Exam Cram.*

Question 39

Answer c is correct. A gateway is commonly used as a "translator" to connect dissimilar networks. Because a PC-based network uses a different data structure than an IBM mainframe, a "translator" or gateway is needed for communication. A gateway converts packets from one network into a recognizable format that the underlying network will understand. In this example, Microsoft's SNA Server could be used as a gateway to connect these networks together. A gateway functions at the application layer of the OSI model. The term "gateway," as it is used in this example, is different than a "default gateway" that is specified as a configuration parameter when using the TCP/IP protocol. A default gateway is the IP address of the router to which TCP/IP clients send remote packets. A repeater and a hub simply boost a signal's strength.

For more information, see Chapter 8 of *Network+ Exam Cram*.

Question 40

Answer b is correct. A hub can be used to connect networks that use dissimilar media, like twisted-pair and coaxial cable. An MAU is used to connect computers in IBM Token Ring networks. An MAU contains a logical "ring" that travels around the network and is used by computers to send data. A multiplexer is a device used to combine signals into one channel and is more commonly associated with a T1 WAN connection.

For more information, see Chapter 2 of *Network+ Exam Cram*.

Question 41

Answers a and b are correct. Project 802 modified the Data Link layer of the OSI model by dividing it into two sublayers: Logical Link Control (LLC) and media access control (MAC). Standards for Ethernet (CSMA/CD) networks are defined in 802.3. CSMA/CD refers to the type of access method used by Ethernet 802.3 networks. The LLC, as specified in 802.2, defines the use of service access points (SAPs) used to transfer information over a network.

For more information, see Chapter 8 of *Network+ Exam Cram*.

Question 42

Answer d is correct. A baseline of system performance can be a valuable tool to a network administrator. Establishing a baseline involves tracking the performance of key network components at varied intervals. When new components are added to a network or when network performance begins to slow, new performance readings should be taken. This new information can be compared to the baseline of system performance to assist an administrator in determining what device(s) are causing the performance levels to decline.

For more information, see Chapter 12 of *Network+ Exam Cram*.

Question 43

Answer d is correct. The Open System Interconnection (OSI) model defines standards for networking based on a seven-layer model. All of the components used in networking (hubs, bridges, routers, cables, protocols, and so on) conform to various layers of the OSI model by "residing" at one or more of these seven layers. Routing refers to the path traveled by packets throughout a network. The primary device used for this is a router. A router operates at the Network layer of the OSI model. A router manages network traffic by reading the network, or IP address, of the packets it receives. The reason a router can read network or IP addresses is because it resides at the same layer of the OSI model as network protocols. Examples of Network layer protocols are IP (part of the TCP/IP protocol suite used by Unix, Microsoft, Novell NetWare 5, and the Internet), IPX (part of the IPX/SPX protocol suite used by Novell NetWare), and NWLink (Microsoft's NT implementation of the IPX/SPX protocol).

For more information, see Chapter 8 of *Network+ Exam Cram.*

Question 44

Answer c is correct. All routers contain routing tables. The routing table in a router contains the information it uses to send, or "route," network traffic. A routing table can be either static or dynamic. With static routing, all information in the routing table must be entered manually. Static routes entered in a routing table do not change. Dynamic routing, as the name implies, allows a router to automatically update its routing table. It does this by "talking" to other routers, checking various paths, counting distances between routes, and so on. Dynamic routes can change as needed. Routing Information Protocol for Internet Protocol (RIP for IP) and Routing Information Protocol for Internetwork Packet Exchange (RIP for IPX) are some examples of the types of methods that can be used when employing dynamic routing.

For more information, see Chapter 4 of *Network+ Exam Cram.*

Question 45

Answer b is correct. A UNC name is a standard for connecting to shared resources on a network. A UNC is comprised of two key elements: a computer name and a share name. All computers in a network must have a computer name to identify themselves. When sharing a resource (a printer, files, CD-ROM, and so on), the shared resource must also be assigned a name, known as a "share" name. Connecting to a shared resource using a UNC simply involves specifying these two parameters in the format "\\computer name\share name". For example, to connect to a directory that has been assigned the share name DATAFILES on the computer named SALES the UNC to connect to this resource would be \\SALES\DATAFILES.

For more information, see Chapter 12 of *Network+ Exam Cram*.

Question 46

Answer b is correct. The TCP/IP protocol is a popular communication protocol used on the Internet and supported in Microsoft and NetWare 5 networks. TCP/IP is a configurable protocol, and all computers wishing to utilize it must have the correct settings. All computers using TCP/IP must have a unique IP address, a subnet mask, and if used in a WAN, a default gateway. An IP address identifies a TCP/IP host on the network and contains two important elements: a network ID and a host ID. The network ID of an IP address identifies the network the host is on. (For example, all users in a single location are said to be on the same network and, therefore, will all have the same network ID in their IP address.) The host ID of an IP address identifies the host, or individual computer, on a TCP/IP network. It is the host ID portion of an IP address that is the unique part. Therefore, in a single TCP/IP network, users will all have the same network ID and different (unique) host IDs. IP addressing is similar to the way houses are addressed on your block. Many people live on Maple Street (network ID), but only one person lives at 21 Maple Street (host ID). A subnet mask is a required parameter for all TCP/IP hosts. A subnet mask is used to distinguish the network ID in an IP address from the host ID. When a computer using TCP/IP needs to communicate with another TCP/IP host, it uses the subnet mask to determine if the destination computer is local (on my network) or remote (on a different network). If the subnet mask determines the destination host is local, it simply places the packet on the cable for delivery. If the subnet mask determines the host it needs to communicate with is remote (on another network), it sends it to its default gateway. A default gateway is only required to be configured on TCP/IP hosts that need to communicate outside of their local network or in a WAN. A default gateway is the IP address of the router used by the local network to connect to another network in the outside world, like the Internet or another branch office location. A default gateway is not a required parameter when using TCP/IP in a LAN, because all computers are on the same network and have the same network ID.

For more information, see Chapter 4 of *Network+ Exam Cram*.

Question 47

Answer c is correct. The TCP/IP protocol is a popular communication protocol used on the Internet and supported in Microsoft and NetWare 5 networks. TCP/IP is a configurable protocol, and all computers wishing to utilize it must have the correct settings. All computers using TCP/IP must have a unique IP address, a subnet mask, and if used in a WAN, a default gateway. An IP address identifies a TCP/IP host on the network, and contains two important elements: a network ID and a host ID. The network ID of an IP address identifies the network the host is on. (For example, all users in a single location are said to be on the same network and, therefore, will all have the same network ID in their IP address.) The host ID of an IP address identifies the host, or individual computer, on a TCP/IP network. It is the host ID portion of an IP address that is the unique part. Therefore, in a single TCP/IP network, users will all have the same network ID and different (unique) host IDs. IP addressing is similar to the way houses are addressed on your block. Many people live on Maple Street (network ID), but only one person lives at 21 Maple Street (host ID). A subnet mask is a required parameter for all TCP/IP hosts. A subnet mask is used to distinguish the network ID in an IP address from the host ID. When a computer using TCP/IP needs to communicate with another TCP/IP host, it uses the subnet mask to determine if the destination computer is local (on my network) or remote (on a different network). If the subnet mask determines the destination host is local, it simply places the packet on the cable for delivery. If the subnet mask determines the host it needs to communicate with is remote (on another network), it sends it to its default gateway. A default gateway is only required to be configured on TCP/IP hosts that need to communicate outside of their local network or in a WAN. A default gateway is the IP address of the router used by the local network to connect to another network in the outside world, like the Internet or another branch office location. A default gateway is not a required parameter when using TCP/IP in a LAN, because all computers are on the same network and have the same network ID.

For more information, see Chapter 4 of *Network+ Exam Cram*.

Question 48

Answer c is correct. Dynamic Host Configuration Protocol (DHCP) is used to automatically configure TCP/IP configuration information on TCP/IP hosts. All computers using TCP/IP must have a unique IP address, a subnet mask, and if used in a WAN, a default gateway. In large networks, it can be time-consuming to configure these settings on each computer one at a time. In these instances, a DHCP server can be used to automatically provide the clients on the network with this information. A DHCP server can provide clients with a unique IP address, a subnet mask, a default gateway, and many other TCP/IP parameters automatically. In order for DHCP to assign unique IP addresses to hosts, it must be configured with a scope. A DHCP scope is the range of IP addresses it uses to distribute to hosts requesting an IP address. To configure a DHCP scope, two parameters must be specified: the "From" address and the "To" address. It is the addresses within this range, or scope, that a DHCP server will assign to clients. Windows Internet Naming Service (WINS) and Domain Name System (DNS) are used for name resolution in a TCP/IP network.

For more information, see Chapter 10 of *Network+ Exam Cram.*

Question 49

Answer d is correct. WINS is used in Microsoft networks to provide name resolution of NetBIOS names to IP addresses. Microsoft networks utilize the NetBIOS API when communicating. NetBIOS is an API that provides the "base" that Microsoft networks are built on. WINS will resolve, or associate, a NetBIOS name to its IP address. All computers running TCP/IP specify a hostname that is used to identify themselves on the network. When TCP/IP hosts communicate, their IP addresses are resolved, or associated, with their hostnames. DNS performs this hostname to IP address name resolution. The main difference between the name resolution services of WINS and DNS are the type of names they resolve. WINS resolves NetBIOS names to IP addresses, while DNS resolves hostnames—Fully Qualified Domain Names (FQDNs) to IP addresses. All Internet addresses (**www.anything.com**, .org, **.net,** and so on) are examples of FQDN names.

For more information, see Chapter 4 of *Network+ Exam Cram.*

Question 50

Answers a and c are correct. A HOSTS file is a local file on every TCP/IP computer that resolves hostnames or domain names to IP addresses. Entries in a HOSTS file must be made manually in the file on each user's computer. An entry in a local HOSTS file would contain two basic parts: the IP address of a host and the hostname. HOSTS files cannot resolve NetBIOS names to IP addresses. That functionality is provided by WINS or a local LMHOSTS file.

For more information, see Chapter 4 of *Network+ Exam Cram.*

Question 51

Answer a is correct. TCP and UDP are part of the TCP/IP protocol suite. Transmission Control Protocol (TCP) is a connection-oriented protocol that provides guaranteed delivery of packets between hosts. TCP also ensures that packets will be delivered to the destination host in the same order they were sent. User Datagram Protocol (UDP) is a connectionless protocol that does not guarantee delivery of packets. UDP is primarily used by TCP/IP utilities and for broadcasting packets in a TCP/IP network.

For more information, see Chapter 4 of *Network+ Exam Cram*.

Question 52

Answer a is correct. Post Office Protocol (POP3) and Simple Mail Transfer Protocol (SMTP) are common protocols used with Internet email. POP3 is used to retrieve Internet mail from a mail server. SMTP is used to send outgoing Internet mail to a mail server. Both SMTP and POP3 are part of the TCP/IP protocol suite. DCHP and WINS have nothing to do with Internet email.

The key points to remember about these protocols are:

➤ You send mail using SMTP.

➤ You receive mail using POP3.

➤ Your POP3 server is your incoming mail server.

➤ Your SMTP server is your outgoing mail server.

For more information, see Chapter 4 of *Network+ Exam Cram*.

Question 53

Answer a is correct. Simple Network Management Protocol (SNMP) is commonly used to monitor a TCP/IP network. SNMP can report on the traffic and components of a TCP/IP network and provide administrators with statistical data. SNMP is implemented using agents and managers. SNMP agents are programs installed on TCP/IP computers in the network. With these agents in place, SNMP management software, installed on a TCP/IP computer, can be used to gather information from these agents on the status of the network. The information and settings used by an SNMP manager when communicating with an SNMP agent are stored in a Management Information Base (MIB). POP3 is a protocol used to retrieve incoming Internet mail. TCP is a connection-oriented protocol that provides guaranteed delivery of packets. SMTP is a protocol used to send outgoing Internet mail.

For more information, see Chapter 4 of *Network+ Exam Cram*.

Question 54

Answer c is correct. File Transfer Protocol (FTP) is used to transfer files between hosts on a TCP/IP network. Although FTP is commonly used on the Internet to upload and download files, it is equally effective when used in an intranet environment. SNMP is commonly used to monitor a TCP/IP network. SNMP can report on the traffic and components of a TCP/IP network and provide administrators with statistical data. POP3 is a protocol used to retrieve incoming Internet mail. TCP is a connection-oriented protocol that provides guaranteed delivery of packets. SMTP is a protocol used to send outgoing Internet mail.

For more information, see Chapter 4 of *Network+ Exam Cram*.

Question 55

Answer c is correct. Internet Protocol (IP) is a key component of the TCP/IP protocol suite. IP resides at the Network layer of the OSI model. IP addresses packets to identify a host at the Network layer. Your IP address, or network address, is the address added by IP. A router, which is commonly used to connect TCP/IP networks, also resides at the Network layer of the OSI model and therefore is capable of reading the IP address of a packet. SNMP is commonly used to monitor a TCP/IP network. SNMP can report on the traffic and components of a TCP/IP network and provide administrators with statistical data. TCP is a connection-oriented protocol that provides guaranteed delivery of packets between hosts. TCP also ensures that packets will be delivered to the destination host in the same order they were sent. UDP is a connectionless protocol that does not guarantee delivery of packets. UDP is primarily used by TCP/IP utilities and for broadcasting packets in a TCP/IP network. SMTP is a protocol used to send outgoing Internet mail.

For more information, see Chapter 4 of *Network+ Exam Cram*.

Question 56

Answers a, b, and c are correct. Small Computer System Interface (SCSI) is a parallel interface standard for attaching peripheral devices to a computer. There are many variations of SCSI. In general SCSI supports the use of Centronics

50, 68 HP, and DB-25 connectors when attaching an external SCSI device to a PC. Dual RJ-11 connectors are used to connect telephone line to a modem card.

For more information, see Chapter 14 of *Network+ Exam Cram*.

Question 57

Answer b is correct. TCP/IP addresses are divided into three main classes: Class A, Class B, and Class C. The address range for each address class is as follows:

➤ **Class A** IP addresses that *begin* with numbers from 1 to 126.

➤ **Class B** IP addresses that *begin* with numbers from 128 to 191. (Note: 127 is not used in IP addressing; it is reserved for localhost.)

➤ **Class C** IP addresses that *begin* with numbers from 192 to 223.

When looking at any IP address, it is the number in the *first* octet that determines the address class of that address. Note the following examples.

➤ The IP address 3.100.32.7 is a Class A address because it *begins* with 3, a number between 1 and 126.

➤ The IP address 145.100.32.7 is a Class B address because it *begins* with 145, a number between 128 and 191.

➤ The IP address 210.100.32.7 is a Class C address because it *begins* with 210, a number between 192 and 223.

For more information, see Chapter 4 of *Network+ Exam Cram*.

Question 58

Answer b is correct. All routers contain routing tables. The routing table in a router contains the information it uses to send, or "route," network traffic. A routing table can be either static or dynamic. With static routing, all information in the routing table must be entered manually. Dynamic routing, as the name implies, allows a router to automatically update its routing table. It does this by "talking" to other routers, checking various paths, counting distances between routes, and so on. Therefore, dynamic routing requires less administration than static routing.

For more information, see Chapter 4 of *Network+ Exam Cram*.

Question 59

Answer a is correct. All computers using TCP/IP must have a unique IP address, a subnet mask, and if used in a WAN, a default gateway. An IP address identifies a TCP/IP host on the network and contains two important elements: a network ID and a host ID. The network ID of an IP address identifies the network the host is on. (For example, all users in a single location are said to be on the same network and, therefore, will all have the same network ID in their IP address.) The host ID of an IP address identifies the host, or individual computer, on a TCP/IP network. It is the host ID portion of an IP address that is the unique part. Therefore, in a single TCP/IP network, users will all have the same network ID and different (unique) host IDs. The subnet mask is used to "mask" the network portion of an IP address, with the number 255, so IP can determine if the destination host is local or remote. A default subnet mask refers to the subnet mask that is used by a particular TCP/IP address class in a single subnet environment, like a LAN. because each address class uses a different number of octets for the network ID, and the subnet mask "masks" the network portion of an IP address, the default subnet mask will be different for each class of IP addresses. The number 255 is the number reserved in TCP/IP for use by the default subnet mask. A default subnet mask will use 255s over the network portion of an IP address, and 0s over the host portion of an IP address.

IP address Class A

➤ Address range is from 1 to 126. Example: 2.45.65.8 is a Class A address. It begins with 2—a number *between* 1 and 126.

➤ Uses the first octet for the network ID, and the last 3 octets for the host ID. Example: The network ID of IP address 2.45.65.8 is 2 because it is a Class A address, and Class A uses the first octet for the network ID. The host ID is 45.65.8.

➤ Default subnet mask is 255.0.0.0. A default subnet mask uses 255 to mask the network portion of an IP address and 0 to mask the host portion of an IP address.

IP address Class B

➤ Address range is from 128 to 191. Example: 162.45.65.8 is a Class B address. It begins with 162—a number between 128 and 191.

➤ Uses the first two octets for the network ID and the last two octets for the host ID. Example: The network ID of IP address 162.45.65.8 is 162.45 because it is a Class B address, and Class B uses the first two octets for the network ID. The host ID is 65.8.

➤ Default subnet mask is 255.255.0.0. A default subnet mask uses 255 to mask the network portion of an IP address and 0 to mask the host portion of an IP address.

IP address Class C

➤ Address range is from 192 to 223. Example: 202.85.65.8 is a Class C address. It begins with 202—a number between 192 and 223.

➤ Uses the first three octets for the Network ID and the last octet for the host ID. Example: The network ID of IP address 202.85.65.8 is 202.85.65 because it is a Class C address, and Class C uses the first three octets for the network ID. The host ID is 8.

➤ Default subnet mask is 255.255.255.0. A default subnet mask uses 255 to mask the network portion of an IP address and 0 to mask the host portion of an IP address.

For more information, see Chapter 4 of *Network+ Exam Cram*.

Question 60

Answer c is correct. A port number is one of the items specified by TCP/IP hosts to establish a connection. Port numbers for common TCP/IP utilities are said to have well-known port numbers. A well-known port number is the port number that will be used when no port number is specifically designated. The most important port numbers to know are:

➤ **HTTP** Hypertext Transfer Protocol, the protocol used by the Web, uses port 80.

➤ **FTP** File Transfer Protocol, used to transfer files (upload/download), uses port 21.

➤ **SMTP** Simple Mail Transfer Protocol, used to send outgoing Internet mail, uses port 25.

➤ **POP3** Post Office Protocol, used to retrieve incoming Internet mail, uses port 110.

When using any of these well-known utilities, the port number does not need to be specified; it is assumed the default will be used. Windows Sockets is an example of the use of a port number. Windows Sockets is a "session" established between two TCP/IP computers. The "socket" created between hosts is used for reliable communication. To create a socket, hosts specify an IP address, the type of service (UDP, TCP), and a port number. If a different port

number is to be used other than the well-known number, it must be specifically designated and must be a number over 1,024. (The number 1,024 and
numbers under it are used for well-known programs).

For more information, see Chapter 4 of *Network+ Exam Cram*.

Question 61

Answer b is correct. Providing some form of security to an internal network
when connecting to the Internet should be a primary concern of a network
administrator. An IP proxy, or proxy server, is a common tool used to provide
this type of security.

An IP proxy, or proxy server (same thing), serves two main purposes:

➤ Firewall protection to protect users on the local network from the
intrusion of the Internet

➤ Improved Internet performance by increasing the speed that users on
the local network retrieve Web pages

An IP proxy can provide firewall security to protect users on the local network
from the intrusion of the Internet. (A firewall is defined as any configuration,
hardware or software, that protects users on a local network from the intrusion
of the Internet.) When an IP proxy is used as a firewall, it typically will be a
dedicated server that is configured with two network adapter cards. One network card will be used for an Internet connection, known as the external network
adapter, and the other will be used for the connection to the local network,
known as the internal network adapter. In this firewall configuration, the only
computer connected to the Internet is the proxy server through this dedicated
external network card. For clients to access the Internet, they must configure
their Web browsers to send all Internet requests to the IP proxy. When a client
requests an Internet address, the request goes to the proxy server, and the proxy
server retrieves the information from the Web site on behalf of the client. The
proxy server "acts" like the client when retrieving this information, so the only
IP address used in making all requests is the proxy server's external network
adapter address. All internal IP addresses will not be seen by any Internet networks. For additional security, the proxy server can be configured to deny access
to Web sites or protocols for both incoming and outgoing requests.

A proxy server also provides improved Internet performance. Because an IP
proxy retrieves Web pages on behalf of all users in a local network, it places all
these pages in its local cache (memory). This way, if a user requests an Internet
address that was previously retrieved by the proxy server, the proxy server will

give the user the page contained in its local cache. The process of providing users with cached Web pages is much faster than the standard means of requesting/retrieving the information from the Web site on the Internet.

A DHCP server is used to automatically assign IP addresses to clients in a TCP/IP network, and POP3 is used to retrieve incoming Internet mail. Neither have anything to do with security.

For more information, see Chapter 6 of *Network+ Exam Cram*.

Question 62

Answer b is correct. The OSI model defines standards for networking based on a seven-layer model. All of the components used in networking (hubs, bridges, routers, cables, protocols, and so on) conform to various layers of the OSI model by "residing" at one or more of these seven layers. A redirector resides at the Presentation layer of the OSI model. In order for a computer to access a network resource, it must have the appropriate redirector installed. A redirector is a Presentation layer component that takes a request made on the local computer and "redirects" it out onto the network. A computer can access the resources of another computer on the network provided it has the appropriate redirector installed. An example of a redirector would be the Microsoft redirector for connecting Windows 95 computers to NetWare servers. This redirector, called Client for NetWare Networks, is included with Windows 95. Installing the redirector Client for NetWare Networks on a Windows 95 computer will allow it to access resources on a NetWare server.

For more information, see Chapter 8 of *Network+ Exam Cram*.

Question 63

Answer a is correct. An LMHOSTS file is used to resolve NetBIOS names to IP addresses. AN LMHOSTS file performs the same type of name resolution as WINS. A key difference between an LMHOSTS file and WINS is that an LMHOSTS file is a file that exists locally on all computers in a network, and entries must be manually added. WINS will run as a service on a single NT server, and its information is dynamically updated by the client computers in a network. Microsoft networks utilize the NetBIOS API when communicating. NetBIOS is an API that provides the "base" that Microsoft networks are built on. For this reason, the name of a Microsoft computer is said to be the NetBIOS name of that computer. WINS will resolve, or associate, a NetBIOS name to its IP address so that computers can communicate with each other. Though there are many types of NetBIOS names used in Microsoft networking (user name, domain name, groups, and so on), the most common NetBIOS name is the computer name.

For more information, see Chapter 4 of *Network+ Exam Cram*.

Question 64

Answer c is correct. IP is a key component of the TCP/IP protocol suite. IP resides at the Network layer of the OSI model. IP addresses packets to identify a host at the Network layer. Your IP address, or network address, is the address added by IP. A router, which is commonly used to connect TCP/IP networks also resides at the Network layer of the OSI model and therefore is capable of reading the IP address of a packet. SNMP is commonly used to monitor a TCP/IP network. SNMP can report on the traffic and components of a TCP/IP network and provide administrators with statistical data. TCP is a connection-oriented protocol that provides guaranteed delivery of packets between hosts. TCP also ensures that packets will be delivered to the destination host in the same order they were sent. UDP is a connectionless protocol that does not guarantee delivery of packets. UDP is primarily used by TCP/IP utilities and for broadcasting packets in a TCP/IP network. SMTP is a protocol used to send outgoing Internet mail.

For more information, see Chapter 4 of *Network+ Exam Cram*.

Question 65

Answer d is correct. TCP/IP contains various command-line utilities used for troubleshooting/diagnosing a TCP/IP network. The key commands to know are **ARP, NBTSTAT, TRACERT,** and **NETSTAT.**

➤ **ARP** Address Resolution Protocol resolves, or associates, an IP address to a MAC address. A MAC address, also known as a hardware address, is the permanent address "burned" into every network adapter card by the manufacturer. The TCP/IP command **ARP –a** will display the local computer's ARP cache, which is a list of all the IP addresses that have been resolved by ARP, along with the corresponding MAC address.

➤ **NETSTAT** A TCP/IP command-line utility used to display protocol statistics about the current TCP/IP connection. **NETSTAT** can be used to display information about the port number (80 for HTTP, 21 for FTP, and so on) and protocol (UDP, TCP) used in a given TCP/IP connection.

➤ **NBTSTAT** A TCP/IP command-line utility that displays the current TCP/IP NetBIOS name information. Microsoft networks commonly use NetBIOS names when communicating. To communicate using TCP/IP, NetBIOS names must be resolved, or associated, with their IP address. This name resolution can take place via WINS, broadcast, or LMHOSTS files. The **NBTSTAT** command can be used to display the NetBIOS names used by the local computer, **NBTSTAT –n**, as well as provide a list of how NetBIOS name resolution is taking place, either by WINS or by broadcast, **NBTSTAT –r**.

➤ **TRACERT** A TCP/IP command used to trace a route to a remote host. **TRACERT** is used to determine the route a packet travels on the way to the destination computer. Typing "TRACERT" and the destination IP address will trace the path the packet travels to its destination.

For more information, see Chapter 4 of *Network+ Exam Cram*.

Question 66

Answer b is correct. TCP/IP contains various command-line utilities used for troubleshooting/diagnosing a TCP/IP network. The key commands to know are **ARP, NBTSTAT, TRACERT,** and **NETSTAT**.

➤ **ARP** Address Resolution Protocol resolves, or associates, an IP address to a MAC address. A MAC address, also known as a hardware address, is the permanent address "burned" into every network adapter card by the manufacturer. The TCP/IP command **ARP –a** will display the local computer's ARP cache, which is a list of all the IP addresses that have been resolved by ARP, along with the corresponding MAC address.

➤ **NETSTAT** A TCP/IP command-line utility used to display protocol statistics about the current TCP/IP connection. **NETSTAT** can be used to display information about the port number (80 for HTTP, 21 for FTP, and so on) and protocol (UDP, TCP) used in a given TCP/IP connection.

➤ **NBTSTAT** A TCP/IP command-line utility that displays the current TCP/IP NetBIOS name information. Microsoft networks commonly use NetBIOS names when communicating. To communicate using TCP/IP, NetBIOS names must be resolved, or associated, with their IP address. This name resolution can take place via WINS, broadcast, or LMHOSTS files. The **NBTSTAT** command can be used to display the NetBIOS names used by the local computer, **NBTSTAT –n**, as well as provide a list of how NetBIOS name resolution is taking place, **NBTSTAT –r**.

➤ TRACERT A TCP/IP command used to trace a route to a remote host. **TRACERT** is used to determine the route a packet travels on the way to the destination computer. Typing "TRACERT" and the destination IP address will trace the path the packet travels to its destination.

For more information, see Chapter 4 of *Network+ Exam Cram*.

Question 67

Answer c is correct. Thicknet attaches to a network adapter card by using a vampire tap into the Thicknet, and a drop cable to the network card. The connector at the end of a drop cable is an AUI 15-pin connector. An AUI is also called a DIX connector, named after the companies that developed it (Digital, Intel, and Xerox).

For more information, see Chapter 2 of *Network+ Exam Cram*.

Question 68

Answer c is correct. The PING utility is a very useful tool when troubleshooting a TCP/IP network. PING is used to test for connectivity between hosts on a TCP/IP network. The syntax for the **PING** command is simple: Type PING and the IP address of the computer you want to connect to and press Enter. PING will then attempt a connection to this host. If PING is successful, this verifies that the TCP/IP connection between these computers is valid. If PING is unsuccessful, this verifies that there is no communication between these hosts using TCP/IP. The **IPCONFIG** (NT Server and Workstation) and **WINIPCFG** (Windows 95/98) commands are used to display IP configuration information. The TCP/IP command **ARP –a** will display the local computer's ARP cache, which is a list of all the IP addresses that have been resolved by ARP, along with the corresponding MAC address. ARP is not used to test connectivity.

For more information, see Chapter 4 of *Network+ Exam Cram*.

Question 69

Answer a is correct. The **ARP** command was used in this example. Notice it displays the IP address and MAC address, which is exactly what the ARP utility is used for. TCP/IP contains various command-line utilities used for troubleshooting/diagnosing a TCP/IP network. The key commands to know are **ARP, NBTSTAT, TRACERT**, and **NETSTAT**.

➤ **ARP** Address Resolution Protocol resolves, or associates, an IP address to a MAC address. A MAC address, also known as a hardware address, is the permanent address "burned" into every network adapter card by the manufacturer. The TCP/IP command **ARP –a** will display the local computer's ARP cache, which is a list of all the IP addresses that have been resolved by ARP, along with the corresponding MAC address.

➤ **NETSTAT** A TCP/IP command-line utility used to display protocol statistics about the current TCP/IP connection. **NETSTAT** can be used to display information about the port number (80 for HTTP, 21 for FTP, and so on) and protocol (UDP, TCP) used in a given TCP/IP connection.

➤ **NBTSTAT** A TCP/IP command-line utility that displays the current TCP/IP NetBIOS name information. Microsoft networks commonly use NetBIOS names when communicating. To communicate using TCP/IP, NetBIOS names must be resolved, or associated, with their IP address. This name resolution can take place via WINS, broadcast, or LMHOSTS files. The **NBTSTAT** command can be used to display the NetBIOS names used by the local computer, **NBTSTAT –n**, as well as provide a list of how NetBIOS name resolution is taking place, **NBTSTAT –r**.

➤ **TRACERT** A TCP/IP command used to trace a route to a remote host. **TRACERT** is used to determine the route a packet travels on the way to the destination computer. Typing "TRACERT" and the destination IP address will trace the path the packet travels to its destination.

For more information, see Chapter 4 of *Network+ Exam Cram*.

Question 70

Answer c is correct. The **NBTSTAT** command was used in this example. Notice it displays NetBIOS Local Name Table, which is one use for the NBTSTAT utility. This output was produced using NBTSTAT with the **–n** switch. TCP/IP contains various command-line utilities used for troubleshooting/diagnosing a TCP/IP network. The key commands to know are **ARP, NBTSTAT, TRACERT,** and **NETSTAT**.

➤ **ARP** Address Resolution Protocol resolves, or associates, an IP address to a MAC address. A MAC address, also known as a hardware address, is the permanent address "burned" into every network adapter card by the manufacturer. The TCP/IP command **ARP –a** will display the local computer's ARP cache, which is a list of all the IP addresses that have been resolved by ARP, along with the corresponding MAC address.

➤ **NETSTAT** A TCP/IP command-line utility used to display protocol statistics about the current TCP/IP connection. **NETSTAT** can be used to display information about the port number (80 for HTTP, 21 for FTP, and so on) and protocol (UDP, TCP) used in a given TCP/IP connection.

➤ **NBTSTAT** A TCP/IP command-line utility that displays the current TCP/IP NetBIOS name information. Microsoft networks commonly use NetBIOS names when communicating. To communicate using TCP/IP, NetBIOS names must be resolved, or associated, with their IP address. This name resolution can take place via WINS, broadcast or LMHOSTS files. The NBTSTAT command can be used to display the NetBIOS names used by the local computer, **NBTSTAT –n**, as well as provide a list of how NetBIOS name resolution is taking place, **NBTSTAT –r**.

➤ **TRACERT** A TCP/IP command used to trace a route to a remote host. **TRACERT** is used to determine the route a packet travels on the way to the destination computer. Typing "TRACERT" and the destination IP address will trace the path the packet travels to its destination.

For more information, see Chapter 4 of *Network+ Exam Cram*.

Question 71

Answer a is correct. Both NT Server and Novell NetWare are server operating systems, so both are viable solutions to the operating system requirement. Windows 95 is not a server operating system; it is a client operating system. The only choice that meets the fault tolerance requirement is answer a. Fault tolerance is the ability to recover from a single hard disk failure. A standard created for implementing fault tolerant strategies is known as RAID. A mirror set, or RAID 1, is created using two disks, with one disk acting as a "mirror" of the other, providing redundancy. A stripe set without parity, or RAID 0, is created by combining equal areas of free space on 2 to 32 disks to form one logical drive. Stripe sets without parity provide faster read performance, since all disks can be read simultaneously, but they do not provide fault tolerance.

For more information, see Chapter 3 of *Network+ Exam Cram*.

Question 72

Answer a is correct. Both Point-to-Point Protocol (PPP) and Serial Line Internet Protocol (SLIP) are used as dial-up protocols when using a modem to connect to a remote network or the Internet. PPP is a newer, more efficient dial-up protocol than SLIP. PPP automatically obtains configuration parameters with the remote server on connection. This simplifies the configurations required when making a remote connection; SLIP must be configured manually with these parameters. Another key difference between PPP and SLIP is the number of communication protocols supported. PPP supports IPX/SPX, AppleTalk, TCP/IP, and NetBEUI. SLIP only supports the use of the TCP/IP protocol.

For more information, see Chapter 4 of *Network+ Exam Cram*

Question 73

Answer a is correct. PPTP is used to create Virtual Private Networks (VPNs). A VPN is a private network that uses the Internet to make a connection. Users from each private network establish an Internet connection locally and use the network capabilities of the Internet to connect to each other. Because the Internet is a public network, connecting two private networks together in this manner does pose some security risks. To provide security for VPNs over the Internet, the PPTP protocol is used. With PPTP enabled, the only packets that will be allowed into members of the VPN are PPTP packets. This provides an extra measure of security against potential hackers PPP is the more efficient dial-up protocol than SLIP. **PING** is used to test for connectivity between TCP/IP hosts. There is no such thing as to PinPoint (PP) the TimePeriod (TP) elapsed during a datagram transmission.

For more information, see Chapter 6 of *Network+ Exam Cram*.

Question 74

Answer d is correct. Integrated Services Digital Network (ISDN) is a digital dial-up service that can send voice and data signals at 128Kbps (128,000 bits per second). ISDN uses two 64K channels, called "B" channels, when transmitting. ISDN uses a terminal adapter (TA) to connect to a computer in place of a modem. This is because the transmission is digital over ISDN and does not have to be "modulated," or converted, to analog as is the case with regular phone line. Public Switched Telephone Network (PSTN), also known as Plain Old Telephone Service (POTS) is the standard dial-up analog phone line used to send voice and data. PSTN can transmit data up to 28,800Bps. (The new 56Kbps standard achieves faster transmission speeds over 28.8Kbps by using digital lines and a technique known as data compression.) PSTN uses a modem (modulate/demodulate) to connect to a computer. A modem converts, or modulates, a computer's digital signal to analog for transmission over PSTN, and the receiving computer's modem will demodulate that signal, or convert it from analog to a digital signal.

For more information, see Chapter 6 of *Network+ Exam Cram*.

Question 75

Answer a is correct. There are two common security models a network administrator can employ to control users' access to network resources: share-level security and user-level security. When using share-level security, passwords are assigned to resources. An example of share-level security is sharing a printer and assigning a password to that printer. When users need to connect to the printer, they will have to enter the password set on the printer in order to access it. The share-level security model is considered a less secure method than user-level security, because users are more likely to tell others the password to access a resource than they are to give away their own username and password. In user-level security, permissions are assigned to users. An example of user-level security is sharing a printer and assigning permissions to users to access this resource. For users to access this printer, their user account must have permissions to access it. Remember: share-level security assigns passwords to resources (printers, files, programs, and so on). User-level security assigns permissions to users. Answer d is incorrect because NASIRD does not exist.

For more information, see Chapter 7 of *Network+ Exam Cram*.

Network+
Practice Test #4

Question 1

Which of the following is used to provide security for sensitive data during transmission over a network by making the data unreadable to potential "hackers" who tap into network cable?

- ○ a. Data encryption
- ○ b. User-level security
- ○ c. Share-level security
- ○ d. Data Eletro Propagation (DEP)

Question 2

Which connectivity device would you use to connect computers in a 10BaseT network?

- ○ a. Hub
- ○ b. MAU
- ○ c. Router
- ○ d. Repeater

Question 3

Which TCP/IP utility is used to resolve hostnames or domain names to IP addresses?

○ a. WINS

○ b. DNS

○ c. DHCP

○ d. None of the above

Question 4

You are troubleshooting a Windows NT Server computer on your network. The computer is using TCP/IP as the only protocol. You need to display the IP address, subnet mask, and default gateway parameters that this computer is using. You also need to know the IP address of the WINS and DNS servers that this computer is using. What TCP/IP command-line utility can give you this information?

○ a. WINIPCFG /ALL

○ b. IPCONFIG /ALL

○ c. IPCONFIG

○ d. None of the above

Question 5

You are using the Internet to download files. You connect to an FTP site and download 30 files. When you connect to the site, you do not specify a port number. You notice the FTP protocol is being used, but you do not see any port number. You know that FTP is a well-known protocol and uses a port number. What port number is being used to make this connection?

○ a. 21

○ b. 25

○ c. 80

○ d. 110

Question 6

What is the IP address class for address 1.200.200.17?

O a. Class A

O b. Class B

O c. Class C

O d. Class A and B

Question 7

The Amazon Coffee Company is having problems with its 10Base2 network and has asked for your help. The network of 300 users was working fine until the company attempted to expand it to include 200 users on an upper floor of its building. Someone ran a single segment of Thinnet coaxial cable between floors over a distance of 200 meters. After doing this and verifying all connections, the network was not functioning properly. Which of the following is the most likely reason this network is malfunctioning?

O a. You cannot use Thinnet coaxial cable in a 10Base2 network.

O b. A 10Base2 network cannot support more than 400 users.

O c. You cannot use Thinnet coaxial cable more than 185 meters in a single segment.

O d. You must use shielded Thinnet coaxial cable for cable runs between floors.

Question 8

Helena's Flowers has a network of 30 computers. Twenty of these computers are running Windows 9X, nine are running Windows NT Workstation, and one computer is running Windows NT Server. The Windows NT Server computer controls users' access to all network resources. Which of the following best describes the type of network Helena has employed?

O a. This is a server-based network.

O b. This is a peer-to-peer network.

O c. This is a token ring network.

O d. It is impossible to tell what type of network this is. There is not enough information given.

Question 9

Which of the following is true about the difference between routable and nonroutable protocols?

○ a. Nonroutable protocols can be used in a LAN, and routable protocols can be used in a WAN and a LAN.

○ b. Nonroutable protocols can be used in a WAN, and routable protocols can only be used in a LAN.

○ c. Nonroutable protocols cannot be used in Ethernet networks, and routable protocols can be used in Ethernet networks.

○ d. Nonroutable protocols can be used in a WAN, and routable protocols cannot be used in a LAN.

Question 10

You are configuring the settings for TCP/IP on your California-based network. Users need to use TCP/IP to communicate with each other in the local network and also to several branch office locations in Florida, Texas, and Utah. Your network connects to these locations through a router in your office. What TCP/IP parameters must you configure on each computer in this scenario? [Choose the three best answers]

❑ a. Subnet mask

❑ b. Default gateway

❑ c. A unique IP address for each computer

❑ d. The same IP address on every computer

Question 11

Which of the following statements are true regarding the difference between the CSMA/CD and token passing access methods? [Choose the two best answers]

❑ a. CSMA/CD is used in Ethernet networks; token passing is used in the ring topology.

❑ b. CSMA/CD is used in the ring topology; token passing is used in Ethernet networks.

❑ c. Networks using CSMA/CD can have packet collisions; token passing networks do not have packet collisions.

❑ d. Networks using token passing can have packet collisions; CSMA/CD networks do not have packet collisions.

Question 12

You are discussing the TCP/IP protocol with your colleagues. Lillian says that UDP is a connection-oriented protocol, and TCP is connectionless. Marcus disagrees and says it's the other way around; TCP is connection-oriented and UDP is connectionless. They both turn to you to resolve the dispute. What will you reply?

- O a. Tell Marcus he is right; TCP is a connection-oriented protocol, and UDP is connectionless.

- O b. Tell Lillian she is right; UDP is connection-oriented, and TCP is connectionless.

- O c. Tell them they are both wrong; TCP and UDP have nothing to do with TCP/IP.

- O d. Tell them they are both right; TCP and UDP do exactly the same thing.

Question 13

You are working phone support at the help desk of your company. A user calls from home complaining that he cannot send his Internet email. The user has no problems retrieving Internet email messages, but cannot send any messages. The user says everything was working fine until he altered the configuration settings in his email client. The user cannot remember if he changed his POP3 server information or his SMTP server information. Based on the information, what can you tell the user?

- O a. You probably changed your POP3 server information.

- O b. You probably changed your SMTP server information.

- O c. You probably changed both your SMTP and your POP3 server information.

- O d. You probably changed some other parameter; SMTP and POP3 have nothing to do with Internet email.

Question 14

What is the IP address Class for address 121.200.200.17?

○ a.   Class A

○ b.   Class B

○ c.   Class C

○ d.   Class A and B

Question 15

You are the network administrator for Harvey's Golf. Recently, you have experienced problems with data loss. You decide to implement a fault tolerance strategy on all your servers, in addition to doing a daily tape backup. Which of the following methods provide fault tolerance?

○ a.   Implement volume sets on all servers.

○ b.   Implement mirror sets on all servers.

○ c.   Implement a stripe set without parity on all servers.

○ d.   Implement RAID 0 on all servers.

Question 16

Which of the following best describes the function of data encryption?

○ a.   Data encryption is used to improve the transmission speed at which a network performs.

○ b.   Data encryption is uñld to provide security for sensitive data during transmission over network media.

○ c.   Data encryption is used when user-level security cannot be implemented.

○ d.   Data encryption is only suitable for LANs.

Question 17

You administer a server-based network of 20 computers. All servers are located in a small utility room. Lately, network performance has become erratic, and the servers are failing intermittently. You go into the utility room and observe the room temperature to be 90 degrees Fahrenheit, and the humidity level is 65 percent. What observations can you make about the room conditions these servers are in?

- ○ a. These conditions are suitable for computers.
- ○ b. These conditions are not suitable for computers. The room is too cold.
- ○ c. These conditions are not suitable for computers. The room is too hot.
- ○ d. These conditions are not suitable for computers. The humidity is too high.

Question 18

Which of the following best describes the function of DHCP?

- ○ a. DHCP is used for name resolution on a TCP/IP network.
- ○ b. DHCP is used to automatically configure TCP/IP information on hosts in a TCP/IP network.
- ○ c. DHCP is not used in TCP/IP.
- ○ d. DHCP is used for name resolution on the Internet.

Question 19

You are the administrator of a network that contains 75 computers configured in a star topology. The network is using twisted-pair cable and is spread out over several floors. Mary, one of the users on the first floor, experiences a system crash and turns off her computer. Which of the following best describes the effect this has on the other users of the network?

○ a. All users will not be able to communicate until Mary's computer is fixed.

○ b. All users will be able to communicate whether or not Mary's computer is turned back on and whether or not the cable is plugged into her network adapter card.

○ c. All users will not be able to communicate until Mary's computer is turned back on.

○ d. All users will be able to communicate whether or not Mary's computer is turned back on as long as the network cable is still attached to her computer.

Question 20

Which of the following statements is true regarding the "10" in 10BaseT, 10Base2, and 10Base5?

○ a. The "10" refers to the number of networks supported.

○ b. The "10" refers to the transmission speed (10Mbps).

○ c. The "10" refers to the Ethernet document conference number of this standard.

○ d. The "10" refers to the number of connectivity devices (routers, hubs, bridges, and so on) supported.

Question 21

The IEEE (Institute of Electrical and Electronics Engineers, Inc.) publishes standards used in networking. A subgroup of IEEE is Project 802, which defines network standards for the physical components of a network. Which of the following statements are true of Project 802 standards? [Choose the two best answers]

❏ a. Project 802.3 defines standards for CSMA/CD (Ethernet).

❏ b. Project 802.2 defines standards for the LLC (Logical Link Control).

❏ c. Project 802.3 defines standards for token ring networks.

❏ d. Project 802.5 defines standards for CSMA/CD (Ethernet).

Question 22

You are brought in as a consultant to assist in implementing TCP/IP for a large network. The network consists of 747 computers, all of which require communication with each other, as well as with other offices through a router. The company asks you to configure TCP/IP configuration information on all clients.

Required result:

- All client computers should have their IP address information dynamically assigned.

Optional desired results:

- You need to provide for efficient name resolution of hostnames to IP addresses.

- You need to provide for efficient name resolution of NetBIOS names to IP addresses.

Proposed solution:

- Implement DHCP, DNS, and WINS.

Which of the following is true about the proposed solution?

○ a. The proposed solution meets the required result and both optional desired results.

○ b. The proposed solution meets the required result and only one of the optional desired results.

○ c. The proposed solution meets the required result and none of the optional desired results.

○ d. The proposed solution does not meet the required or any of the optional desired results.

Question 23

What is the IP address class for address 128.2.20.1?

○ a. Class A

○ b. Class B

○ c. Class C

○ d. Class A and B

Question 24

Which network topology relies on the computers to act as repeaters and counts on them to boost a token around the network?

○ a. Bus

○ b. Star

○ c. Ring

○ d. Mesh

Question 25

Performing regular tape backups are an important part of data protection. Which of the following backup methods will reset or clear the archive bit of files?

○ a. Full backup and incremental

○ b. Incremental, differential, and full backup

○ c. Differential and full backup

○ d. Incremental and differential

Question 26

Alanis has two computers that need to be networked together. The computers each have a 10BaseT network adapter card installed. She does not have a hub. Which of the following best describes how Alanis should proceed?

- ○ a. To connect two 10BaseT computers together, she will have to purchase a hub.

- ○ b. To connect two 10BaseT computers together, at least three crossover cables and a hub are required.

- ○ c. To connect two 10BaseT computers together, a crossover cable can be used to connect two 10BaseT computers together without the use of a hub.

- ○ d. To connect two 10BaseT computers together, a null modem cable can be used to connect the 10BaseT ports together without the use of a hub.

Question 27

Which of the following is the correct UNC command to access a network directory with the share name CLIENTS that is located on a computer named MEMPHIS?

- ○ a. \\MEMPHIS\CLIENTS
- ○ b. \MEMPHIS\\CLIENTS
- ○ c. \\CLIENTS\MEMPHIS
- ○ d. \CLIENTS\\MEMPHIS

Question 28

Novell NetWare 4 is a popular network operating system that is based on what standard?

- ○ a. TCP/IP
- ○ b X.300
- ○ c. 500.X
- ○ d. X.500

Question 29

Which of the following statements is true about the difference between 100BaseT and 100Base VG-AnyLAN?

- ○ a. 100BaseT transmits at 100Mbps; 100Base VG-AnyLAN transmits at 56Kbps.
- ○ b. 100Base VG-AnyLAN uses demand priority as an access method; 100BaseT uses CSMA/CD as an access method.
- ○ c. 100BaseT supports category 5 UTP, and 100Base VG-AnyLAN does not.
- ○ d. 100Base VG-AnyLAN uses CSMA/CD as an access method; 100BaseT uses demand priority as an access method.

Question 30

What is the access method used in a 100Base VG-AnyLAN network?

- ○ A. CSMA/CD
- ○ B. CSMA/CA
- ○ C. Demand priority
- ○ D. Token passing

Question 31

What is the name of the tool used in NT Server to view server error logs?

- ○ a. NT Administrator
- ○ b. User Manager for Domains
- ○ c. User Administrator
- ○ d. Event Viewer

Question 32

You are configuring a Windows 95 computer to be able to remotely access an Internet server. The connection will be made through a modem. You need to select a dial-up protocol to use for this connection. You want to select the most efficient dial-up protocol that supports the greatest number of communication protocols. Which dial-up protocol will you select?

○ a. PPP

○ b. SLIP

○ c Both PPP and SLIP, because they are the same

○ d. PPTP

Question 33

You are configuring a newly purchased Windows 95 computer that will be added to your network. You install and configure the devices as follows:

- NIC card—IRQ 5
- Modem—IRQ 11
- Sound card—IRQ 7
- Scanner—IRQ 5

Which of the following *best* describes this configuration?

○ a. It will work fine.

○ b. It will not work; the network card has an IRQ conflict with the sound card.

○ c. It will not work; the network card has an IRQ conflict with the scanner.

○ d. There is no way to tell if there are any configuration conflicts unless it is attached to the network.

Question 34

You need to implement a new security model for your network. Controlling users' access to resources is important, so you want to select a security model that will provide the greatest amount of security. Which of the following security models is the most secure?

○ a. User-level security

○ b. No Access User Implemented Resource Distribution (NAUIRD)

○ c. Password-protected, share-level security

○ d. Share-level security

Question 35

If a network cable is said to support baseband transmission, what does that tell you about how data will travel across this cable?

○ a. Cables that support baseband can transmit bidirectionally using digital signals.

○ b. Cables that support baseband can transmit unidirectionally using digital signals.

○ c. Cables that support baseband can transmit bidirectionally using analog signals.

○ d. Cables that support baseband can transmit unidirectionally using digital signals.

Question 36

What are the two most popular protocols used to send and receive Internet email?

○ a. POP3 and SMTP

○ b. POP3 and SNMP

○ c. SMTP and SNMP

○ d. POP3 and POP4

Question 37

Which component of the TCP/IP protocol stack does not guarantee that packets will be received in the same order they were sent?

○ a. UDP

○ b. TCP

○ c. Both a and b

○ d. None of the above

Question 38

What network topology is characterized by computers connecting to a hub, with the hubs handling termination of the signal?

○ a. Bus

○ b. Star

○ c. Token ring

○ d. Token bus

Question 39

When connecting an external modem to a computer, the modem is attached to a serial port. What chip in the computer controls the serial port?

○ a. The Plug and Play BIOS

○ b. The UART chip

○ c. The AURT chip

○ d. The CHIPS Ahoy chip

Question 40

A modem is typically used to connect computers over analog phone lines. Which of the following correctly describes how a modem's speed is measured?

○ a. Bps

○ b. PPS

○ c. DDS

○ d. PPP

Question 41

> What is the maximum distance a computer can be away from the hub in a 10BaseT topology using a single segment length of cable?
>
> ○ a. 100 meters
>
> ○ b. 185 meters
>
> ○ c. 500 meters
>
> ○ d. 1,000 meters

Question 42

> The IPX/SPX protocol is commonly used in Novell NetWare network. Like TCP/IP, the IPX/SPX protocol also uses an addressing scheme to identify the computers on a network. Which of the following statements is true about the internal network address used in an IPX/SPX address?
>
> ○ a. The internal network address must be different for all computers running IPX/SPX.
>
> ○ b. The internal network address must be the same for all computers running IPX/SPX.
>
> ○ c. The internal network address is only used when communicating in a WAN.
>
> ○ d. None of the above.

Question 43

> Which of the following network topologies does not transmit data electronically?
>
> ○ a. 10BaseFL
>
> ○ b. 10Base2
>
> ○ c. 10Base5
>
> ○ d. 100BaseT

Question 44

Which of the following is not considered a network operating systems?

○ a. Windows NT

○ b. Novell NetWare

○ c. DOS

○ d. OS/2

Question 45

You have been asked to implement a network for the Caruso Realty Company. Its network consists of 20 Microsoft computers. The company has just installed a router in the office that it wants to use to connect to its home office in Sioux City, Iowa. You suggest the company use the TCP/IP protocol for all communication. What TCP/IP parameters will you need to configure for this network?

○ a. An IP address, a subnet mask, and a default gateway

○ b. An IP address only

○ c. An IP address and a subnet mask only

○ d. This is not possible; Microsoft computers do not support the TCP/IP protocol

Question 46

Which network topology features the use of a token to pass network traffic?

○ a. Bus

○ b. Star

○ c. Ring

○ d. Ethernet

Question 47

Your network is a LAN of 152 computers in a single subnet and uses TCP/IP as the communication protocol. Your computer is configured with the IP address 1.2.3.4. What is the correct default subnet mask for this network?

○ a. 255.255.0.0

○ b. 255.0.0.0

○ c. 255.255.255.0

○ d. 255.255.255.255

Question 48

What type of cable is used in 10Base5 networks?

○ a. Thinnet coaxial

○ b. Thicknet coaxial

○ c. Twisted-pair

○ d. Shielded twisted-pair

Question 49

Your network consists of five servers and 60 clients' computers. Due to recent problems with data loss, your company has decided to implement fault tolerance on all servers. Which of the following provide fault tolerance? [Choose the two best answers]

❑ a. RAID 0

❑ b. RAID 1

❑ c. RAID 5

❑ d. Volume set

Question 50

What computer industry acronym (or acronyms) is used to describe regular analog phone line?

○ a. POTS

○ b. PSTN

○ c. Both a and b

○ d. ISDN

Question 51

Which of the following correctly states an advantage of a star topology over a bus topology?

○ a   A star topology uses no hubs and is therefore less expensive to implement than a bus topology.

○ b. A star topology can use coaxial cable; a bus topology cannot.

○ c. A bus topology is easier to troubleshoot than a star topology, especially in larger networks.

○ d. A star topology is easier to troubleshoot than a bus topology, especially in larger networks.

Question 52

Which of the following correctly states a benefit of segmenting a network?

○ a. Segmenting a network is done to provide security.

○ b. Segmenting a network is done to allow for data encryption across a LAN.

○ c. Segmenting a network is done to improve overall network performance by controlling network traffic.

○ d. Segmenting a network is done to connect fiber-optic networks to coaxial networks.

Question 53

Which of the following devices can be used to segment a network?

○ a. Multiplexer

○ b. Hub

○ c. Bridge

○ d. Repeater

Question 54

Which of the following are Microsoft operating systems? [Choose the two best answers]

❑ a. NT Server

❑ b. Unix

❑ c. NetWare

❑ d. Windows 95

Question 55

The main difference between category 3 twisted-pair and category 5 twisted-pair is what?

○ a. Category 5 twisted-pair can travel further in a single segment than category 3 twisted-pair.

○ b. Category 3 twisted-pair can travel further in a single segment than category 5 twisted-pair.

○ c. Category 3 twisted-pair provides more resistance to interference than category 5 twisted-pair.

○ d. Category 5 twisted-pair supports faster transmission speeds than category 3 twisted-pair.

Question 56

A protocol acts as a "language" enabling computers to communicate. Which of the following statements correctly matches the operating system with its native protocol? [Choose the two best answers]

❑ a. IPX/SPX is commonly used in Novell NetWare networks.

❑ b. IPX/SPX is commonly used in Unix networks.

❑ c   TCP/IP is commonly used in Unix networks.

❑ d. UPX is commonly used in Microsoft networks.

Question 57

What is the maximum total length allowed in a 10Base2 network?

○ a. 925 meters

○ b. 185 meters

○ c. 1,000 meters

○ d. 100 meters

Question 58

What is the maximum total length allowed in a 10Base5 network?

○ a. 500 meters

○ b. 2,500 meters

○ c. 185 meters

○ d. 925 meters

Question 59

You are installing a network adapter card in a computer that will be part of your network. Which of the following statements are true of the configuration of this network adapter card? [Choose the two best answers]

❑ a. The network adapter card must be configured with a unique IRQ number.

❑ b. The network adapter card must be configured with the same IRQ as the hub (or hubs) in your network.

❑ c. The network adapter must have a unique MAC address.

❑ d. The network adapter must have the same MAC address as the other computers in the local network.

Question 60

What is the access method used in a 10Base2 network?

○ a. CSMA/CD

○ b. CSMA/CA

○ c. Demand priority

○ d. Token passing

Question 61

Which of the following network cable types is impervious to electrical interference?

○ a. Shielded twisted-pair

○ b. Thicknet coaxial

○ c. Fiber optic

○ d. Thinnet coaxial

Question 62

You are the network administrator for your company. The daily tape backup you now perform does not allow you to recover from data loss fast enough. To address this problem, you decide to implement fault tolerance. Which of the following is a good fault tolerance solution?

○ a. Volume set

○ b. Mirror set

○ c. Stripe set without parity

○ d. RAID 0

Question 63

Which of the following topologies is the least expensive to implement?

○ a. Bus

○ b. Star

○ c. Ring

○ d. Mesh

Question 64

What is the access method used in an Apple network?

○ a. CSMA/CD

○ b. CSMA/CA

○ c. Demand priority

○ d. Token passing

Question 65

Which of the following are Ethernet networks? [Choose the three best answers]

❑ a. 10BaseT

❑ b. 10Base2

❑ c. 100Base VG-AnyLAN

❑ d. 100 BaseT

Question 66

On what layer of the OSI model does a gateway reside?

- ○ a. Physical
- ○ b. Presentation
- ○ c. Application and has access to all layers
- ○ d. Network

Question 67

Which of the following dialup protocols supports TCP/IP as its *only* communication protocol?

- ○ a. PPP
- ○ b. SLIP
- ○ c. Both PPP and SLIP
- ○ d. Neither SLIP nor PPP can be used as dial-up protocols

Question 68

A virus is a destructive program that gets onto a computer without the user's knowledge. Which of the following best describes a "stealth" virus?

- ○ a. A stealth virus is a relatively harmless virus.
- ○ b. A stealth virus tries to "hide" from view and do its damage in the background.
- ○ c. A stealth virus is only a threat to Apple computers.
- ○ d. A stealth virus is only a threat to Microsoft computers.

Question 69

You are troubleshooting a computer on your network. The computer is using TCP/IP as the only protocol. You need to know if this computer is performing NetBIOS name-to-IP address resolution by broadcast. What TCP/IP command-line utility can give you this information?

○ a. ARP

○ b. TRACERT

○ c. NBTSTAT

○ d. NETSTAT

Question 70

What network topology is characterized by the use of an MAU?

○ a. Bus

○ b. Star

○ c. Token ring

○ d. Token bus

Question 71

Your network is a LAN of 30 computers in a single subnet and uses TCP/IP as the communication protocol. Your computer is configured with the IP address 211.105.250.172. What is the correct default subnet mask for this network?

○ a. 255.255.0.0

○ b. 255.0.0.0

○ c. 255.255.255.0

○ d. 255.255.255.255

Question 72

The manner in which data flows on a network cable can be defined as either baseband or broadband. Which of the following best describes the manner of data flow in an Ethernet network?

○ a. Ethernet networks use baseband as analog signaling.

○ b. Ethernet networks use broadband as digital signaling.

○ c. Ethernet networks use baseband as digital signaling.

○ d. Ethernet networks use broadband as analog signaling.

Question 73

You have configured your NT Server computer to function as a router in your TCP/IP network. What must you install on the NT Server to enable it to perform dynamic routing?

○ a. Install POP3.

○ b. Install RIP for IPX.

○ c. Install RIP for IP.

○ d. Do nothing. NT Server will automatically perform dynamic routing.

Question 74

Which of the following is the correct UNC command to access a network printer with the share name HAWK that is located on a computer named EYE?

○ a. \\EYE\HAWK

○ b. \HAWK\EYE

○ c. \\EYE\\HAWK

○ d. \HAWK\\EYE

Question 75

A common fault tolerance strategy is disk duplexing. Which of the following statements correctly describes disk duplexing?

○ a. Disk duplexing provides fault tolerance and requires two disks and two disk controllers.

○ b. Disk duplexing provides fault tolerance and requires two disks and one disk controller.

○ c   Disk duplexing provides fault tolerance and requires three disks and two controllers.

○ d. Disk duplexing does not provide fault tolerance and requires one disk and one controller.

Network+
Answer Key #4

1. a	16. b	31. d	46. c	61. c
2. a	17. c	32. a	47. b	62. b
3. b	18. b	33. c	48. b	63. a
4. b	19. b	34. a	49. b, c	64. b
5. a	20. b	35. a	50. c	65. a, b, d
6. a	21. a, b	36. a	51. d	66. c
7. c	22. a	37. a	52. c	67. b
8. a	23. b	38. b	53. c	68. b
9. a	24. c	39. b	54. a, d	69. c
10. a, b, c	25. a	40. a	55. d	70. c
11. a, c	26. c	41. a	56. a, c	71. c
12. a	27. a	42. a	57. a	72. c
13. b	28. d	43. a	58. b	73. c
14. a	29. b	44. c	59. a, c	74. a
15. b	30. c	45. a	60. a	75. a

Question 1

Answer a is correct. Data encryption is the process of making data unreadable during transmission over network media. Encrypted data cannot be understandable to hackers who attempt to capture network traffic from a cable. When encryption is used, a "key" is required to decrypt the data into a readable form. Encryption is commonly used when transmitting sensitive information. An example of a data encryption method is Secure Sockets Layer (SSL). SSL can be used to provide data encryption between a Web browser and an Internet server and is frequently used when conducting financial transactions over the Internet, like transmitting your credit card information to a Web server to make a purchase. In this scenario, user-level and share-level security will not help if someone is "tapping" into your network cable and reading data. Data encryption is implemented separately than user-level or share-level security. Data Eletro Propagation (DEP) does not exist.

For more information, see Chapter 7 of *Network+ Exam Cram*.

Question 2

Answer a is correct. A hub is commonly used to connect computers in 10BaseT, 10Base5, and 10Base2 networks. A hub operates at the Physical layer of the OSI model and can be used to connect dissimilar media (Thinnet coaxial and Thicknet coaxial), but it cannot make decisions on how to send network traffic. A hub simply passes traffic out all ports. A Multistation Access Unit (MAU) is used to connect computers in IBM Token Ring networks. A router is more commonly used to connect local access networks (LANs) together into a wide area network (WAN). A router looks similar to a hub, but unlike a hub, it can "route" network traffic, identify packets by network address, and filter out unnecessary packets. A repeater is a device used to connect segments of Thinnet coaxial cable. A repeater simply connects cable together and boosts the signal. Most hubs can act as repeaters, boosting the signals they pass.

For more information, see Chapter 2 of *Network+ Exam Cram*.

Question 3

Answer b is correct. Domain Name System, also called Domain Name Service (DNS), is used to provide name resolution of hostnames or domain names to IP addresses in a TCP/IP network. Dynamic Host Configuration Protocol (DHCP) is used to automatically assign IP addresses to clients. Windows Internet Naming Service (WINS) is used to resolve NetBIOS names to IP addresses.

For more information, see Chapter 4 of *Network+ Exam Cram*.

Question 4

Answer b is correct. While IPCONFIG and WINIPCFG are both used to display TCP/IP configuration information, NT Server and NT Workstation utilize IPCONFIG, not WINIPCFG. Windows 95 supports the **WINIPCFG** command to display TCP/IP configuration information. The IPCONFIG utility will display the IP address, subnet mask, and default gateway parameters. Typing "IPCONFIG /ALL" will display additional TCP/IP parameters, such as the IP address of the DNS, WINS, and DHCP servers being used by the client. **WINIPCFG** will display the IP address, subnet mask, and default gateway parameters and also DNS, WINS, and DHCP information after clicking on the More Info button.

For more information, see Chapter 4 of *Network+ Exam Cram.*

Question 5

Answer a is correct. A port number is one of the items specified by TCP/IP hosts to establish a connection. Port numbers for common TCP/IP services are said to have well-known port numbers. A well-known port number is the port number that will be used when no port number is specifically designated. The most important port numbers to know are:

➤ **HTTP** Hypertext Transfer Protocol, the protocol used by the Web, uses port 80.

➤ **FTP** File Transfer Protocol, used to transfer files (upload/download), uses port 21.

➤ **SMTP** Simple Mail Transfer Protocol, used to send outgoing Internet mail, uses port 25.

➤ **POP3** Post Office Protocol, used to retrieve incoming Internet mail, uses port 110.

When using any of these well-known services, the port number does not need to be specified, as it is assumed the default will be used. Windows Sockets is an example of the use of a port number. Windows Sockets is a "session" established between two TCP/IP computers. The "socket" created between hosts is used for reliable communication. To create a socket, hosts specify an IP address, the type of service (UDP or TCP), and a port number. If a different port number is to be used other than the well-known number, it must be specifically designated and must be a number over 1,024. (The number 1,024 and numbers below are used for well-known services.)

For more information, see Chapter 4 of *Network+ Exam Cram.*

Question 6

Answer a is correct. TCP/IP addresses are divided into three main classes: Class A, Class B, and Class C. The address range for each address class is as follows:

➤ **Class A** IP addresses that *begin* with numbers from 1 to 126.

➤ **Class B** IP addresses that *begin* with numbers from 128 to 191 (note: 127 is not used in IP addressing; it is reserved for localhost).

➤ **Class C** IP addresses that *begin* with numbers from 192 to 223.

When looking at any IP address, it is the number in the *first* octet that determines the address class of that address. For example:

➤ The IP address 3.100.32.7 is a Class A address because it *begins* with 3, a number between 1 and 126.

➤ The IP address 145.100.32.7 is a Class B address because it *begins* with 145, a number between 128 and 191.

➤ The IP address 210.100.32.7 is a Class C address because it *begins* with 210, a number between 192 and 223.

An IP address is made up of a network ID and a host ID. The network ID identifies the network a user is on, and the host ID identifies the user. An IP address is specified using four individual numbers separated by periods. Each one of these "sections" is known as an octet (because it contains eight bits). Each address class uses different combinations of octets to specify a network ID and host ID. The configuration is as follows:

➤ **Class A** Uses the first octet for the network ID and the last three octets for the host ID. Example: IP address 2.3.45.9 is a Class A address (it begins with 2, a number between 1 and 126). The network ID of this IP address is 2, and the host ID is 3.45.9, because a Class A address uses the first octet for the network ID and the last three octets for the host ID.

➤ **Class B** Uses the first *two* octets for the network ID and the last two octets for the host ID. Example: IP address 167.211.32.5 is a Class B address (it begins with 167, a number between 128 and 191). The network ID of this IP address is 167.211, and the host ID is 32.5, because a Class B address uses the first two octets for the network ID and the last two octets for the host ID.

➤ **Class C** Uses the first *three* octets for the network ID and the last octet for the host ID. Example: IP address 200.3.11.75 is a Class C address (it begins with 200, a number between 192 and 223). The network ID of this IP address is 200.3.11 and the host ID is 11, because a Class C address uses the first three octets for the network ID and the last octet for the host ID.

For more information, see Chapter 4 of *Network+ Exam Cram*.

Question 7

Answer c is correct. In this scenario, the cable run of 200 meters has exceeded the maximum single-segment length of Thinnet coaxial. Ethernet 10Base2 uses Thinnet coaxial cable in a bus topology. 10Base2 transmits at 10Mbps, and single segment can travel 185 meters. The total number of users supported in a 10Base2 network is 1,024. The proper way to extend this network would be to use two segments of Thinnet, connected by a repeater. A hub can act as a repeater.

For more information, see Chapter 2 of *Network+ Exam Cram*.

Question 8

Answer a is correct. A server-based network features a server that is used to centrally manage the clients in a network. Popular server operating systems are Novell NetWare and Microsoft's NT Server. A peer-to-peer network is comprised of computers that are all running client operating systems, such as Windows 9X or Microsoft's NT Workstation. Because all computers in a peer-to-peer network utilize a client operating system, they are all considered to be equal, or "peers," of one another.

For more information, see Chapter 3 of *Network+ Exam Cram*.

Question 9

Answer a is correct. A protocol is the "language" computers use to communicate. The most common communication protocols in use can be divided into two categories: routable and nonroutable. A routable protocol is one that resides at the Network layer of the OSI model, so its packets can be read by a router and is therefore suitable for WAN communication. This does not, however, limit routable protocols to just WANs. They can (and are very frequently) used in LAN environments. A nonroutable protocol is a protocol that does not reside at the Network layer of the OSI model. Because a nonroutable protocol does not reside at the Network layer, its packets cannot be read by a router. This limits a nonroutable protocol to LAN use only. Examples of Network layer, or routable, protocols are IP (part of the TCP/IP protocol suite used by Unix, Microsoft, Novell NetWare 5, and the Internet), IPX (part of the IPX/SPX protocol suite used by Novell), and NWLink (Microsoft's Windows NT implementation of the IPX/SPX protocol). Examples of nonroutable protocols are NetBEUI (a small, fast, nonroutable protocol used in Microsoft networks), and Local Area Transport (LAT, from Digital Equipment Corp).

For more information, see Chapter 4 of *Network+ Exam Cram*.

Question 10

Answers a, b and c are correct. The TCP/IP protocol is a popular communication protocol used on the Internet and supported in Microsoft and NetWare 5 networks. TCP/IP is a configurable protocol, and all computers wishing to utilize it must have the correct settings. All computers using TCP/IP must have a unique IP address, a subnet mask, and if used in a WAN, a default gateway. An IP address identifies a TCP/IP host on the network and contains two important elements: a network ID and a host ID. The network ID of an IP address identifies the network the host is on. (For example, all users in a single location are said to be on the same network and therefore will all have the same network ID in their IP address.) The host ID of an IP address identifies the host, or individual computer, on a TCP/IP network. It is the host ID portion of an IP address that is the unique part. Therefore, in a single TCP/IP network, users will all have the same network ID and different (unique) host IDs. IP addressing is similar to the way houses are addressed on your block. Many people live on Maple Street (network ID), but only one person lives at 21 Maple Street (host ID). A subnet mask is a required parameter for all TCP/IP hosts. A subnet mask is used to distinguish the network ID in an IP address from the host ID. When a computer using TCP/IP needs to communicate with another TCP/IP host, it uses the subnet mask to determine if the destination computer is local (on my network) or remote (on a different network). If the subnet mask determines the destination host is local, it simply places the packet on the cable for delivery. If the subnet mask determines the host it needs to communicate with is remote (on another network), it sends it to its default gateway. A default gateway is only required to be configured on TCP/IP hosts that need to communicate outside of their local network or in a WAN. A default gateway is the IP address of the router used by the local network to connect to another network in the outside world, like the Internet or another branch office location. A default gateway is not a required parameter when using TCP/IP in a LAN, because all computers are on the same network and have the same network ID.

For more information, see Chapter 4 of *Network+ Exam Cram*.

Question 11

Answers a and c are correct. In a ring topology, all computers are connected to an MAU. Inside this MAU is a logical "ring" that contains a "token" used by computers to transmit data. A ring topology uses token passing as an access method, and provides equal access for all computers through the use of a "token." This token travels around the ring, roughly at the speed of light, and each computer acts as a repeater for it. To send data, a computer accesses the token and places data in it. Because there is only one token on the cable at all times, there cannot be any collisions of packets on the cable. The Ethernet standard for bus and star topologies utilizes an access method known as Carrier Sense Multiple Access/Collision Detection (CSMA/CD). When using CSMA/CD, computers must first check to see the cable is free before sending data, and only one computer at a time can place data on the cable. For this reason, CSMA/CD is considered a "contention" method of access, meaning that computers must compete with one another for access to the network. If two computers sense the cable is free at the same time, they will both place data on the cable simultaneously, and a collision will occur. In the event of a collision with CSMA/CD, packets are retransmitted.

For more information, see Chapter 2 of *Network+ Exam Cram*.

Question 12

Answer a is correct. TCP and UDP are part of the TCP/IP protocol suite. Transmission Control Protocol (TCP) is a connection-oriented protocol that provides guaranteed delivery of packets between hosts. TCP also ensures that packets will be delivered to the destination host in the same order they were sent. User Datagram Protocol (UDP) is a connectionless protocol that does not guarantee delivery of packets. UDP is primarily used by TCP/IP utilities and for broadcasting packets in a TCP/IP network.

For more information, see Chapter 4 of *Network+ Exam Cram*.

Question 13

Answer b is correct. Based on the fact that the user can retrieve mail but not send it, he probably changed his SMTP server information. If the user had changed both his POP3 and SMTP settings, he would not be able to send or receive mail. POP3 and SMTP are common protocols used with Internet email. Post Office Protocol (POP3) is used to retrieve Internet mail from a mail server. Simple Mail Transfer Protocol (SMTP) is used to send outgoing Internet mail to a mail server. Both SMTP and POP3 are part of the TCP/IP protocol suite. The key points to remember about these protocols are:

➤ You send mail using SMTP.

➤ You receive mail using POP3.

➤ Your POP3 server is your incoming mail server.

➤ Your SMTP server is your outgoing mail server.

For more information, see Chapter 6 of *Network+ Exam Cram*.

Question 14

Answer a is correct. TCP/IP addresses are divided into three main classes: Class A, Class B, and Class C. The address range for each address class is as follows:

➤ **Class A** IP addresses that *begin* with numbers from 1 to 126.

➤ **Class B** IP addresses that *begin* with numbers from 128 to 191. (Note: 127 is not used in IP addressing, it is reserved for localhost.)

➤ **Class C** IP addresses that *begin* with numbers from 192 to 223.

When looking at any IP address, it is the number in the *first* octet that determines the address class of that address. For example:

➤ The IP address 3.100.32.7 is a Class A address because it *begins* with 3, a number between 1 and 126.

➤ The IP address 145.100.32.7 is a Class B address because it *begins* with 145, a number between 128 and 191.

➤ The IP address 210.100.32.7 is a Class C address because it *begins* with 210, a number between 192 and 223.

An IP address is made up of a network ID and a host ID. The network ID identifies the network a user is on, and the host ID identifies the user. An IP address is specified using four individual numbers separated by periods. Each one of these "sections" is known as an octet (because it contains eight bits). Each address class uses different combinations of octets to specify a network ID and host ID. The configuration is as follows:

➤ **Class A** Uses the first octet for the network ID and the last three octets for the host ID. Example: IP address 2.3.45.9 is a Class A address (it begins with 2, a number between 1 and 126). The network ID of this IP address is 2, and the host ID is 3.45.9, because a Class A address uses the first octet for the network ID, and the last three octets for the host ID.

➤ **Class B** Uses the first *two* octets for the network ID and the last two octets for the host ID. Example: IP address 167.211.32.5 is a Class B address (it begins with 167, a number between 128 and 191). The network ID of this IP address is 167.211, and the host ID is 32.5, because a Class B address uses the first two octets for the network ID and the last two octets for the host ID.

➤ **Class C** Uses the first *three* octets for the network ID and the last octet for the host ID. Example: IP address 200.3.11.75 is a Class C address (it begins with 200, a number between 192 and 223). The network ID of this IP address is 200.3.11 and the host ID is 11, because a Class C address uses the first three octets for the network ID and the last octet for the host ID.

For more information, see Chapter 4 of *Network+ Exam Cram*.

Question 15

Answer b is correct. Fault tolerance refers to the ability of a system to recover from a single hard disk failure. Standards for implementing fault tolerance are defined by Redundant Arrays of Independent Disks (RAID). A mirror set, defined as RAID level 1, consists of two disks: a primary and a mirror. When data is written to the primary member of a mirror set, it also is written to the mirrored copy, providing fault tolerance. If the primary member of a mirror set fails, the mirrored disk can replace it. A volume set is created by combining 2 to 32 areas of free disk space into one logical drive. A stripe set without parity, defined by RAID level 0, is created by combining the free disk space of 2 to 32 disks into a single logical drive, where data is written evenly across all members of the set. Implementing a stripe set can improve performance, because members of the set can be read simultaneously. Stripe sets without parity and volume sets do not provide fault tolerance, meaning that if a single disk in a volume set or stripe set without parity fails, all data will be lost.

For more information, see Chapter 5 of *Network+ Exam Cram*.

Question 16

Answer b is correct. Data encryption is the process of making data unreadable during transmission over network media. Encrypted data cannot be understandable to hackers who attempt to capture network traffic from a cable. When encryption is used, a "key" is required to decrypt the data into a readable form. Encryption is commonly used when transmitting sensitive information. An example of a data encryption method is Secure Sockets Layer (SSL). SSL can be used to provide data encryption between a Web browser and an Internet server and is frequently used when conducting financial transactions over the Internet, like transmitting your credit card information to a Web server to make a purchase. In this scenario, user-level and share-level security will not help if someone is "tapping" into your network cable and reading data. Data encryption is not limited to LANs and is implemented separately than user-level or share-level security. Data encryption does not improve network performance.

For more information, see Chapter 7 of *Network+ Exam Cram*.

Question 17

Answer c is correct. Generally speaking, computers like similar temperature conditions that people do. Room temperature should not be extreme, and the ideal temperature should be on the cool side. Humidity should be kept at approximately 50 to 70 percent. If humidity is too low, the instances of electrostatic discharge (ESD) will be increased, due to the "dryness" of the particles in the air. An ESD shock can cause a computer to intermittently fail or cause more serious damage. High humidity produces excessive moisture in the air that could cause condensation to develop on the electrical components inside a computer and cause a short.

For more information, see Chapter 13 of *Network+ Exam Cram*.

Question 18

Answer b is correct. DHCP is used to automatically configure TCP/IP configuration information on TCP/IP hosts. All computers using TCP/IP must have a unique IP address, a subnet mask, and if used in a WAN, a default gateway. In large networks, it can be time-consuming to configure these settings on each computer one at a time. In these instances, a DHCP server can be used to automatically provide the clients on the network with this information. A DHCP server can provide clients with a unique IP address, a subnet mask, a default gateway, and many other TCP/IP parameters automatically. In order for DHCP to assign unique IP addresses to hosts, it must be configured with a scope. A DHCP scope is the range of IP addresses it uses to distribute to hosts requesting an IP address. To configure a DHCP scope, two parameters must be specified: the "From" address and the "To" address. It is the addresses within this range, or scope, that a DHCP server will assign to clients.

For more information, see Chapter 4 of *Network+ Exam Cram*.

Question 19

Answer b is correct. In a star topology, computers are connected to a hub, and the hub handles termination. The failure of a single computer wired in a star topology will only affect that computer. This is also true for a cable break. Therefore, all users will be able to communicate in this scenario whether or not the problem with Mary's computer is physical or software related.

For more information, see Chapter 2 of *Network+ Exam Cram*.

Question 20

Answer b is correct. The "10" designation refers to the transmission speed supported in Mbps, or megabits per second. A megabit is one million bits. The standards for Ethernet are documented in IEEE 802.3.

For more information, see Chapter 2 of *Network+ Exam Cram*.

Question 21

Answers a and b are correct. The Open System Interconnection (OSI) model defines standards for networking based on a seven-layer model. All of the components used in networking (hubs, bridges, routers, cables, protocols, and so on) conform to various layers of the OSI model by "residing" at one or more of these seven layers. Project 802 modified the Data Link layer of the OSI model by dividing it into two sublayers: Logical Link Control (LLC) and Media Access Control (MAC). Standards for Ethernet (CSMA/CD) networks are defined in 802.3. CSMA/CD refers to the type of access method used by Ethernet 802.3 networks. The LLC, as specified in 802.2, defines the use of service access points (SAPs) used to transfer information over a network. Standards for token ring networks are defined by 802.5 specifications.

For more information, see Chapter 8 of *Network+ Exam Cram*.

Question 22

Answer a is correct. The proposed solution in this case meets the required result and both optional desired results. The required result is met by implementing DHCP. DHCP is used to automatically configure TCP/IP configuration information on TCP/IP hosts. In large networks, it can be time-consuming to configure TCP/IP settings on each computer one at a time. In these instances, a DHCP server can be used to automatically provide the clients on the network with this information. The first optional desired result is met by implementing DNS. DNS provides name resolution in a TCP/IP network by resolving a TCP/IP computer's hostname to its IP address. The second optional desired result is met by implementing WINS. WINS is used in Microsoft networks to provide name resolution of NetBIOS names to IP addresses. Microsoft networks utilize the NetBIOS application programming interface (API) when communicating. NetBIOS is an API that provides the "base" that Microsoft networks are built on. WINS will resolve, or associate, a NetBIOS name to its IP address. There are many types of NetBIOS names used in Microsoft networking (computer name, username, domain name, and so on). Novell NetWare supports the use of NetBIOS applications, which are programs that support the NetBIOS API.

For more information, see Chapter 4 of *Network+ Exam Cram*.

Question 23

Answer b is correct. TCP/IP addresses are divided into three main classes: Class A, Class B, and Class C. The address range for each address class is as follows:

➤ **Class A** IP addresses that *begin* with numbers from 1 to 126.

➤ **Class B** IP addresses that *begin* with numbers from 128 to 191. (Note: 127 is not used in IP addressing, it is reserved for localhost.)

➤ **Class C** IP addresses that begin with numbers from 192 to 223.

When looking at any IP address, it is the number in the *first* octet that determines the address class of that address. For example:

➤ The IP address 3.100.32.7 is a Class A address because it *begins* with 3, a number between 1 and 126.

➤ The IP address 145.100.32.7 is a Class B address because it *begins* with 145, a number between 128 and 191.

➤ The IP address 210.100.32.7 is a Class C address because it *begins* with 210, a number between 192 and 223.

An IP address is made up of a network ID and a host ID. The network ID identifies the network a user is on, and the host ID identifies the user. An IP address is specified using four individual numbers separated by periods. Each one of these "sections" is known as an octet (because it contains eight bits). Each address class uses different combinations of octets to specify a network ID and host ID. The configuration is as follows:

➤ **Class A** Uses the first octet for the network ID and the last three octets for the host ID. Example: IP address 2.3.45.9 is a Class A address (it begins with 2, a number between 1 and 126). The network ID of this IP address is 2, and the host ID is 3.45.9, because a Class A address uses the first octet for the network ID, and the last three octets for the host ID.

➤ **Class B** Uses the first *two* octets for the network ID and the last two octets for the host ID. Example: IP address 167.211.32.5 is a Class B address (it begins with 167, a number between 128 and 191). The network ID of this IP address is 167.211, and the host ID is 32.5, because a Class B address uses the first two octets for the network ID and the last two octets for the host ID.

➤ **Class C** Uses the first *three* octets for the network ID and the last octet for the host ID. Example: IP address 200.3.11.75 is a Class C address (it begins with 200, a number between 192 and 223). The network ID of this IP address is 200.3.11 and the host ID is 11, because a Class C address uses the first three octets for the network ID and the last octet for the host ID.

For more information, see Chapter 4 of *Network+ Exam Cram*.

Question 24

Answer c is correct. In a ring topology, all computers are connected to an MAU. Inside this MAU is a logical "ring" that contains a "token" used by computers to transmit data. A ring topology uses token passing as an access method. With token passing, all computers act as repeaters and are counted on to "boost" the token around the network. Therefore, if one computer in a token ring network fails, it will miss its turn to boost the token, decreasing network performance. To return the network back to normal performance, the failed computer must be dropped from the ring by the MAU. To accomplish this, all other computers will start "beaconing," or signaling, the MAU that they are still active. This allows the MAU to identify the failed computer and drop it from the ring. The bus, star, and mesh topologies are all known as passive topologies, meaning that computers are not relied on to boost a signal, so the failure of a single computer will not affect the network.

For more information, see Chapter 2 of *Network+ Exam Cram*.

Question 25

Answer a is correct. A full backup and incremental backup will clear, or reset, the archive bit of files.

The attribute of a file used to determine its backup status is known as the archive bit. The archive bit attribute of a file can be one of two values: "set" or "cleared" (reset). When a full or incremental backup is performed, the backup program clears, or resets, the archive bit. When files that have been backed up are changed, the program that modifies the file will "set" the archive bit. The process of "setting" the archive bit of modified files allows the backup program to determine if a file has changed since the last time a backup was performed. There are three important backup methods to be aware of: differential, incremental, and full backup.

➤ **Differential** A differential backup will back up files that have their archive bit "set," but does not clear the archive bit. Restoring data from a differential backup only requires two tapes: the original full backup and the last differential backup. Differential back up is faster than a full backup.

➤ **Incremental** An incremental backup will back up files that have their archive bit "set" and then clears the archive bit. Restoring data from an incremental backup requires many tapes: the original full backup tape and all incremental backups performed since the full backup. An incremental backup is the fastest way to perform a daily tape backup.

➤ **Full backup** Backs up all files regardless of the archive bit attribute and clears the archive bit. Periodic full backups are recommended in addition to either incremental or differential backups. Performing a full backup is the safest but most time consuming of all backup methods.

For more information, see Chapter 5 of *Network+ Exam Cram*.

Question 26

Answer c is correct. A crossover cable is used to connect two (and only two) 10BaseT computers together without the use of a hub. A crossover cable is made from twisted-pair cable with RJ-45 connectors at each end. The send and receive wires are "crossed" to allow the cable to act as a hub. A crossover cable can only be used to connect two computers, and both computers must have a 10BaseT network adapter card. A null modem cable attaches to a serial port, not an RJ-45 10BaseT port.

For more information, see Chapter 2 of *Network+ Exam Cram*.

Question 27

Answer a is correct. A Universal Naming Convention (UNC) name is a standard for connecting to shared resources on a network. A UNC is comprised of two key elements: a computer name and a share name. All computers in a network must have a computer name to identify themselves. When sharing a resource (a printer, a directory of files, a CD-ROM, and so on), the shared resource must also be assigned a name, known as a "share" name. Connecting to a shared resource using a UNC simply involves specifying these two parameters in the format "\\computer name\share name". For example, to connect to a printer that has been assigned the share name PRINTER1 on the computer named USER1, the UNC to connect to this resource would be \\USER1\PRINTER1.

For more information, see Chapter 12 of *Network+ Exam Cram*.

Question 28

Answer d is correct. Novell NetWare is a popular network operating system that uses NetWare Directory Services (NDS). NDS is an object-oriented database that organizes network resources into a hierarchical, tree-like structure. From this NDS tree, users can access the resources on a NetWare network. NDS is based on a standard known as X.500. X.500 is an OSI standard for file and directory services in networking. Windows 95, NT Server, and NT Workstation are all Microsoft operating systems.

Microsoft's NT Server is a popular network operating system that utilizes the concept of a "domain" to organize a network. A domain is a logical grouping of computers with centralized resources and security. Windows 95 and Windows NT Workstation are Microsoft desktop operating systems designed to run on client computers. These client computers can be members of an NT Server domain.

For more information, see Chapter 3 of *Network+ Exam Cram*.

Question 29

Answer b is correct. 100BaseT and 100Base VG-AnyLAN are two totally different topologies. 100BaseT is an Ethernet standard that supports categories 3, 4, and 5 twisted-pair cable. (Although categories 3 and 4 are supported, category 5 is required for 100Mbps transmission.) 100BaseT uses CSMA/CD as an access method. An access method is a standard that defines how a packet is placed on a network cable. With CSMA/CD, computers "listen" to the cable, and when they sense it is free, a packet is sent. 100Base VG-AnyLAN is know by several names: VG, AnyLAN, 100VG-AnyLAN, and 100BaseVG. It supports categories 3, 4, and 5 twisted-pair cable and requires special hubs and network cards to be implemented. The access method used by 100Base VG-AnyLAN is known as " demand priority." The demand priority access method relies on these special hubs to control access to the network cable.

For more information, see Chapter 2 of *Network+ Exam Cram.*

Question 30

Answer c is correct. An access method defines rules for how data is placed on a network cable. Demand priority is the access method used in 100Base VG-AnyLAN networks. The access method used in 10Base2, 10BaseT, and 10Base5 networks is CSMA/CD. Carrier Sense Multiple Access/Collision Avoidance (CSMA/CA) is used in Apple networks. Token passing is the access method used in token ring networks.

For more information, see Chapter 2 of *Network+ Exam Cram.*

Question 31

Answer d is correct. Windows NT uses Event Viewer to record failed system events. Event Viewer contains three logs: the system log to record service failures, the application log to record program failures, and the security log to record the results of security auditing. These server error logs can be useful to an administrator when troubleshooting. User Manager for Domains is the tool used in NT to manage user accounts. The other answers are not valid.

For more information, see Chapter 3 of *Network+ Exam Cram.*

Question 32

Answer a is correct. Both Point-to-Point Protocol (PPP) and Serial Line Internet Protocol (SLIP) are used as dial-up protocols when using a modem to connect to a remote network or to the Internet. PPP is a newer, more efficient dial-up protocol than SLIP. PPP automatically obtains configuration parameters with the remote server on connection. This simplifies the configurations required when making a remote connection; SLIP must be configured manually with these parameters. Another key difference between PPP and SLIP is the number of communication protocols supported. PPP supports IPX/SPX, AppleTalk, TCP/IP, and NetBEUI. SLIP only supports the use of the TCP/

IP protocol. Point-to-Point Tunneling Protocol (PPTP) is used for secure communications over the Internet, not as a dial-up protocol.

For more information, see Chapter 6 of *Network+ Exam Cram*.

Question 33

Answer c is correct. An Interrupt Request Line (IRQ) is a "line" of communication that a hardware device uses to communicate with a processor. All devices in a computer require a unique IRQ. (There are some exceptions to this rule, but stick with the rule on your exam.) The computer does not have to be connected to the network to see if there are internal device conflicts. Windows 95 includes a tool, Device Manager, that is used for this purpose.

For more information, see Chapter 14 of *Network+ Exam Cram*

Question 34

Answer a is correct. There are two common security models a network administrator can employ to control users' access to network resources: share-level security and user-level security. When using share-level security, passwords are assigned to *resources*. An example of share-level security is sharing a printer and assigning a password to that printer. When users need to connect to the printer, they will have to enter the password set on the printer in order to access it. The share-level security model is considered a less secure method than user-level security, because users are more likely to tell others the password to access a resource than they are to give away their own username and password. In user-level security, permissions are assigned to users. An example of user-level security is sharing a printer and assigning permissions to users to access this resource. In order for users to access this printer, their user account must have permissions to access it. Remember: share-level security assigns passwords to *resources* (printers, files, programs, and so on); user-level security assigns permissions to *users*. Answer b does not exist.

For more information, see Chapter 7 of *Network+ Exam Cram*.

Question 35

Answer a is correct. The manner in which data flows on a network cable can be defined as either baseband or broadband. Baseband, as used by Ethernet 802.3, uses digital signaling over a single frequency. Baseband can send information bidirectionally and utilizes repeaters to boost a signal. Broadband uses analog signaling over a range of frequencies. Broadband sends information unidirectionally and uses amplifiers to boost a signal.

For more information, see Chapter 2 of *Network+ Exam Cram.*

Question 36

Answer a is correct. POP3 and SMTP are common protocols used with Internet email. POP3 is used to retrieve Internet mail from a mail server. SMTP is used to send outgoing Internet mail to a mail server. Both SMTP and POP3 are part of the TCP/IP protocol suite. DCHP and WINS have nothing to do with Internet email.

The key points to remember about these protocols are:

➤ You send mail using SMTP.

➤ You receive mail using POP3.

➤ Your POP3 server is your incoming mail server.

➤ Your SMTP server is your outgoing mail server.

The Simple Network Management Protocol (SNMP) is used to gather TCP/IP statistical data, not to send Internet mail.

For more information, see Chapter 4 of *Network+ Exam Cram.*

Question 37

Answer a is correct. TCP and UDP are part of the TCP/IP protocol suite. TCP is a connection-oriented protocol that provides guaranteed delivery of packets between hosts. TCP also ensures that packets will be delivered to the destination host in the same order they were sent. UDP is a connectionless protocol that does not guarantee delivery of packets. UDP is primarily used by TCP/IP utilities and for broadcasting packets in a TCP/IP network.

For more information, see Chapter 4 of *Network+ Exam Cram.*

Question 38

Answer b is correct. In a star topology, each computer is connected to a hub. The hub handles termination and distributes packets to all segments. Hubs may be connected together, or "daisy chained," to expand a star topology. A bus topology features a single segment of computers in a continuous, single line that is terminated at both ends. A token ring topology uses a device that looks similar to a hub, known as an MAU, to connect computers together. There is no such thing as a token bus topology.

For more information, see Chapter 2 of *Network+ Exam Cram*.

Question 39

Answer b is correct. Serial ports are controlled by a chip called the universal asynchronous receiver/transmitter (UART) chip. The UART chip manages serial communication by establishing the protocol used in the communication throughout the serial port. The other choices are invalid.

For more information, see Chapter 6 of *Network+ Exam Cram*.

Question 40

Answer a is correct. Modem speed is measured in bits per second (bps). A modem that transmits at 28,800bps is said to transmit data at a rate of 28,800 bits per second. The other choices are not valid.

For more information, see Chapter 6 of *Network+ Exam Cram*.

Question 41

Answer a is correct. In a 10BaseT topology, all computers connect to a hub using twisted-pair cable. Because the maximum single-segment length of twisted-pair cable is 100 meters, that is the furthest a computer can be away from a hub. Thinnet can travel up to 185 meters in a single segment. Thicknet coaxial cable can travel up to 500 meters in a single segment.

For more information, see Chapter 2 of *Network+ Exam Cram*.

Question 42

Answer a is correct. The IPX/SPX protocol is commonly used in Novell NetWare networks. IPX/SPX addresses are comprised of two elements: an external network address and an internal address. The external network address, also known as the network number, used in IPX/SPX identifies the network a computer is part of, similar to the network ID used by TCP/IP. For example, all users in a single location using IPX/SPX will all have the same external network address, because they are all on the same network. The external network address is specified by the system administrator. The internal address, also known as the node address, is used by IPX/SPX to uniquely identify an individual computer, similar to the host ID used in TCP/IP. The internal address must be unique to each computer and, for this reason, is usually the MAC address of the computer that is running IPX/SPX. (The MAC address is the hardware address that is "burned" on every network adapter card by the manufacturer.) The internal address is generated automatically by IPX/SPX when it is installed. A network ID and a subnet mask are TCP/IP parameters and are not used in IPX/SPX addressing.

For more information, see Chapter 4 of *Network+ Exam Cram.*

Question 43

Answer a is correct. The 10BaseFL topology features the use of fiber-optic cable to send a signal. Fiber-optic cable transmits data as pulses of light, not electricity. All of the other topologies feature cable that uses copper wire to electronically transmit a signal.

For more information, see Chapter 2 of *Network+ Exam Cram.*

Question 44

Answer c is correct. Microsoft's Windows NT, Novell's NetWare, and OS/2 are all network operating systems. DOS is not considered a network operating system. Novell NetWare is a popular network operating system that uses NetWare Directory Services (NDS). NDS is an object-oriented database that organizes network resources into a tree-like structure. From this NDS tree, users can access the resources on a NetWare network. NDS is based on a standard known as X.500. X.500 is an OSI standard for file and directory services in networking. Windows 95, NT Server, and NT Workstation are all Microsoft operating systems. Microsoft's NT Server is a popular network operating system that utilizes the concept of a "domain" to organize a network. A domain is a logical grouping of computers with centralized resources and security. OS/2 is an IBM network operating system that can run DOS and Windows programs.

For more information, see Chapter 3 of *Network+ Exam Cram.*

Question 45

Answer a is correct. The TCP/IP protocol is a popular communication protocol used on the Internet and supported by all Microsoft operating systems and Novell NetWare 5 networks. TCP/IP is a configurable protocol, and all computers wishing to utilize it must have the correct settings. All computers using

TCP/IP must have a unique IP address, a subnet mask, and if used in a WAN, a default gateway. An IP address identifies a TCP/IP host on the network, and contains two important elements: a network ID and a host ID. The network ID of an IP address identifies the network the host is on. (For example, all users in a single location are said to be on the same network and, therefore, will all have the same network ID in their IP address.) The host ID of an IP address identifies the host, or individual computer, on a TCP/IP network. It is the host ID portion of an IP address that is the unique part. Therefore, in a single TCP/IP network users will all have the same network ID and different (unique) host IDs. IP addressing is similar to the way houses are addressed on your block. Many people live on Maple Street (network ID), but only one person lives at 21 Maple Street (host ID). A subnet mask is a required parameter for all TCP/IP hosts. A subnet mask is used to distinguish the network ID in an IP address from the host ID. When a computer using TCP/IP needs to communicate with another TCP/IP host, it uses the subnet mask to determine if the destination computer is local (on my network) or remote (on a different network). If the subnet mask determines the destination host is local, it simply places the packet on the cable for delivery. If the subnet mask determines the host it needs to communicate with is remote (on another network), it sends it to its default gateway. A default gateway is only required to be configured on TCP/IP hosts that need to communicate outside of their local network or in a WAN. A default gateway is the IP address of the router used by the local network to connect to another network in the outside world, like the Internet or another branch office location. A default gateway is not a required parameter when using TCP/IP in a LAN, because all computers are on the same network and have the same network ID.

For more information, see Chapter 4 of *Network+ Exam Cram*.

Question 46

Answer c is correct. A ring topology provides equal access for all computers through the use of a "token." This token travels around the ring, roughly at the speed of light, and each computer acts as a repeater for it. To send data, a computer accesses the token and places data in it. The Ethernet standard for bus and star topologies utilizes the CSMA/CD access method. When using CSMA/CD, computers must first check to see if the cable is free before sending, and only one computer at a time can place data on the cable. For this reason, CSMA/CD is considered a "contention" method of access, meaning that computers must compete with one another for access to the network.

For more information, see Chapter 2 of *Network+ Exam Cram*.

Question 47

Answer b is correct. All computers using TCP/IP must have a unique IP address, a subnet mask, and if used in a WAN, a default gateway. An IP address identifies a TCP/IP host on the network and contains two important elements: a network ID and a host ID. The network ID of an IP address identifies the network the host is on. (For example, all users in a single location are said to be on the same network and, therefore, will all have the same network ID in their IP address.) The host ID of an IP address identifies the host, or individual computer, on a TCP/IP network. It is the host ID portion of an IP address that is the unique part. Therefore, in a single TCP/IP network users will all have the same network ID and different (unique) host IDs. The subnet mask is used to "mask" the network portion of an IP address, with the number 255, so IP can determine if the destination host is local or remote. A default subnet mask refers to the subnet mask that is used by a particular TCP/IP address class in a single subnet environment, like a LAN. Because each address class uses a different number of octets for the network ID, and the subnet mask "masks" the network portion of an IP address, the default subnet mask will be different for each class of IP addresses. The number 255 is the number reserved in TCP/IP for use by the default subnet mask. A default subnet mask will use 255s over the network portion of an IP address and 0s over the host portion of an IP address.

For more information, see Chapter 4 of *Network+ Exam Cram*.

Question 48

Answer b is correct. 10Base5 uses Thicknet coaxial cable in a bus topology. Thicknet coaxial cable is one-half inch in diameter with a copper core and can carry a signal up to 500 meters in a single segment. Thinnet is used in 10Base2 networks. Twisted-pair and shielded twisted pair are used in 10BaseT networks.

For more information, see Chapter 2 of *Network+ Exam Cram*.

Question 49

Answers b and c are correct. Fault tolerance is the ability to recover from a single hard disk failure. A standard created for implementing fault-tolerant strategies is known as RAID. A volume set is created by combining areas of free space from one or more hard disks into one logical drive. Volume sets do not provide fault tolerance. In fact, if one member of a volume set fails, all data is lost. A mirror set, or RAID 1, is created using two disks, with one disk acting as a "mirror" of the other, providing redundancy. In the event of a single disk failure in a mirror set, the other disk may be used. Disk duplexing is a physical form of RAID 1 mirroring and requires two physical disks and two disk controllers to be implemented. A stripe set with parity, or RAID 5, is created by combining equal areas of free space on 3 to 32 disks to form one logical drive. If one member of a stripe set with parity fails, the failed member can be "regenerated" using the parity information that is stored on the remaining members of the set. A stripe set without parity, or RAID 0, is created by combining equal areas of free space on 2 to 32 disks to form one logical drive. Stripe sets without parity do not provide fault tolerance.

For more information, see Chapter 5 of *Network+ Exam Cram*.

Question 50

Answer c is correct. Public Switched Telephone Network (PSTN), also known as Plain Old Telephone Service (POTS), is the standard dial-up analog phone line used to send voice and data. PSTN can transmit data up to 28,800bps. (The new 56Kbps standard achieves faster transmission speeds over 28.8Kbps by using digital equipment and data compression.) PSTN uses a modem (modulate/demodulate) to connect to a computer. A modem converts, or modulates, a computer's digital signal to analog for transmission over PSTN, and the receiving computer's modem will demodulate that signal, or convert it from analog to a digital signal. Integrated Services Digital Network (ISDN) is a digital dial-up service that can send voice and data signals at 128Kbps (128,000 bits per second).

For more information, see Chapter 6 of *Network+ Exam Cram*.

Question 51

Answer d is correct. A star topology features the use of a hub to connect computers. If a single computer is disconnected from the hub, only that computer is affected, as opposed to a bus network where the failure of the cable at any point will take the entire network down. This makes a star topology easier to troubleshoot than a bus topology. Both a bus and star can use coaxial cable.

For more information, see Chapter 2 of *Network+ Exam Cram*.

Question 52

Answer c is correct. Segmenting a network is the process of dividing a network into separate parts to improve performance. A bridge is a common device used to segment a network. A bridge can read the hardware address of packets, and use that information to distribute packets, eliminating unnecessary traffic. A bridge can read hardware addresses because it resides at the same layer of the OSI model as a network adapter card driver (the Data Link layer). Segmenting a network can greatly improve network performance because network traffic will be more evenly distributed and unnecessary traffic eliminated. Segmenting a network will not provide security. Data encryption is not provided by segmenting a network. The process of segmenting a network is independent of the type of media used in a network.

For more information, see Chapter 2 of *Network+ Exam Cram.*

Question 53

Answer c is correct. Segmenting a network is the process of dividing a network into separate parts to improve performance. A bridge is a common device used to segment a network. A bridge can read the hardware address of packets, and use that information to distribute packets, eliminating unnecessary traffic. A bridge can read hardware addresses because it resides at he same layer of the OSI model as a network adapter card driver (the Data Link layer). A multiplexer is used to combine multiple connections into a single one. A hub cannot segment a network, because it only passes traffic out all ports. A repeater cannot segment a network, because it only boosts a signal's strength. A hub and a repeater both reside at the Physical layer of the OSI model, and have no access to any packet information.

For more information, see Chapter 2 of *Network+ Exam Cram.*

Question 54

Answers a and d are correct. Microsoft operating systems include Windows NT Server and Workstation, Windows 9X, 3.X, and DOS. Unix is not a Microsoft operating system. NetWare is Novell's network operating system.

For more information, see Chapter 3 of *Network+ Exam Cram.*

Question 55

Answer d is correct. Twisted-pair cable is the most common, least expensive cable used in networking today. All categories of twisted-pair can carry a signal 100 meters in a single-segment length. Category 3 twisted-pair supports transmission speeds up to 10Mbps. Category 5 twisted-pair supports transmission speeds up to 100Mbps. Shielded twisted pair provides a greater resistance to electrical interference than unshielded twisted pair.

For more information, see Chapter 2 of *Network+ Exam Cram*.

Question 56

Answers a and c are correct. IPX/SPX is a routable protocol commonly used in Novell NetWare networks. TCP/IP is an industry-standard protocol that got its start in Unix networks. There is no such protocol as UPX.

For more information, see Chapter 4 of *Network+ Exam Cram*.

Question 57

Answer a is correct. A 10Base2 network uses Thinnet coaxial cable. A single segment length of Thinnet coaxial cable can travel up to 185 meters. The maximum length of a 10Base2 network is 925 meters, according to a specification known as the 5-4-3 rule. The 5-4-3 rule states that by specification, only five segments of Thinnet coaxial cable can be used to extend the length of a 10Base2 network, using four repeaters, and only three segments can have computers attached to them. Therefore, the total maximum length of a 10Base2 network is 925 meters (185x5).

For more information, see Chapter 2 of *Network+ Exam Cram*.

Question 58

Answer b is correct. A 10Base5 network uses Thicknet coaxial cable. A single segment length of Thicknet coaxial cable can travel up to 500 meters. The maximum length of a 10Base5 network is 2500 meters, according to a specification known as the 5-4-3 rule. The 5-4-3 rule states that by specification, only five segments of Thicknet coaxial cable can be used to extend the length of a 10Base5 network, using four repeaters, and only three segments can have computers attached to them. Therefore, the total maximum length of a 10Base5 network is 2,500 meters (500x5).

For more information, see Chapter 2 of *Network+ Exam Cram*.

Question 59

Answers a and c are correct. When installing a network adapter card, it must be configured to use a unique IRQ. An IRQ is a number that identifies a device to the CPU. All network adapter cards come preconfigured with a MAC address. The MAC address is the permanent address "burned" on every network adapter card by the manufacturer and must be unique for all network cards.

For more information, see Chapter 14 of *Network+ Exam Cram.*

Question 60

Answer a is correct. An access method defines rules for how data is placed on a network cable. The access method used in 10Base2, 10BaseT, and 10Base5 networks is CSMA/CD. CSMA/CA is used in Apple networks. Demand priority is the access method used in 100Base VG-AnyLAN networks. Token passing is the access method used in token ring networks.

For more information, see Chapter 2 of *Network+ Exam Cram.*

Question 61

Answer c is correct. Fiber-optic cable is an extremely fast, secure media that can transport a signal. Fiber optic sends a signal as a pulse of light, so it is impervious to electrical interference. Data traveling through a fiber-optic cable cannot be tapped and read. Thicknet (500 meters), Thinnet (185 meters), and twisted-pair (100 meters) all utilize copper wire to transmit a signal and are therefore all susceptible to electrical interference.

For more information, see Chapter 2 of *Network+ Exam Cram.*

Question 62

Answer b is correct. Fault tolerance refers to the ability of a system to recover from a single hard disk failure. Standards for implementing fault tolerance are defined by RAID. A mirror set, defined as RAID level 1, consists of two disks: a primary and a mirror. When data is written to the primary member of a mirror set, it also is written to the mirrored copy, providing fault tolerance. If the primary member of a mirror set fails, the mirrored disk can replace it. A volume set is created by combining 2 to 32 areas of free disk space into one logical drive. A stripe set without parity, defined by RAID level 0, is created by combining the free disk space of 2 to 32 disks into a single logical drive, where data is written evenly across all members of the set. Stripe sets without parity and volume sets do not provide fault tolerance, meaning that if a single disk in a volume set or stripe set without parity fails, all data will be lost.

For more information, see Chapter 5 of *Network+ Exam Cram.*

Question 63

Answer a is correct. A bus topology is the least expensive to implement, because no hubs are required. A mesh topology features multiple links that can provide alternate routes to a host in the event of a single line failure. Because of these multiple links, the cost of implementing a mesh topology is greater than any other networking topology. The star (hub) and ring (MAU) topologies are more expensive to implement than a bus, because they both require connectivity devices in addition to cabling, but they cost less than a mesh topology to implement.

For more information, see Chapter 2 of *Network+ Exam Cram.*

Question 64

Answer b is correct. An access method defines rules for how data is placed on a network cable. CSMA/CA is used in Apple networks. The access method used in 10Base2, 10BaseT, and 10Base5 networks is CSMA/CD. Demand priority is the access method used in 100Base VG-AnyLAN networks. Token passing is the access method used in token ring networks.

For more information, see Chapter 2 of *Network+ Exam Cram.*

Question 65

Answers a, b, and d are correct. Standards for Ethernet networks are defined in project 802.3. Ethernet networks include 10Base2, 10Base5, 10BaseT, and 100BaseT. 100Base VG-AnyLAN is not an Ethernet standard network.

For more information, see Chapter 2 of *Network+ Exam Cram.*

Question 66

Answer c is correct. The OSI model defines standards for networking based on a seven-layer model. All of the components used in networking (hubs, bridges, routers, cables, protocols, and so on) conform to various layers of the OSI model by "residing" at one or more of these seven layers. A gateway is used to connect dissimilar networks, like a PC network to an IBM mainframe network. A gateway resides at the Application layer of the OSI model and has access to all seven layers.

For more information, see Chapter 8 of *Network+ Exam Cram.*

Question 67

Answer b is correct. Both PPP and SLIP are used as dial-up protocols when using a modem to connect to a remote network or the Internet. SLIP only supports the use of the TCP/IP protocol. PPP is a newer, more efficient dial-up protocol than SLIP. PPP automatically obtains configuration parameters with the remote server on connection. This simplifies the configurations required when making a remote connection. SLIP must be configured manually with these parameters. Another key difference between PPP and SLIP is the number of communication protocols supported. PPP supports IPX/SPX, AppleTalk, TCP/IP, and NetBEUI. SLIP only supports the use of the TCP/IP protocol.

For more information, see Chapter 6 of *Network+ Exam Cram*.

Question 68

Answer b is correct. A stealth virus can be very destructive to any computer. It gets into a computer and hides in the background while it does its damage. No virus is harmless.

For more information, see Chapter 13 of *Network+ Exam Cram*.

Question 69

Answer c is correct. TCP/IP contains various command-line utilities used for troubleshooting/diagnosing a TCP/IP network. The key commands to know are **ARP, NBTSTAT, TRACERT,** and **NETSTAT**.

➤ **ARP** Address Resolution Protocol resolves, or associates, an IP address to a MAC address. A MAC address, also known as a hardware address, is the permanent address "burned" into every network adapter card by the manufacturer. The TCP/IP command **ARP –a** will display the local computer's ARP cache, which is a list of all the IP addresses that have been resolved by ARP, along with the corresponding MAC address.

➤ **NETSTAT** A TCP/IP command-line utility used to display protocol statistics about the current TCP/IP connection. **NETSTAT** can be used to display information about the port number (80 for HTTP, 21 for FTP, and so on) and protocol (UDP or TCP) used in a given TCP/IP connection.

➤ **NBTSTAT** A TCP/IP command-line utility that displays the current TCP/IP NetBIOS name information. Microsoft networks commonly use NetBIOS names when communicating. To communicate using TCP/IP, NetBIOS names must be resolved, or associated, with their IP address. This name resolution can take place via WINS, broadcast, or LMHOSTS files. The **NBTSTAT** command can be used to display the NetBIOS names used by the local computer, **NBTSTAT –n**, as well as provide a list of how NetBIOS name resolution is taking place, **NBTSTAT –r**.

For more information, see Chapter 4 of *Network+ Exam Cram*.

Question 70

Answer c is correct. A token ring topology uses a device that looks similar to a hub, known as an MAU, to connect computers together. In a star topology, each computer is connected to a hub. The hub handles termination and distributes packets to all segments. A bus topology features a single segment of computers in a continuous, single line, with termination at both ends. There is no such thing as a token bus topology.

For more information, see Chapter 2 of *Network+ Exam Cram*.

Question 71

Answer c is correct. All computers using TCP/IP must have a unique IP address, a subnet mask, and if used in a WAN, a default gateway. An IP address identifies a TCP/IP host on the network and contains two important elements: a network ID and a host ID. The network ID of an IP address identifies the network the host is on. (For example, all users in a single location are said to be on the same network and, therefore, will all have the same network ID in their IP address.) The host ID of an IP address identifies the host, or individual computer, on a TCP/IP network. It is the host ID portion of an IP address that is the unique part. Therefore, in a single TCP/IP network, users will all have the same network ID and different (unique) host IDs. The subnet mask is used to "mask" the network portion of an IP address, with the number 255, so IP can determine if the destination host is local or remote. A default subnet mask refers to the subnet mask that is used by a particular TCP/IP address class in a single subnet environment, like a LAN. Because each address class uses a different number of octets for the network ID, and the subnet mask "masks" the network portion of an IP address, the default subnet mask will be different for each class of IP addresses. The number 255 is the number reserved in TCP/IP for use by the default subnet mask. A default subnet mask will use 255s over the network portion of and IP address and 0s over the host portion of an IP address.

For more information, see Chapter 4 of *Network+ Exam Cram*.

Question 72

Answer c is correct. The manner in which data flows on a network cable can be defined as either baseband or broadband. Baseband, as used by Ethernet networks, uses digital signaling over a single frequency. Baseband can send information bidirectionally and utilizes repeaters to boost a signal. Broadband uses analog signaling over a range of frequencies. Broadband sends information unidirectionally and uses amplifiers to boost a signal.

For more information, see Chapter 2 of *Network+ Exam Cram*.

Question 73

Answer c is correct. A Windows NT Server computer can perform routing functions to segment a network. Installing and configuring multiple adapters and selecting the Enable IP Forwarding option in TCP/IP Properties will allow NT Server to act as a router with a static routing table. With static routing, all information must be manually added to the routing table. Dynamic routing, as the name implies, allows a router to automatically update its routing table. Routing Information Protocol for Internet Protocol (RIP for IP) and Routing Information Protocol for Internetwork Packet Exchange (RIP for IPX) are some examples of the types of methods that can be used when employing dynamic routing. Although both RIP for IP and RIP for IPX will allow NT Server to perform dynamic routing; in this example, the only protocol used is TCP/IP, so only RIP for IP is required. POP3 is used to retrieve Internet mail and has nothing to do with routing tables.

For more information, see Chapter 4 of *Network+ Exam Cram*.

Question 74

Answer a is correct. A UNC name is a standard for connecting to shared resources on a network. A UNC is comprised of two key elements: a computer name and a share name. All computers in a network must have a computer name to identify themselves. When sharing a resource (a printer, files, CD-ROM, and so on), the shared resource must also be assigned a name, known as a "share" name. Connecting to a shared resource using a UNC simply involves specifying these two parameters, in the format "\\computer name\share name". For example, to connect to a directory that has been assigned the share name DATAFILES on the computer named SALES, the UNC to connect to this resource would be \\SALES\DATAFILES.

For more information, see Chapter 12 of *Network+ Exam Cram*.

Question 75

Answer a is correct. Fault tolerance is the ability to recover from a failure. A standard created for implementing fault-tolerant strategies on disks is known as RAID. A mirror set, or RAID 1, is created using two disks, with one disk acting as a "mirror" of the other, providing redundancy. Disk duplexing is a physical form of RAID 1 mirroring and requires two physical disks and two disk controllers to be implemented.

For more information, see Chapter 5 of *Network+ Exam Cram*.

"*Taking an exam without an Exam Cram book is worse than going to work without my trousers!*"

— *Christian, U.K.*

ISBN: 1-57610-449-4
$99.99 U.S.
Available Now

ISBN: 1-57610-289-0
$29.99 U.S.
Available Now

"Thank you for writing and making available the valuable **Exam Cram** series of books. I not only passed the NT Server 4 in the Enterprise exam but also scored very high. I give credit to the very readable and understandable **Exam Cram** books."
 —**Richard Peppel**

"I just wanted to thank you for writing the **Exam Cram** series of books. I have used them solely for studying for my tests (five in all.) I find that **Exam Cram** makes for a passing grade."
 —**Jack R. Watson**

"The **Exam Crams** are by far the best studying companions! Since discovering your study guides, I have been able to cut my study time in half. Thank you!"
 —**Michael Dominguez, MCSE**

Certification Insider™ Press

CORIOLIS™

CERTIFIED CRAMMER SOCIETY

PHI SLAMMA CRAMMA

A breed apart, a cut above the rest—a true professional. Highly skilled and superbly trained, certified IT professionals are unquestionably the world's most elite computer experts. In an effort to appropriately recognize this privileged crowd, The Coriolis Group is proud to introduce the Certified Crammer Society. If you are a certified IT professional, it is our pleasure to invite you to become a Certified Crammer Society member.

Membership is free to all certified professionals and benefits include a membership kit that contains your official membership card and official Certified Crammer Society blue denim ball cap emblazoned with the Certified Crammer Society crest—proudly displaying the Crammer motto "Phi Slamma Cramma"—and featuring a genuine leather bill. The kit also includes your password to the Certified Crammers-Only Web site containing monthly discreet messages designed to provide you with advance notification about certification testing information, special book excerpts, and inside industry news not found anywhere else; monthly Crammers-Only discounts on selected Coriolis titles; *Ask the Series Editor* Q and A column; cool contests with great prizes; and more.

GUIDELINES FOR MEMBERSHIP

Registration is free to professionals certified in Microsoft, A+, or Oracle DBA. Coming soon: Sun Java, Novell, and Cisco. Send or email your contact information and proof of your certification (test scores, membership card, or official letter) to:

Certified Crammer Society Membership Chairperson
THE CORIOLIS GROUP, LLC
14455 North Hayden Road, Suite 220, Scottsdale, Arizona 85260-6949
Fax: 480.483.0193 • Email: ccs@coriolis.com

APPLICATION

Name:

Address:

Society Alias:

Choose a secret code name to correspond with us and other Crammer Society members. Please use no more than eight characters.

Email:

CORIOLIS HELP CENTER

Here at The Coriolis Group, we strive to provide the finest customer service in the technical education industry. We're committed to helping you reach your certification goals by assisting you in the following areas.

Talk to the Authors

We'd like to hear from you! Please refer to the "How to Use This Book" section in the "Introduction" of every Exam Cram guide for our authors' individual email addresses.

Web Page Information

The Certification Insider Press Web page provides a host of valuable information that's only a click away. For information in the following areas, please visit us at:
www.coriolis.com/cip/default.cfm

- Titles and other products
- Book content updates
- Roadmap to Certification Success guide
- New Adaptive Testing changes
- New Exam Cram Live! seminars
- New Certified Crammer Society details
- Sample chapters and tables of contents
- Manuscript solicitation
- Special programs and events

Contact Us by Email

Important addresses you may use to reach us at The Coriolis Group.

eci@coriolis.com

To subscribe to our FREE, bi-monthly online newsletter, *Exam Cram Insider*. Keep up to date with the certification scene. Included in each *Insider* are certification articles, program updates, new exam information, hints and tips, sample chapters, and more.

techsupport@coriolis.com

For technical questions and problems with CD-ROMs. Products broken, battered, or blown-up? Just need some installation advice? Contact us here.

ccs@coriolis.com

To obtain membership information for the *Certified Crammer Society*, **an exclusive club for the certified professional.** Get in on members-only discounts, special information, expert advice, contests, cool prizes, and free stuff for the certified professional. Membership is FREE. Contact us and get enrolled today!

cipq@coriolis.com

For book content questions and feedback about our titles, drop us a line. This is the good, the bad, and the questions address. Our customers are the best judges of our products. Let us know what you like, what we could do better, or what question you may have about any content. Testimonials are always welcome here, and if you send us a story about how an Exam Cram guide has helped you ace a test, we'll give you an official Certification Insider Press T-shirt.

custserv@coriolis.com

For solutions to problems concerning an order for any of our products. Our staff will promptly and courteously address the problem. Taking the exams is difficult enough. We want to make acquiring our study guides as easy as possible.

Book Orders & Shipping Information

orders@coriolis.com

To place an order by email or to check on the status of an order already placed.

coriolis.com/bookstore/default.cfm

To place an order through our online bookstore.

1.800.410.0192

To place an order by phone or to check on an order already placed.

What's On The CD-ROM

The *Network+ Practice Tests Exam Cram*'s companion CD-ROM contains one practice exam. This exam is built using an interactive format that allows you to practice in an exam environment similar to CompTIA's own testing format.

System Requirements

Software

➤ Your operating system must be Windows 95/98 or NT 4.

➤ Internet Explorer or Netscape Navigator with Java capabilities is needed to complete the projects included in this book. (The software is not provided on this CD-ROM.)

Hardware

➤ Minimum of a 486/66 MHz processor is recommended.

➤ 16MB RAM is the minimum requirement.